D1345409

THE 100 BEST CHILDREN'S BOOKS

THE 100 BEST CHILDREN'S BOOKS

by

BRIAN ALDERSON

G

GALILEO PUBLISHERS, CAMBRIDGE

16 Woodlands Road
Great Shelford
Cambridge CB22 5LW
UK
www.galileopublishing.co.uk

Distributed in the USA by:
SCB Distributors
15608 S. New Century Drive
Gardena, CA 90248-2129

ISBN 978-1-903385-98-2

First published in the UK 2019

Printed in the UK

CONTENTS

★
remembering
as always
Christopher John and Thomas Bembo
★

INTRODUCTION

C hildren's books and their students sit well below the salt at the table of literature. Truth to tell they do not really belong there at all but at a table of their own. Although often referred to as a genre of the larger assembly they are really a separate literature *sui generis* and have a multiplicity of genres of their own. Some of these, like nursery rhymes or nonsense or folktales or movable books, barely figure in adult literary studies and one of them – picture books – is itself multi-generic. Furthermore, the linguistic capacity of the literature can spread from the completely wordless (an example is included among our one hundred books below) to five hundred-page novels which nonetheless claim a child readership, several examples of which may also be found here.

That this large territory has been inadequately mapped over the three centuries of its existence is understandable insofar as the adult community of readers and scholars have mostly passed beyond it as a subject of direct relevance to their cultural lives. True, they may have varying degrees of interest in their roles as parents, teachers, collectors or specialist librarians (now seemingly a dying breed) but that will often be incidental to more central concerns. Additionally, although a strong case can be made for seeing publishers and the book trade as the founders and the foremost influencers of the books laid before children, their participation as editors, designers, publicists is often focused on their position in the market rather than on any dispassionate interest in the subject itself.

Although for historians there was a notable attempt by a bookseller/publisher, Benjamin Tabart, in 1801 to summarize for his customers in over eighty pages the variety of books for children and young people that he stocked (not just his own products[1]), it was not until much later that a first concerted effort to survey the field was undertaken by the author Charlotte Yonge, who, as a writer for children, can be found here at our item 13. In 1869 *Macmillan's Magazine* ran three articles by her on 'Children's Literature of the Last Century'[2] and twenty years later she produced what might almost be deemed a forerunner to the present work: *What Books to Lend and What to Give.* This was a bound volume of 126 pages introducing, categorizing, briefly annotating and indexing some 955 books, magazines and 'penny readings'. It was undertaken on behalf of the National Society for Promoting Religious Education (an organisation much concerned with the administration of the new Church of England schools that were arriving after the 1870 Education Act). 'Most of the books I have personally proved', she says, adding the proviso, relevant now as then, that 'many readers will be disappointed at omissions, but it is quite impossible to answer for all the books in existence'. And it was a list of recommendations ('*not* an advertisement') and it is cheering to find that, among much theology and educational works, she commended the 'exceedingly droll mishaps' subsisting in one of the less well-known items in the present list (no.22). However, 'tales that have any dissenting bias or which appear to involve false doctrine, are of course, omitted'.

Other evaluations of children's literature that followed Miss Yonge's make for amusing and not irrelevant consultation. Lilian Stevenson's (wait for it) *A Child's Bookshelf: suggestions on Children's Reading, with an Annotated List of Books on Heroism, Service, Patriotism, Friendliness, Joy and Beauty* (SCM, 1917), acknowledges Yonge as 'still very useful' and while coloured by the war going on around its selection, it offers notes on almost as many books as she did in

1   See the description and part of his Introduction in Marjorie Moon's *Benjamin Tabart's Juvenile Library.* (Winchester: St Paul's Bibliographies, 1990).

2   The articles were republished in nos. 2, 3 and 4 of *Signal; approaches to children's literature* (Stroud: Thimble Press, May, 1970-January, 1971).

multiple categories 'intended to help those who desire to build up a good library for their children's home use'. (The Bishop of Wakefield in a Foreword, pragmatically extends that to 'Training Colleges and schools of every grade'.) By way of modification she appends a list of nothing less than 'A Hundred Books with which to Begin'; (It would not do as a model here since it has many open choices: 'A picture book about the Empire'; 'One of Andrew Lang's fairy books' and it leaves the last four to be 'filled up according to taste'... 'Do not forget a painting book!').'

Both the systematic listing of recommended children's books and the employment of a hundred examples gained a professionally-grounded status thirty-three years later in the work of Kathleen Lines. She was a librarian trained in Canada where – as also in the United States – both the collecting and discussion of children's books was taken more seriously than in Britain, but after moving to England she became involved as an advisor on the subject. In 1950 she organised a major exhibition at the National Book League, whose 294-page catalogue, *Four to Fourteen,* stands as a major commentary on the publishing scene of the period. (When, in 1954, I accidentally found myself employed by a bookseller who specialised in supplying children's books to schools and public libraries I found that his showroom had been entirely stocked by the books recommended in *Four to Fourteen*).

In 1958 Miss Lines was commissioned to edit a *Sunday Times* 'special survey' of The 100 Best Books for Children and a form of audience participation was devised. In the weeks before the list went into print, the newspaper published the titles of ninety-nine of the exhibits and readers were asked to send in on a postcard their suggestions for the hundredth. Over a hundred answers were received and Miss Lines preserved the cards, which make for amusing reading. One contributor demanded that the Bible should go in while a group of cards with the same postmark called, in the same handwriting, for the inclusion of Beverly Nicholls' *The Tree that Sat Down*. The winner by many furlongs was Hodgson Burnett's *The Secret Garden.*

This event long preceded Neil MacGregor's exhibition at the British Museum of *A History of the World in One Hundred Objects,* whose influence has by now surely inspired more than a hundred lists of this that and the other. Children's books have returned as a subject, most notably in an elaborately staged show at New York's Grolier Club, curated by Chris Loker, with a splendidly detailed bibliographic catalogue edited by Jill Shefrin: *One Hundred Books Famous in Children's Literature.* (The exhibition was one of an historic series of 'Grolier One Hundreds' which, for all we know, may have influenced Dr MacGregor.) The British Library has also joined in with a book which is valuable chiefly in illustrating the near-contempt in which children's literature may be held in Britain, even by publishers with a reputation for scholarly work. Its title is misleading: *A History of Children's Literature in 100 Books,* for the one hundred are pegs on a washing-line from which dangle a miscellany of choices in comprehensive disorder and with amateur descriptions which are often erroneous.

With that as an Awful Warning I must now proceed to the criteria for my choice of the one hundred books before you here, a central problem with which derives from the word 'best' in my title. To begin with, as already noted, the body of work is vast and consists of many genres and levels of discourse with 'bests' all over the place. My choice has thus been restricted, in accordance with earlier lists in this series, to works of fiction published up to the year 2000, some here of foreign origin. They give hospitality (with one or two exceptions) to a single story aimed at a child readership (i.e. omitting short story collections). Traditional narratives, usually lacking a specific author and often published as collections anyway, are excluded, but several translations of original works are present and regular attention has been paid to illustrations, upon which many books may be as much dependent for their total effect as their texts. Some of these are, of course, illustrated by their own authors and (with others too) may call upon the reader to look at an accompanying image. I have noted in the captions both artist and reproductive process, a practice almost universally omitted from literature studies.

Much debate can be engendered over the selection of the hundred books, which, it must be emphasised, are drawn primarily from the ranks of those intended for pre-pubescent *children* and not from today's omnipresent helpmeets for adolescent catchers in the rye. My consciousness of many readers' likely unfamiliarity with the course of children's book publishing has led me to adopt a chronological sequence so that the bestness of my authors of choice may not always lie in their absolute literary accomplishment but in their importance as waymarks in the development of a literature during its formative decades. Thus *The History of Little Goody Two-Shoes* is, *sub specie aeternitatis*, no more than comical rubbish but a work full of resonance in the history of its genre.

It may well be objected that my inclusion of these earlier books (although most of them are still in print in one form or another, or else accessible through internet services) has resulted in the exclusion of the work of many twentieth century writers for children more worthy of attention. Admitting the impossibility of 'answering for all the books in existence', is there still not a hint of unfairness in the omission of many well-loved friends? The nearest that I can get to doing a deal on the matter is to note that my pre-twentieth century inclusions amount to the sum of thirty-four (including some surely indispensable classics) but that if I were to leave them all out I would have room for that number of modern contestants and I therefore append, as a frustrating extra, that number of writers who might have been included.

Aside from what is essentially a numerical question, explanations still need to be given as to my criteria for selecting both the writers and the books of the one hundred and that in turn demands consideration of an everlasting problem which further exemplifies the fundamental distinction between the treatment of literature for the young and for adults. So far as reading is concerned, pre-pubertal children are at the mercy of a community where the books are written, published, distributed and judged by people who are not children (and, many of whom, what's more, have only the vaguest knowledge of the literature in question). What store may be set on judgments made thus all along the line which may determine what the child is offered? Is not Samuel Johnson right in saying that the best encouragement to choice is to let a child loose in, say, a well-stocked shop (as occurred with him), a procedure evidenced to perfection by Eleanor Farjeon among the thrilling, uncoordinated heaps in her *Little Bookroom*?

Ah, but these days we need to be more discriminating than that in our methods. The twentieth century owners of the resources sufficient for the exercise, the public librarians, have certainly proved the most knowledgeable in administering them but that has not stopped (indeed it has stimulated) debates about the guidance of the unformed tastes of their young customers. The perception by that omniverous reader, John Rowe Townsend, that the guides in charge may be roughly divided into 'child people', who prioritize the likelihood of child response in judging a book, or 'book people', who look to the book itself as a foundation has long been a useful distinction for observers of critical fashion and in recent decades, with the arrival of Children's Literature as an element in university curricula, that comparatively simple division has been subject to the refinements of Theory, which is put in to the pot, rather like Anglo-Saxon in the former English syllabi, to make the subject look more worthy of study. 'Criticism is the Theory of Literature: Theory is the Criticism of Literature', cries Roderick McGillis in *The Routledge Companion to Children's Literature,* a work whose index carries no entry for Beatrix Potter but eighteen for Jacques Lacan.

In a note in that book, its editor, David Rudd, records a piece of journalism by myself in 1969 that has rather dogged any reputation I might myself have as a critic: 'The Irrelevance of Children to the Children's Book Reviewer'. It placed me firmly in the camp as a 'book person' whose rather simple-minded philosophy has continued down to the editing of this book. What I have been looking for in the authors that I have chosen is a distinctiveness in their writing which brings it close to that of the told story, one of those *'Tales of Tom Thumbe* in the old time[3] [which] have been the reuiuers of drouzy age at mid night … [or] compasses the Christmas fire-block till the Curfew bell rings candle out'. Almost all the books of my team will sound as well read aloud as they may be read on the printed page (or perhaps better).

With that as a general criterion, there is the further decision

---

3   From R[ichard] J[ohnson's] introduction to the story, whose printing in 1630 was the first known of an English folktale.

that I have had to make as to the choice of story that best exhibits their powers. Here I have now and again perversely chosen a book which I would not adjudge their 'best' but which allows a discussable element of their style. In some cases too – Peter Dickinson, say, or Jan Mark or William Mayne – 'best' cannot be assigned since their craft extends to such a variety of wondrous narratives that I have tended to choose the first or an early work from which the oeuvre as a whole has blossomed.

Townsend's dichotomy of 'child people' and 'book people' probably owes its origins to critical arguments that stemmed from the growing attention paid to children's books from the 1930s onward. Discrimination was being called for between those books that had market appeal ('children love them') or were deemed to have a desirable didacticism ('that will improve their attitudes') and those books that may be perceived by the critic to have a degree of authorial originality or narrative complexity which make the child (and usually the adult critic too) aware of a distinctive potential in the goods on offer.

The point was well made by Joan Aiken in 'A Free Gift', an essay (or what she called 'a rambling series of disjointed remarks') that was included in a volume on 'writers and writing for children': *The Thorny Paradise*, edited by Edward Blishen in 1986[4]. Here she calculated that pre-pubescent children might be able to read at most six hundred books in their years of growth, a quantity which would include books as they learned to read, picture books, educational books and favourites read over and over again. Among that quantity she guessed that there might be a deal of what she called, in a term borrowed from Saki, 'Filboid Studge' – a breakfast food so dull and tasteless that everybody thought it must be good for them – truck by celebrities or household names which offer no nourishment, or debased versions of the classics (look at the catastrophies that have attended the commercialisation of Beatrix Potter or Winnie-the-Pooh).

Children of course are unlikely to be aware of the critical distinctions that are being made and the 'book person' can be

4   The passage is excerpted from her wise (and highly entertaining) *The Way to Write for Children*, Elm Tree Books, 1982.

faced with difficulties in making known the potential of their recommendations. (How many of the hundred titles here will be known to, let alone read by, the non-specialist audience for whom Filboid Studge offers a ready-made product?)

There is a meeting-ground in the business of selection where choice can be dictated by the children themselves through their liking and enthusiasm for fictional groupings. With due encouragement, committed young readers may build up a knowledge and critical judgment of their own within some category of the large roster of family stories, animal stories – sub-section on horses, although hunting is now banned (but you will find an example of the infamous theme here) – school stories, holiday adventure stories, historical stories, etc. etc.

These categories are not set in concrete and themes may interpenetrate but almost a third have elements of the fantastic to them, although 'fantasy' itself may vary from *Kunstmärchen* (MacDonald), adventures towards a goal (Bunyan), there and back again (Tolkien), wild comedy (Lindsay), or tales resonant through an original vision (I think that my two favourites in the whole hundred are Masefield's *Midnight Folk* and De la Mare's *Three Mulla-Mulgars*). The next largest category consists of those realistic tales devoted to aspects of family life that may be prevalent at the time of writing (Edgeworth at one end and Jacqueline Wilson at the other, although one could subsume here ten or so school and holiday adventure stories); similarly, it's not easy to distinguish between adventure stories like those stemming from *Robinson Crusoe* and those exploring a set historical period as a site for narrative (Sutcliff or – another favourite – *Ransom for a Knight*).

It is also interesting to note the strong showing of male authors among the fantasy writers and that of women among the stories of family life and associated topics. (In the past, surveyors of the field were prone to divide readership into books favoured by boys and those favoured by girls. It is probably anathema to do that now but a judgment from someone more competent than I would be worth hearing on, say, the response of boy readers to those little women or to the heroinic Tracy Beaker, or girl readers to Bevis or Biggles.)

Regardless of all that partial tallying though, may I be allowed to hope that my hundred authors, taken as a whole, may spread a wider knowledge of the artistry that is present among those dining at the children's table – with no Filboid Studge?

ACKNOWLEDGMENTS

In many cases my treatment of a book has derived from my earlier journalistic essay in a series on children's classics, written for the periodical *Books for Keeps*. The ploy has allowed for an approach governed by the demands of the subject of each article rather than a set-piece approach and the additional Commentaries give room to varieties of related bibliographical gossip. I am, though, very grateful to Andrea Reece, the editor of *BfK* for allowing me to draw upon my work there.

At the outset of my labours I benefited greatly from the wise advice of my dear friend, the late Marilyn Edwards, whose early death brought a too precipitate end to much energetic and entertaining argufying. In the final stages of composition I also enjoyed help from Paula Wride of Seven Stories, my grand-daughter Naomi who carried out a vital piece of research for me at the British Library when I was unable to get there, and my son Nicholas, who solved many baffling problems arising from my incompetence in matters electronic.

Three hand-coloured etchings by Isaac Taylor on one leaf of plate paper, inserted with many others throughout the book.

-1-

THE PILGRIM'S PROGRESS
BY JOHN BUNYAN (1678)

'… so I awoke, and behold it was a Dream.'

That's a customary cop-out, Master Bunyan. It is unlikely that you ever came across such a thing as the fourteenth century French spiritual romance by Guillaume de Guileville: *Le Pèlerinage de l'Homme*, which has some parallels to your great book, and also sets out its enormous text in the guise of a dream. This was derived from the earlier *Romance of the Rose* and bespeaks 'dream' as the heart of literary fantasy so that long after Christian wends his way to the Celestial City, it is in a dream that Alice Liddell finds herself in Wonderland, or Kay Harker battles the wicked Abner Brown in *The Box of Delights*.

No claim could be made for Bunyan that he conceived his adventure as a theological tract for children, but many testimonies to its appeal to them can rest upon the state of storytelling at the time of its publication. In 1678 the concept of books directed at, and published for, a child readership, was just emerging thanks largely to the Calvinist desire to save their souls from Hell. Such things were tough going however, (*A Token for Children*, a bestseller of 1671, dated 1672, which lasted into Victorian times, dealt with 'the holy lives and joyful deaths' of small children) and it is not difficult to believe that an adventure fantasy, however many sermons it might contain, would make an attractive alternative, especially at a time when the craft of the novel was yet to be fashioned.

A glimpse of the evidence for child use may be had from the publication in 1825 of Isaac Taylor's *Bunyan Explained to a Child*. The Rev'd Taylor was himself a dissenting minister and he acknowledges that Bunyan's book 'takes great hold of children long before they can enter into its spiritual meaning' and in fifty-one short sections he takes them through the episodes of the story, glossing what he takes to be Bunyan's spiritual reading of the events and adding, in each instance, a little hymn of his own composition to reinforce the message. (Unfortunately, these are no easier for the reader to follow than Bunyan's prose – and they lack its rugged force.)

Although the procedure can't help but coarsen both the argument and the rhetoric of the original, it does systematically recapitulate each incident and allows the child more easily to see the disparate incidents of the plot. For the reverend author was an artist and engraver as well as minister (father too of the famous Ann and Jane Taylor whose *Original Poems for Infant Minds* of 1804-5 was popular for a hundred years) and each of his fifty-one numbered sections is illustrated with a vignette picturing the action, with a pictorial route map at the start. (An elaborate fold-out road map had figured as the frontispiece to an edition of Bunyan's book in 1775.) Thus Taylor graphically sums up the narrative appeal of the story's function as an adventure along with the fantasy of the topography and the dangers that Pilgrim encounters: the Slough of Despond, say, or the Valley of the Shadow Death, or Vanity Fair and Doubting Castle.

Taylor's generous procession of images may also offer a ground for speculating on the long-term 'gratification' which he saw the *Progress* as offering children. While the conversational language could easily have made it a book that could be read aloud serially in families, printed copies with illustrations might also serve as a guide to those dramatic passages where events supersede doctrine or saintly reflection. Several illustrated editions were published in the eighteenth century, with the elementary metal-cuts by John Sturt predominating in many cheap, often provincial, editions. None were intended for child readers (unless you count chapbooks as such) and the first so intended was perhaps the oddest, as well as the rarest, ever published. It came from the Holborn Hill shop of William Darton in 1823 and consists of twelve leaves, measuring 85x105mm and printed on one side of the paper only. The whole story is told in 547 words which are engraved round six finely hand-coloured engravings, for it was also issued as a print. Encompassing Part I of the *Progress,* it would have been a costly purchase (at a shilling a time) in its pink paper wrappers and you could buy Part II and the spurious Part III in a companion volume for the same price.

Commentary

The Victorian period saw the arrival of a plenitude of editions, often heavily illustrated, which children might read (I myself still remember with horror Frederick Barnard's picture of the Man with the Muck-Rake, from Part II, in a Partridge edition belonging to a Victorian great-aunt) and both Robert Louis Stevenson and Edward Ardizzone record their liking for the tiny vignettes by Eunice Bagster that illustrated the popular Bagster edition of 1845. It may well be that, throughout the twentieth century, versions for children greatly outnumbered those for adults, even though they might be 'retold for little folks' in a picture book illustrated by Helen Stratton (1909), or as a simplified version by John Fuller, with four fine scraperboard drawings by Biro (1951), or later modified in a large colourful album illustrated by Pat Marriott, or rewritten on a larger scale as *Quest and Conquest* by James Reeves with drawings by Joanna Troughton (1976).

-2-

TALES OF THE FAIRYS
BY THE COMTESSE D'AULNOY (1698)

'Give me a ballad … some book that tells of old fables …' wrote John Bunyan in *A Few Sighs from Hell* in 1658. He was reprobating the reading follies of his youth when he was diverted by some of the shrivelled, and not always polite, remnants of the old romances that found their way into the penny histories and the penny merriments that were the staple of the chapbook trade.

At a time when the reading child was being catered for by educational works, manuals on courtesy and evangelical tracts, almost the only source for imaginative sustenance lay in the 'old fables' which were, (and continued to be for a century or more) condemned by the social arbiters of the day. Certainly there was a powerful imaginative presence in those oral tales that were told to 'old and young' but these were told out loud in who-knows-what tedious or naughty versions dependent on the circumstances of their telling.

Then suddenly, at the court of Louis XIV, a French revolution occurred. On the one hand, in 1697, Charles Perrault brought into print the *Contes de ma Mère l'Oye* – the tales of Mother Goose – which recorded with great skill what eight of those old oral tales might have sounded like. Meanwhile a fashion sprang up for inventing similarly fantastical tales for the diversion of a courtly audience. *Les Contes nouveaux, ou les fées à la mode,* written out at length, not re-told, by the Comtesse D'Aulnoy, were the best-known and the most numerous of these. Sixteen were published in 1698 with another half dozen a year later.

Perhaps it was their aristocratic origin, perhaps their narrative contrivances, very different from those of Mother Goose, that gave these stories social respectability and led to their almost instantaneous translation into English in 1698 as *Tales of the Fairys* (it would take another thirty years before the arrival of the more truly vernacular fantasies of Perrault). Admittedly these were short fictions rather than book-length tales, and primarily conceived as a fashionable court entertainment, but in a time of the dearth of imaginative stimulus, who (except Zeals of the Land Busies) could forgive children for taking to them as an alternative to Improvement.

Often known as *Kunstmärchen* or 'invented fairytales' the Comtesse's efforts may be seen as the first of a genre of storytelling which would later have a fruitful place in the annals of children's fiction. There is a multiplicity of evidence in their plots that the Comtesse is drawing upon traditional motifs (the queen longing for a child, the king sending out three sons to seek their fortune, the animal helpers ...) and one can only speculate on what sources she may have known. By far the richest could have been the sequence of folktales relayed, Boccaccio fashion, in the five days' entertainment of Basile's *Lo Cunto de li Cunti,* or *Pentamerone,* many of whose tales have cognates in the Grimm tales, except that they were all printed in an impossible Neapolitan dialect, hardly known to fashionable French ladies and not translated, even into Italian, until 1757.

To present readers, and quite possibly to the non-courtly public of 1700, the *Tales of the Fairys* quickly outstayed their welcome and must be praised for their imaginative potential rather than their often long-winded and silly plots. (Within a couple of years they were also up against the dramatic arrival, in Paris, of the first ever revisions of the tales from the Orient: the *Thousand Nights and One Night*.) As a result, heavily abridged versions for children occurred in the eighteenth century, perhaps got together as the *Tales of Mother Bunch* (thus twinning Mother Goose) or as truncated single stories such as *The White Cat* or *The Yellow Dwarf*. The latter may be found in Iona and Peter Opie's *Classic Fairy Tales*, although it is not a traditional tale and ends, unusually, with the death of the hero and heroine at the hands of the villain. Andrew Lang, who should have known better, includes a number of D'Aulnoy's tales in the *Blue* and *Red Fairy Books* (1889 and 1890) but he was not responsible for the hacking around of the texts that went on in that series which, for D'Aulnoy, was done by one Minnie Wright, and for much else by his put-upon wife. Perhaps the only volume that aims to give a complete translation of the stories for children was that done by Miss Annie Macdonell and 'Miss Lee', a weighty tome, introduced by Thackeray's daughter and illustrated with many wash-drawings by a little-known artist, Clinton Peters, in 1892.

Commentary

The earliest native English folktale to appear in print was that referred to above on p.12: *The History of Tom Thumbe,* in 1621. As a folktale though, its text is not a definitive authorial work and that is the feature that distinguishes it from a *Kunstmärchen* which – in theory anyway – is the composition of a single voice. As such, the frequent presence of such inventions as an element in the corpus of the best children's novels gives the role a more vital and continuing form than may be the case with 'adult' fiction where, aside from dystopias and scientific fantasies, 'realism' tends to prevail.

-3-

THE LIFE AND STRANGE SURPRIZING
ADVENTURES OF ROBINSON CRUSOE,
OF YORK, MARINER ... AS TOLD BY HIMSELF
BY DANIEL DEFOE (1719)

'Poor Robin Crusoe! Where are you, Robin Crusoe? Where are
you? Where have you been?'

Thus spoke Poll, the parrot, when the shipwrecked mariner
returns to his homely bower after a day or two's survey of his island
kingdom. Perhaps we can concur with Poll, not so much because
of the fate that had brought her master to his lonely residence or
for his eight and twenty years, two months and nineteen days of
practising survival techniques, but more for what has happened
during the three hundred since Daniel Defoe gave the world an
account of his 'strange surprizing' adventures.

There had been nothing like it before. That a life, seemingly so
exactly minuted, could be a work of fiction – the first modern
novel as it happens – was altogether strange and surprising in itself.
Whether true, as some believed, or not, the tale was met with
wonderment and instant bestsellerdom when it came out in April
1719. At least four editions of the book went through the press
before the year was done and Mr Crusoe, a shrewd enough business
man, saw to it that some *Further Adventures* got into print within
five months of the first volume. Unfortunately the book pirates
were active alongside the maritime ones and poor Robin found
the first assailants of his success in coffee-house abridgements and
serialisations in the weekly press, unprotected by those wishing to
control runaway journalists.

The graphic instancy of his story as well as its immediate
newsworthiness would surely have penetrated the neglected
world of the child-reader along with the busy one of adults. (In
1728 little Jemmy Yorke only agreed to suffering an anal clyster
on promise that he should have a copy of *Robinson Crusoe* as a
reward.) Like their elders, they suddenly discovered the potential
of a written *story* as a source of entertainment and, with nothing to

speak of devised for them by the publishers at that time, they look to have tackled the substantial volumes of the original or its re-workings with readerly zest. It was not until mid-century that the one-, two- or even three hundred pages of *Robinson Crusoe* were shrunk down to a twenty four-page chapbook. (And once done, such drastic shortenings became legion, many – from Plymouth to Glasgow – using the same abridgments and hacking out the same illustrations.)

Poor Robin indeed, he didn't just create a story but a genre. Jean-Jacques Rousseau can hardly be blamed for requiring his Emil's first book to be *Robinson Crusoe*, an example of practical resourcefulness, free of the corruptions of civilised life, but would-be educators picked up the idea and produced its conversion to a fireside tract. There was the German *Robinson der Jüngere* of 1779-80 by Joachim Campe who had his youthful hero washed up on the island without all the accoutrements that the original gained – a more fully Rousseauesque instruction manual that swept Europe. (Britain had it as *The New Robinson Crusoe*, illustrated by John Bewick no less, but it went everywhere, sometimes being attributed to Defoe himself. An English chapbook for children published in Newcastle round about 1810 begins with Robinson leaving Defoe's York and has him finally arriving at Campe's Hamburg.)

Adventure was nonetheless more profitable than instruction. The first abridgment specifically for children (unlike the chapbooks which were for everybody) was a sixpenny one from the shop in St Paul's Churchyard of that prolific publisher of children's books, John Newbery. It probably came out in 1768, soon after his death but it carries an imprint typical of the Master: 'printed for the inhabitants of the island [Robinson's] and sold by all the booksellers in the world'. It does away with educational and moral reflections, giving rather a selective treatment of Events. Those at the start, when Crusoe is enslaved by the Moors, are, as often, passed over in order to get him to the desert island, and once there, his protracted spell of housekeeping is also much abridged in order to get us to Man Friday, the cannibals and the corpses all over the beach.

Having opened up so exotic a seam, Defoe and Campe came to be seen as a mite circumscribed and, as the trade in children's books grew and flourished, the variants became legion. Whole families are wrecked (Marryat wrote his *Masterman Ready* because he couldn't do with the inaccurate topographies foisted on the Swiss Robinsons by Johann David Wyss [no.8 below]). There were Dog Crusoes, Rival Crusoes, Arctic Crusoes; there were Crag Islands, Invisible Islands and Coral Islands, long before the most famous of them all, the Treasure one by 'Capt. George North', turned up in 1881. And Ro-bin-son himself is often traduced, as was Bunyan's *Pilgrim*, in a Victorian version by Mar-y God-ol-phin, all in short words for the child who is but new to print and can cope with but one syl-lab-le at a time.)

What though of the original? Has any serious attempt been made to offer children a worthy version of the whole of Defoe's great book since the admirable edition edited by Kathleen Lines in 1968 with its masterly line-drawings by Edward Ardizzone? And indeed, how many children would have read that book then or would read it now? It lives only as a name and a theme, fit for pantomimes, or such modern chapbooks as Ladybird's 'I Can Read It [what?] Myself', or as the location of that now-overpopulated site to which celebrities retire in order to play shellac records on a wind-up gramophone.

Commentary

In 1974, Erhard Dahl, a German graduate, undertook a study of the abridgments of *Robinson Crusoe* which had been published in the first hundred years of the book's life. He spent eighteen months in England, combing through collections, eventually producing a catalogue of some 152 separate editions. In a series of exhaustive comparisons he was able to show how most of these belonged within four textual families, with many provincial booksellers simply reprinting versions and their illustrations pinched from competitors. Furthermore, in the case of perhaps fifty of these editions, the targeted reader was a child. How far that audience was catered for on a worldwide scale may be gauged by noting the special collection of 'Robinsonades' held at the International Youth Library in Munich, whose online catalogue runs to 621 items.

-4-

TRAVELS INTO SEVERAL REMOTE NATIONS OF THE WORLD. BY LEMUEL GULLIVER
BY JONATHAN SWIFT (1726)

In 1726 our wandering friends Christian and Robinson were joined by Captain Lemuel Gulliver to make up that trio of English adventurers who were foremost in bringing literary invention to the children of their day, all of whom were much deprived of that commodity. Of the three, the Captain's voyages 'into several remote nations of the world' carry the reader into a territory very different from the spiritual staging-posts of the Pilgrim or the do-it-yourself island economy of the shipwrecked mariner. Shipwrecks abound, certainly, but it is a matter of remarkable coincidence that, in each case, the Captain finds himself a sole survivor, lost from his comrades but among strange congregations of local inhabitants. It is notable too that, although he claims for himself 'a great Facility in learning Languages', his exercise of it in the nations of Lilliput (and Blefuscu), Brobdingnag, Laputa and the land of the Houyhnhnm enables him to discuss decidedly abstruse social and political questions.

Such was the drama of these travellers' tales that their fundamental distinction from their predecessors was at first passed over. 'They will have as great a run as John Bunion' said Swift's friend Arbuthnot and another friend, John Gay, added that 'from the highest to the lowest [the book] is universally read, from the Council-chamber to the Nursery'. But what the Nursery made of it – then as now – is a debatable question.

Samuel Johnson, who was no fan of either Swift or his book, made the obvious point that 'when once you have thought of big men and little men, it is very easy to do all the rest', and that at once singles out the book's most memorable feature; its harking back to the traditional tales of Giants and Tom Thumbs. At a superficial level it is very easy to see the attractions of the Man Mountain's capture by the little people and his later employment as their secret weapon against the Blefuscans. Likewise there are the perpetual dangers among the Brobdingnagians where our hero may be dunked in a bowl of cream or floored by a falling apple. But such graphic occasions (to which may be added the less admissible events of fire-fighting by micturition or a sportive seat astride the nipple of a Queen's waiting-woman) are entirely subsidiary to the author's satiric purposes.

Not for the Nursery are the (failed) Utopian ideals of Lilliput, or the Brobdingnagian condemnation of the pernicious and odious nature of European politics, or the satire on the scientific projectors of Laputa, or even Swift's telling prognostication of our coming Yahoodom. As with the pilgrim and the mariner, it was the stories that mattered and the popular market was filled with abridgments and adaptations, although not so overwhelmingly as with the earlier tales. Almost all dispensed with the third and fourth voyages, which is a continuing practice and not only for young readers (the Folio Society edition of 1948, for instance, illustrated by Edward Bawden, took us only to Lilliput and Brobdingnag). Certainly what looks to be the first volume, as opposed to a chapbook, that was intended for children was the one published by John Newbery's nephew, Francis, round about 1772 and that did not venture into the mysteries of Laputa or the land of the horses and the Yahoos.

Commentary

Although there is no record of John Newbery himself publishing a version of the *Travels* it was typical of his editorial style that he should see the commercial potential of the book's fame. This is manifest in his producing (abortively) the first periodical for children, parts of which found their way into his miscellany *The Lilliputian Magazine* (1752). One of his successors also published a *Lilliputian Masquerade*, celebrating the peace between 'those potent nations, the Lilliputians and the Tommythumbians' (1774) and another was involved with the issue of the (very rare) 'Lilliputian Library', a uniform set of ten books that also made play with the designation.

A library could also be assembled of the many abridgments, school-reader and picture books that continue down to the present time. (Lang idiotically included the trip to Lilliput in *The Blue Fairy Book*.) One of the most recent abridgments is a heavyweight oblong folio *Gulliver* with all four voyages recounted by Martin Jenkins and cumbrously illustrated by the former Children's Laureate, Chris Riddell (2004). By far the most imaginative tribute to Swift's work, though, is to be found in T. H. White's *Mistress Masham's Repose* (1946), whose distinction would qualify it for inclusion in this volume except that the author is represented below with another book [no.59].

-5-

THE GOVERNESS; OR, LITTLE FEMALE ACADEMY…
BY SARAH FIELDING (1749)

The first fight in English children's literature occurred between the young ladies of Mrs Teachum's Academy at the start of 1749. Mrs Teachum had given her nine pupils a bowl of apples while they were sitting in the arbour, but one of these apples was bigger than the rest and before long each girl was laying claim to it. Eventually Jenny Peace, the head girl, chucked the thing over the fence so that nobody got it and mayhem ensued: 'They fell to pulling of Caps, tearing of Hair, and dragging of Cloathes off one another's Backs …'

Well, the first fight is one thing, but the contretemps also takes place on the first pages of the first sustained piece of English storytelling intended for young readers: *The Governess; or, Little Female Academy, being the History of Mrs Teachum and her nine Girls, with their nine Days' Amusement*. Its date of 1749 is notable as being at the end of the decade which first saw children's books becoming a staple of the London booktrade.

A Thomas Boreman, selling what he called his 'Gigantick Histories' from a stall in Guildhall in 1741, is reckoned the pace-setter and he was followed by a heterogeneous body of competitors from other City booksellers who fell to devising little books for the home education of the children of the rising bourgeoisie. They produced one work of genius: the two volumes of *Tommy Thumb's Pretty Song-Book* (1744), the first English nursery-rhyme book (which now survives in only two copies of its second volume and none of its first), but no one up to 1749 had attempted an extended story until Andrew Millar published *The Governess.*

The idea of writing a novel was itself pretty new. *Robinson Crusoe* and *Pamela* had opened up the market and Henry Fielding, with *Shamela,* showed the potential for fun, which he followed with *Tom Jones,* the first novel which still speaks directly to twenty-first century readers. The point is germane, because Sarah Fielding, the author of *The Governess,* was Henry's much-loved sister, and an early 'blue-stocking', whom he had helped to the publication of an earlier novel for an adult readership: *David Simple* (1744).

The verve with which *The Governess* begins is, alas, not sustained. Repenting of their misdeeds, the young ladies (none over eleven years old) are persuaded by Jenny Peace to a programme of reform which is set out as a children's nine-day Decameron. We are given a little biography of each of them before they recount the life-stories that brought them to 'the Care of good Mrs *Teachum*' and these are interspersed with incidents, including a school-trip to a Dairy-House where they are able to 'eat plentifully of Cream, Strawberries, Brown-bread, and Sugar'.

The programme is most notable for including two independent stories which are told to the girls by Jenny with the approval of Mrs T. The first is 'The Story of the cruel Giant BARBARICO, the good Giant BENEFICO and the pretty little Dwarf MIGNON, and the second, which is specifically labelled 'A Fairy Tale', follows a long and meandering course involving a good queen, a wicked queen, an innocent princess and some good and bad fairies. Delightful as these may be to the pupils, who have little seminars on the moral lessons to be learnt from the tales, their significance to the historian is their connection back to the *contes* of the Comtesse D'Aulnoy, so that Jenny Peace is responsible for bringing the first invented fairytales to children's literature.

In its everyday setting and being 'calculated for the Amusement and Instruction of Young Ladies in their Education', *The Governess* anticipates both the intentions and the form of a generation of children's fiction that followed it. Not much is made of the one or two symbolic names given to some of the girls (Dolly Friendly, Lucy Sly) but the practice, that dates back long before Bunyan, is later used by publishers to exhaustion. Patty Prouds and Tommy Lovebooks dominate a scene – doubtless under the eye of Giant Benefico – where Enlightenment manners have taken over from the Calvinism of earlier years.

Commentary

The Governess was the most fully articulated children's fiction of the 1740s but may be seen alongside some earlier harbingers of storytelling being adopted as a means of sugaring the moral pill. In 1746 there was published the two tiny volumes of *A Christmass-Box* from Mary Cooper, the woman who also published *Tommy Thumb's Pretty Song-Book*. Its anonymous author is now known to be Mary Collyer, the wife of a printer who had fallen on hard times, so that she had taken up writing as a means towards subsistence. (Elsewhere she recorded a view of fiction as a help towards practical education.) That may be seen at its crudest in the *Christmass-Box*, which is arguably the first attempt at publishing secular moral fictions for children, although they amount only to short stories depicting childish shortcomings.

That such a purpose was in the air may also be seen in a manuscript story from 1744 that describes itself as *A Very Pretty Story to tell Children when they are five or six years of age*. This was written by a parson's wife, Jane Johnson, for her own children and is the culminating part of an immense and wonderful home-made set of pictures, cards and booklets that she designed as aids to their learning to read. (The whole set is now at the Lilly Library at Bloomington, Indiana, but the *Pretty Story* went walkabout on its own and is now at the Bodleian Library at Oxford which has produced it in facsimile.) For all the charm of Mrs Johnson's characters, there is a terrifying ruthlessness in the fate that she deals out to one of the four participants of the story, a boy who steals and lies in pursuit of a much-desired ivory horse seen at a local fair. Shifting to an Aulnoy-like fantasy, the good children are haled off to spend a happy time at the magical Castle of Pleasure and Delights while the errant youth is condemned to dwell in the hogsty – an experience which leads to his early death. The story met with approbation among its hearers however, for Mrs Johnson records that her two children 'took vast delight in hearing it told over and over again a vast many times'.

Curiously, much of *The Governess* also found its way into the evangelical fiction that emerged via Hannah More and others at the start of the nineteenth century. A leading activist was Martha Maria Sherwood who, in 1820, edited 'a revisal' of a story which she acknowledged as giving 'an exact and lively picture' from the youthful days of the grandmothers and great-grandmothers of contemporary readers. Fielding's text is begirt with much devotional material and Mrs Sherwood has suppressed most of the 'Fairy-tales, since fanciful productions of this sort can never be rendered generally useful'. (The first translations of the Grimm stories would appear a year later.)

–6–

THE HISTORY OF LITTLE GOODY TWO-SHOES
BY GILES JONES[5] (1765)

Online, the Oxford dictionary has it that 'a goody two-shoes' is 'a smugly or obtrusively virtuous person'. But in doing so it sadly maligns the personality of its first owner and its great Begetter.

She was Margery, bereft orphan of Farmer Meanwell and his wife. They had been hounded off their land by the rapacious Sir Timothy Gripe and, destitute and in 'a Place where Doctor James's Fever Powder was not to be had', they had both expired. Margery and her brother Tommy were left to sleep in a barn, living off what hedge-pickings they could find, and while Tommy was accoutred in a pair of shoes, poor Margery had lost one of hers.

5   However, authorship has also been attributed to Oliver Goldsmith or John Newbery.

Rescue came through Mr Smith, 'a very worthy Clergyman', who saw to it that Tommy was kitted out to be a sailor, while Margery was measured up for a proper pair of shoes. And thus it was that, with a cry of 'Two Shoes, Mame, two Shoes!' she paraded around the village 'and by that Means obtained the name of *Goody Two-Shoes*' or even of *Old Two-Shoes*'.

Mrs. MARGERY TWO-SHOES. 79

'See how he sits, a fancy rogue' relief metal cut (35x43mm.) of the dog Jumper on p.79 of *The History of Little Goody Two-Shoes.* London, for T.Carnan, 1783.

Further reference to etymologies will also yield the information that the 'Goody' bit had nothing to do with virtue, smug or otherwise, but was simply the local nickname applied to honoured village goodwives. Nevertheless, our Goody was good-hearted by nature and possessed of a remarkable resilience. For when the odious Gripe (who gets his comeuppance at the end) resumes his persecutions, she takes herself off to another parish, teaches herself to read, and sets herself up as 'a trotting Tutoress'. Armed with what sounds to be a heavy bagful of wooden letters, she tours the neighbourhood and teaches the village children how to read through a play-way scheme of her own invention. (Conservative pundits may be sorry to hear that it seems to be closer to look-and-say than synthetic phonics.)

Great Learning having thus been established as a means of social advancement, Little Goody's story rather fragments itself thereafter until Tommy's return, he having made a large fortune 'beyond Sea'. Random ideas, such as a ghost story to show there's no such thing, are briskly exploited, while irrelevancies such as Rules for the Conduct of Life, and a poem by Addison are interjected, giving the impression of a need to fill up pages rather than tell a coherent tale.

But, first published in 1765 (only one copy of which edition now survives), *Little Goody Two-Shoes* has had lasting fame. It can be seen as one of the first attempts to tell young children a story of contemporary life, while it is also the most celebrated original product of the London bookseller John Newbery, who did more than anyone else to establish children's books as a trade-able form of literature. (Between 1744 and his death in 1767 he published well over fifty of what are often scornfully referred to as 'juveniles', many going into multiple printings.)

Among these, *Goody* was a new phenomenon and was at once greeted as such by encouraging almost instant imitation. It also buzzed with a discursive energy that was typical of Newbery's book-making style. Indeed, a compendium in which it has just made a new and welcome reappearance with all its illustrations includes two other items from his list which well support that contention: *The Fairing*, from around the same date as *Goody*, a rackety, whirligig account of a visit to a fair, and *The Lilliputian Magazine*, a miscellany originating from 1751 [noted above in our *Gulliver* entry] when he attempted the first magazine for children.[6]

Jumbled up though Mrs Goody's progress might be, it carries many entertaining evidences of Mr Newbery's own involvement in the editing. There is a hectoring Introduction on social iniquities addressed to 'Children of six Feet high'. Opportunities are taken to plug other Newbery ventures, not least Dr James's Fever Powder, which might have saved Farmer Meanwell, of which he was sole agent, but other children's books such as the titles of those 'usually read by the Scholars of Mrs Two-Shoes' which were sold at his shop in St Paul's Churchyard. Coverage of her tutorial activities (assisted by a talking raven) make part of the book almost a reading-scheme in itself, while he takes great pleasure in drawing readers' attention

6   *Little Goody Two-Shoes and Other Stories; originally published by John Newbery.* Edited with an introduction by M.O.Grenby. (London: Palgrave Macmillan, 2013).

to the cuts ('by Michael Angelo in the Vatican at Rome'!). 'Pray look at him', he says of a dressed-up Tommy, or 'This is a fine hearse indeed' of what looks to be a very wonky vehicle.

And at the start he is urgent in addressing his work 'to all young Gentlemen and Ladies who are good, or intend to be good' assuring them that it will benefit those:

> Who from a State of Rags and Care,
> And having Shoes but half a Pair,
> Their Fortune and their Fame would fix
> And gallop in a Coach and Six.

Commentary

The authorship of *Goody* is unresolved with modest arguments supporting claims for the journalist brothers, Giles and Griffith Jones, and for Oliver Goldsmith. A coherence in the somewhat hectoring conversationalist style that typifies other Newbery publications also argues for the man himself being a controlling influence. Certainly, his variegated efforts to give child-appeal to his productions, from his famous first compendium of 1744, *A Little Pretty Pocket-Book* onwards bespeak an originality not possessed by the more earnest moralising of *The Governess* [no.5 above] and many successor stories in later decades. For some social critics of our times, his tendency to see Right Morals as a key to enjoying life with a Coach and Six rather than as a good in themselves has led to his being seen as a promoter of Thatcherite Enlightenment economics.

From the start the book was immensely popular. The rarity of all eighteenth-century editions is sufficient testimony of this, along with supplementary evidence of piracies, lookalike stories (such as the *History of Primrose Prettyface*) and its later history as a prompt for many variant uses, from alphabets of *Goody Two-Shoes* and picture-book versions, to plays and pantomimes. During the Second World War a miniature edition was published in a series of booklets for reading in air-raid shelters.

-7-

THE PARENT'S ASSISTANT
BY MARIA EDGEWORTH (1796)

Jane Austen was demonstrably influenced by her writing and Walter
Scott, who admired her Irish setting for *Castle Rackrent*, called her
'the great Maria'. Nowadays, though, Maria Edgeworth's greatness
is manifest chiefly in the jolt that she gave to the composing of
stories for children. She brought a new and unfamiliar humanity
to a genre which, at the end of the eighteenth century, was
dominated by a bevy of mostly female writers who, whatever
their tenderness, were manufacturing their fictions in the pill-
sugaring department.

Unmarried, she might be thought no better qualified than
most of these spinsters and didactic mammas at entertaining the
young, but that would be to discount both her parentage and her
experience. Born in 1767, she was the daughter of the Enlightened
and polyphiloprogenitive Richard Lovell Edgeworth, scion of
the Edgeworths of Edgeworthtown in County Longford and
ultimately the father of twenty-two children by four successive
wives. Being an early member of this brood Maria found herself,
from adolescence onward, both a step-sister and a nurse to them
and since both she and her father were keenly interested in new
ideas on education (they would jointly write the intelligent and
influential *Practical Education* of 1798) she both taught her siblings
and learned from them.

School slates were said to be a key factor in the composition
of Maria's earliest stories, for a story might be written on them,
read to whatever company of children might be present and
then revised in the light of their reactions. Such an oral origin
gave some of the tales from the first a natural speaking rhythm
while talk within the family (and she and her father often noted
children's turns of speech) would give an authenticity to the words
on the page. Take this reply of a bullying housemaid, telling a little
lacemaker to come back later for her payment:

Lord bless my stars! What makes people so poor, I wonders! [...] Call again ! Yes to be sure. I believe that you'd call, call, call twenty times for twopence.

Saved from drowning by a passing chimney-sweep. From an anecdote in 'Harry and Lucy. Part I' in *Early Lessons* Vol.I. Philadelphia: Robert Daesilver, 1823, facing p.31.

That's from 'The Birth-Day Present', one of the stories in the three volumes of Maria's first publication: the unappealingly-titled *The Parent's Assistant* of 1796. Its publication history is complicated but by the time a third edition appeared, in six volumes, in 1800, twenty stories in all had been printed. (Three very short tales for younger children were transferred to a new series of ten volumes called, also unappealingly, *Early Lessons*.) In choice of subject and in length they make up a varied bunch ('Old Poz' is actually a play) and their two longest, 'Lazy Lawrence' and 'Simple Susan', take something of the form of novellas rather than single-incident tales.

'Lazy Lawrence' is set in the vicinity of Bristol, where the Edgeworths had lived for a couple of years, and works on the contrast between Jem, a poor fatherless boy, whose purposeful energies fend off financial calamity, and the indolent Lawrence, whose directionless existence brings him to disaster and the bridewell. Formulaic though it be as a moral tale, it is saved from crassness by Maria's eye for details of daily life, for the more than formulaic depiction of character and by the sheer readability of her storytelling.

These virtues are yet more prominent in 'Simple Susan', which runs to two chapters and has a wider spread of characters. Once again we are in the countryside – this time 'on the borders of Wales' – and among village folk. Destitution is not now at issue so much as rescuing Susan's father, a tenant farmer, first from his being ballotted as a militiaman and second as a victim of unscrupulous actions on the part of a vindictive local lawyer. The tensions of that small drama are mirrored in the bad feeling that exists between the lawyer's daughter and the village children and her jealousy of 'Simple Susan' in particular. All would surely have gone ill were it not for the arrival of a new and beneficent squire and his family who take the role of *dei ex machina*. Susan is, of course, simple only in her unassuming demeanour, for she shows great determination and self-sacrifice in bringing about a happy conclusion, at one point of which Walter Scott was left able 'to do nothing but cry'.

'*The Parent's Assistant*' also saw the early arrival of little Rosamond in the famous story of 'The Purple Jar', with several tiny, insightful adjunct tales, including the wonderfully-crafted 'Birth-Day Present'[7]. But Rosamond, reckoned to be based on Maria herself, would not go away and found herself growing up in episodes interspersed through later story collections down to 1821, when she is on the brink of adolescence. (Victorian publishers sensibly brought the earlier chunks of her biography together in compendia.) The educational content remains – after all, the stories were intended to assist parents in guiding their children – but Rosamond never loses an attractiveness that makes her the first living character in children's literature.

---

7   Barbara Willard chose it for her fine racketty anthology, *Hullabaloo,* with jolly head-pieces by Fritz Wegner (London, Hamish Hamilton, 1969).

Commentary

Almost all Edgeworth's writings for, or about, children were published by Joseph Johnson, one of the booksellers around St Paul's Churchyard (it was he who, to her chagrin, imposed the title of *Parent's Assistant* on her early work). While she must have been one of his most profitable authors, as witness the multiple and confusingly organised editions of her stories put out by him and his successor, he played an important role in encouraging the spread of progressive, if not radical, ideas about children's reading. He was almost a father figure to Mary Wollstonecraft, whose rather forbidding children's book, *Original Stories from Real Life* he published in 1790 and he employed her as both reviewer for his journal *The Analytical Review,* and translator. For him she translated the three volumes of Salzmann's *Elements of Morality* and among the illustrators for that work, as well as for the illustrating of *Original Stories*, he commissioned William Blake. (He was also involved with Blake's abortive efforts to produce a trade edition of that thrilling work, *For Children: the Gates of Paradise.*) Despite that, Johnson seems to have had little interest in book illustration and, apart from a special edition of *The Parent's Assistant,* produced all her books with a sad typographic dullness. (The Americans did much better. A six-volume Philadelphia edition of *Early Lessons* of 1821-3 was furnished with many charming hand-coloured engravings, as exemplified on p.35).

–8–

THE SWISS FAMILY ROBINSON
BY JOHANN DAVID WYSS (1814)

In 1805 William Godwin, famous as a seeker after truth and political justice, became a publisher of children's books. His first wife, Mary Wollstonecraft, had died in 1797, leaving him with their daughter Mary (who would later run off with Shelley and compose *Frankenstein*) and a step-daughter, Fanny, from her liaison with Gilbert Imlay. In 1801 he married again – yet another Mary – and in 1805 they set up in trade as the French and English Juvenile Library in Hanway Street, just off the east end of Oxford Street.

Forever wobbly in its finances, the business nonetheless produced some remarkable books, including the Lambs' *Tales from Shakespeare* (1807) which has never gone out of print, and, likewise, the first translation of a work from Switzerland. This purported to be the journal of a pastor, shipwrecked in the Pacific with his wife and their four sons and left to fend for themselves on a deserted island, a work which it seemed only natural to call *The Family Robinson Crusoe*.

Godwin's devotion to truth however was somewhat compromised on the book's title-page where he declared that the text was 'translated from the German', which was not the case. Certainly it had been originally written in German by one Johann David Wyss and edited by his son in Zürich in two volumes in 1812 and 1813, but it had been immediately translated into French by a Swiss baroness, Mme de Montolieu, who had introduced sundry incidents of her own. In defiance of their title-page, the Godwins had, in fact, translated the first half of Mme de Montolieu's effort, thus initiating what was to become a textual history of Byzantine complexity.[8]

8   A judicious account is given by David Blamires in his *Telling Tales; the impact of Germany on English Children's Books 1780-1918* (Cambridge: Open Book Publishers, 2009).

Success nonetheless attended that first volume in 1814 and four years later the translation was completed and issued under the title by which it has been known ever since: *The Swiss Family Robinson*, and by 1824 when the Godwins went bankrupt, it had already got to a fifth edition. That was not the end though, for the book's popularity encouraged both Wyss's son, Johann Rudolf and Mme.de Montolieu separately, to tack on extensive continuations during the 1820s, and versions of these, rarely acknowledging any author at all and rarely following all the Swiss family's adventures as to either length or content, began to invade the English market.

The ground rules for this do-it-yourself Robinsonade required little of adaptors beyond a succession of quick-fire activities and encounters which brought the home-bound child readers of the nineteenth century face to face with a wild exoticism. The pastor is intrepid in taking his sons exploring across a richly varied topography of what is more or less an archipelago. As a super-Humboldt he can explain every species of animal, vegetable and mineral that they meet with and can turn his hand to anything from raft-making to the building of a staircase inside the tree which is the family's favourite abode. (His regular appeals to his Maker have tended to be skipped by readers and editors alike.) His well-behaved sons are given carefully differentiated characters and his wife is good for preparing a regular 'comfortable supper', sucking-pigs, say, or pigeons preserved in lard.

There has been much deprecation over the impossible, not to say farcical, range of flora and fauna on which Wyss allows his pastor to expatiate. Indeed, Frederick Marryat, who had been asked by his children to write a continuation of the (interminable) story, was so offended at its 'ignorance, or carelessness' that, in *Masterman Ready*, he created a similar narrative but '*based* upon truth' which he saw as a *sine qua non* for child readers. In so devising, he missed the central cause of the Swiss family's popularity which lay in the wild and diverse unpredictability of their adventures. Whether or not the events were introduced with an educational intention – looking after bees, say, or how to make candles, or the nature of cochineal – the speed at which one follows another propels the reader through the family's ten years of island life.

Towards the end the *dramatis personae* is increased by one when an English lady is found to have been also wrecked on one of the islands of the archipelago, she ingeniously sending up smoke signals and attaching a message to the leg of a visiting albatross. She is rescued and joins the company on the main island not long before a ten-tonne brig, flying the Union Jack, anchors in their Bay of Safety. This proves only to be a partial rescue since the pastor, his wife and two of his sons elect to stay on their now very comfortable island, founding the colony of New Switzerland.

Commentary

Although it only contained the first half of the final Swiss version, the Godwins' very readable translation continued to have a life of its own down to the 1840s. Subsequently it was used as the first part of some full translations although tracing the authors responsible for the second half is a vain exercise (see for instance the Godwins and A. N. Other in a handsome twentieth century edition, illustrated by T. H. Robinson, published by Oxford University Press). Other independent versions exist in the sort of confusion that may be seen in comparing two editions from the 1870s (precise dating is difficult). One, 'translated from the best original editions' by Henry Frith is given in fifty-eight chapters over 556 pages, while the other, 'a new translation from the original German', famously edited by the boys' author William H. G. Kingston, has eighteen chapters over 566 more expansively printed pages. Both editions carry many black and white illustrations but these are not by a single artist but put together from stock blocks from various sources. Indeed, a history of the illustrations devised for the dozens of texts in English editions runs from the anonymous and casual to the specific and artistic. The Godwins prepared attractive full-page etchings by J. Dadley after H. Corbould while an edition in the post-Second World War Treasure Library (in fact an early venture by George Weidenfeld) had illustrations in monochrome and colour by Mervyn Peake.

-9-

HOLIDAY HOUSE
BY CATHERINE SINCLAIR (1839)

Escape from Enlightenment ethics and the constrictions of the moral tale was a long time a-coming for the young story-readers of the first decades of the nineteenth century. The tales of Maria Edgeworth and the compendium of stories that made up another bestseller, *Sandford and Merton,* by a fellow Rousseauist, Thomas Day, dominated the fiction market, only to be joined by the doctrinal promotions of the Evangelicals. The Religious Tract Society, founded in 1801, would grow to be the most prolific publisher of children's fiction down to the First World War (we shall meet them again here before long).

Voices were raised in objection, primarily to a prevalent Gradgrindism, long before that pedagogue stood before his blackboard in Coketown. The most specific complaint was that of Edgar Taylor in his aggressive introduction to what may be accounted one of the most truly enlightened children's books ever: his 1823 translation of the *Household Stories* of the Brothers Grimm. Deploring that 'philosophy is made the companion of the nursery' in what he sees as 'an age of reason and not of imagination' he commends both the antiquity of his tales as a sign of the longevity of the appeal of storytelling and confirms this by remarking that his whole project was inspired by the 'eager relish' with which his first efforts were greeted when told to a group of 'young friends'.

For all his espousal of their narrative imagination however, the arrival of the Grimm tales are only a waymark in the progress towards individual fictional inventions. Walter Scott, who had corresponded with the Grimms, was an enthusiast for Taylor's work and had, from *Waverley* onwards, broken a path for the nineteenth century novel to follow, but it took another sixteen years before 'a series of tales' should echo Taylor's criticism and reiterate his strictures by pointing to those wishing 'to stuff children's minds with facts like a cricket-ball' rather than open them to 'appeals

to the heart and excitements to the fancy'. The sentiment comes
from a friend of Scott, the Scottish author Catherine Sinclair, who
includes it in her Preface to *Holiday House*, the 'series of tales' that
was published in Edinburgh in 1839.

It may not be a coincidence that Sinclair attributes the origins
of her endeavour to paint 'that species of noisy, frolicsome,
mischievous children, now almost extinct' to a like experience
to that of Edgar Taylor: the telling of the stories to 'a circle of
joyous eager faces listening with awe' to the exploits of her chosen
heroes, the siblings Harry and Laura. One can easily imagine how
she captured her young audience by retailing incidents of startling
misbehaviour with an amused tolerance rather than a heavy-
handed moral.

Two colour-printed
lithographs by Standidge
& Co. (63x75mm. each)
on plate paper, facing p.49
of *Holiday House*. London:
Simpkin, Marshall and Co.
nd. ca. 1856. The designs
are unrelated to the Sinclair
holographs.

The two children, whose mother is dead and father gone abroad, are looked after by a wondrously indulgent uncle whose tolerance of the frolicsome extends even to Harry setting fire to the house while Laura is cutting off her curls with a pair of scissors. He is inclined to sing comic songs and proffer advice on the lines of 'Never crack nuts with your teeth', an attitude that must have caused grief to the disciplinarian Mrs Crabtree, a forbidding 'governor of the nursery' in all senses, whose job it is to administer both verbal and corporal correction to her charges. About half way through, the narrative swerves into what will be a tragic mode, not long after Uncle David has told a 'nonsensical story about giants and fairies'. That in itself may be seen as a reversion to an older moralism, for it is much akin to the 'fairy tales' we have noted as being invented by Jane Johnson and Sarah Fielding a century before and it is quite a surprise as coming from a jolly uncle who had been inclined to mock the Gradgrinds and 'that old vixen, Mrs Crabtree'.

Kindly and pious Frank, the siblings' much-loved elder brother, now takes something of the focus, leaving school with honour and becoming a midshipman in the Royal Navy. The children are growing up, discovering to their surprised regret, that they now miss Mrs Crabtree, who has been dismissed. And the concluding chapters take on scenes all-too typical of genre fiction related to the wounding and death of Frank. There is much bravery in facing up to the inevitable and what looks to be an authorial cop-out was wisely abandoned. (At least one edition of the story seems to have been sanctioned by Sinclair in which a medico *ex machina* produces 'a powder' which effects a cure for the injured boy.) Sad though the unavoidable conclusion may be, *Holiday House* remains a harbinger of the freeing of children's novels to enter 'the age of imagination'.

Commentary:
There can be little doubt about the oral origins of the stories of *Holiday House*. In 1968 Sotheby's sold the family copy of a first edition of the book, given by Sinclair to her sister Margaret and including thirty-one holograph drawings by the author, and

perhaps others, pasted in to face appropriate passages. All but one relate to the romping stories and from the captions it may be seen that Harry and Laura were originally Tommy and Caroline and that some re-jigging of the narrative must have taken place before publication. The drawings were never used in printed editions, the earliest being unillustrated, with pictures appearing in the third printing of 1839. These consisted of a frontispiece and five inserted plates, with two images per plate lithographed by W. H. Lizars and coloured by hand (as such they count as very early examples of lithography being used in children's book illustration). Over ten thousand copies were sold before Sinclair's death in 1864 (the 'revised edition' with the happy ending came out round about 1862) and from about this time down to at least 1939 many variant editions appeared, mostly from the firms of Ward, Lock & Co. and Blackie & Son who issued immense series of 'classics' for the school-prize market. In 1972 the book was published in a series of Hamish Hamilton Reprints with a fine introduction by Barbara Willard.

–10–

THE SNOW QUEEN
by Hans Christian Andersen
(published in The Shoes of Fortune, 1846)

Hans Christian Andersen has not been very sympathetically treated by his British audience, whether translators, publishers, or children's literature cognoscenti. There is for a start something demeaning about calling his children's stories 'fairytales' – which implies a sloppiness inherent in the term and also a relationship to the anonymous traditional tales recorded by such as Charles Perrault or the Brothers Grimm, which are anchored in no definitive form. Andersen himself divided his tales into '*Eventyr*' a barely translatable term (like the German '*Märchen*') which implies fantasy or 'tales of wonder' or even of 'magic realism' and '*Historier*' or plain 'stories' perhaps with greater attention paid to the real world.

What matters anyway is that these are literary creations, influenced by German writers, like E. T. A. Hoffmann, and their '*Kunstmärchen*'. Some of them may look like traditional tales but the specifics of their plotting and their language are to be respected as individual work – a tenuous requirement in the history of Andersen in English.

The first stories appeared in Copenhagen in 1835 as *Eventyr fortalte for Børn,* a tiny booklet of 'wonder tales told for children' which put down a marker for all that was to follow. One from that book was 'Little Ida's Flowers', an everyday sentimental concoction of Andersen's own; the other three were highly differentiated tales that drew their form from tradition but worked it in a fashion characterised by Andersen's voice and no one else's.

Consider 'The Tinderbox': the plot lies close to the Grimms' 'The Blue Light' (which owes something to 'Aladdin') but elements like the three dogs with their great eyes are pure Andersen as is the colloquial voice of the storyteller. When the old witch pulls the soldier out of the subterranean chambers she demands the tinderbox from him. 'Snik, snak!' he says, 'if you won't tell me what you want it for I'll get my sword and chop off your head':- ' "*Nei!*" sagte Hexen. Saa huggede Soldaten Hovede af hende. Der laae hun …' (' "No!" said the witch. So the soldier chopped off her head. There she lay! …') Similarly unprecedented, in 'The Princess on the Pea' (usually politely translated as '… and the Pea'), is the farce of the king going down to open the town gate when the princess arrives, or the queen's sceptical remark about the princess being genuine: 'Huh, we'll see about that'.

It took eleven years for Andersen to reach England, by which time some thirty-seven *Eventyr* had been published in Denmark, most also having been translated into German. Mary Howitt was responsible for the first selection as *Wonderful Stories for Children* – ten of them, translated from the Danish, replete with errors and misspelling the author's name as 'Anderson' on the title-page (by no means for the only time). One of the ten also turns out to be only half a story, since it wrenches an excerpt out of 'The Flying Trunk', its hilarious original. Worse was to follow, since in that same year four more translations appeared, all of which were translated from the often defective German. They stand witness to a continuing succession of versions down to the present time, which entirely fail to capture the colloquial accents of the original Danish. (Caroline Peachey, who published the second of the 1846 tranche, went on to eventually translate sixty-one stories whose unsatisfactory and clumsy retelling is often still used today.)

Despite several of his novels being written for adult readers (and vast quantities of poetry, plays, travelogues etc.) the world-wide fame which Andersen has enjoyed is entirely due to the 'canon' of his '*eventyr og historier*'. By no means all of these were '*fortalte for Børn*' and it has been estimated that less than half represent the core of his genius as a children's storyteller. They are a greatly varied bunch from the bare two pages of 'The Princess on the Pea' to what are, in effect, novellas, such as the fantasies of 'The Little Mermaid', 'The Marsh King's Daughter' and 'The Ice Maiden'.

'The Snow Queen' is not to be confused with that last story and has been seen by many to be the acme of Andersen's storytelling genius. It was first published in Copenhagen in a collection of '*New Stories*' in 1844 and was one of the stories translated into English (from the German) by Charles Boner in one of the unsatisfactory 1846 volumes, *The Shoes of Fortune*. Andersen called it 'a wonder-tale in seven stories' and it hales from some un-analysable wellspring of fantasy. To say that it tells of the quest of a little town-girl, Gerda, to find and release her friend Kay who has been abducted by the Snow Queen, would be the crudest of descriptions but to venture much further would endanger the numinous quality of the story.

Gerda's journey takes place through what amounts to an anthology of chapbook adventures, all coloured by Andersen's touch. (I was going to qualify that as 'inimitable' except that its influence on the children's stories by Oscar Wilde is unmistakable.) The religiosity of a tract is mingled with episodes involving animal helpers, a beneficent fairy, a prince and princess out of a *conte de fée*, ruthless gypsy highwaymen and two Wise Women of the North. Over all, there looms the power of the Snow Queen, the White Goddess of Reason. It is Andersen's most ambitious and resonant story and stands as a rare example of the imaginative power of children's storytelling.

Commentary

Although Andersen wrote several novels for adults (the English translations of *The Improvisatore* and *Only a Fiddler* in 1845 paved the way for the arrival of the *Eventyr* a year later), his only long story for children was *Lykke-Peer* published in Copenhagen in 1870. It is not part of the 'canon' and never appeared in book-form in Britain but only as a serial in *Aunt Judy's Magazine* (as Luck-Peter) from March to September 1871, translated by Edward Bell and illustrated by A. W. Cooper. Such is Andersen's importance in English children's literature however that the above synopsis of 'The Snow Queen' has been given here to highlight one of his longer, and perhaps his best, story which may certainly be reckoned as much a novella as a fantasy tale.

Calling one of his three autobiographies *The Fairy Tale of my Life*, Andersen anticipates the huge literature that would dwell on his rags-to-riches story. Few critical sources in English, however, expatiate on his anglophone legacy: the immense succession of translations in both magazines and in book form that may appear as either collections or selections, or as private press and picture-book versions of individual stories. The Andersen bi-centenary in 2005 saw several new studies among which *Ugly Ducklings?* by Viggo Hjörnager Pedersen, published by a University Press in Andersen's home town of Odense, undertook a full-scale description of the translations of story collections. My own slender *HCA and His Eventyr in England* (Wormley: Five Owls Press, 1982) attempted a more critical analysis which included picture-book versions.

-11-

THE CHILDREN OF THE NEW FOREST
BY FREDERICK MARRYAT (1847)

Captain Marryat or, sequentially, Midshipman, Lieutenant, Commander, Marryat came somewhat late to writing novels and later still to writing novels for children. His run of rollicking sea- and adventure-stories for a mainly adult readership had almost run its course by 1840 when his children who, it seems, were fans of *The Swiss Family Robinson* requested papa to write them a sequel to that unexhausted kaleidoscope of desert island life.

Papa was appalled. Consulting one of the many varied translations that were coming on the market at that time he saw no good in it: 'Amusing' it may have been but 'it does not adhere to the probable, or even the possible, which should ever be the case in a book, even if fictitious, when written for children'. The want of seamanship was predictable since that occurred regularly in naval writings, but it was 'the ignorance, or carelessness' in matters concerning animal, vegetable and topographic affairs that forbade any attempt at continuation. So he decided to write a fresh account 'in the same style'.

That turned out to be *Masterman Ready; or the Wreck of the Pacific,* the first volume of which was published by Longman in 1841. Marryat saw it as a bow at a venture, promising more if it was successful, and in 1842 two further volumes showed that that had been the case. For all its accuracy though, it shares with its forerunner unappealing moments of piety and didacticism whose continuance in print down to the twentieth century tells more of the moribund nature of 'reward-book' publishing than of a genuine affection on the part of the readers.

Contemporary success, however, pointed a way forward for Marryat as writer and with the publication of *The Children of the New Forest* in two volumes in 1847 he aimed for a less formulaic children's book. It opens in 1647 at the time of the escape of Charles I from detention in Hampton Court, and his presumed flight southwards to the coast.

'The Burning of Arnwood' etched frontispiece (63x95mm.) after Frank Marryat for Vol. I of *The Children of the New Forest* London: H.Hurst nd [1847].

Ruthless Levellers are after him, burning down, in the course of their hunt, the mansion of the Royalist Beverley family at Arnwood, near Lymington, on the off-chance that the King is hiding there. That might have been the end of the story since no quarter was offered and it was assumed that the four Beverley children, all orphans, died in the immolation. But, thanks to that vital ingredient in adventure stories, an overheard conversation, the children are rescued just before the Levellers arrive and are taken into the forest to live with the Beverleys' faithful retainer, Jacob Armitage.

The four children, two boys, aged thirteen and twelve, and two girls, eleven and eight, are biddable learners, despite their rank, and, taking their harbouring in a forest cottage as a bit of a game, adapt themselves to their suddenly restricted fortune. Jacob Armitage, on whose wits they are entirely dependent, is a bit of a Masterman Ready in his bluff practicality, but he is not given so regularly

to homespun theology and his forest skills are the more easily
passed on to his pupils than would be those of the old mariner.
As time goes on, through the development of the children's native
abilities, the cottage retreat becomes something of a successful
smallholding – Edward, the eldest, becoming a great deer-stalker
and thus producer of saleable venison; his brother, Humphrey, a
natural property developer and creator of a little working farm.

The tension between the need for secrecy and some necessary
contacts with the world beyond the cottage eventuates in
Edward's accidental encounter, in the role of Armitage's grandson,
with a newly appointed Parliamentary Intendant of the Forest
and his daughter. Through this the plot opens out to some side-
adventures, with villainy and bloodshed, rather in the style of those
experienced by Mr Midshipman Easy in Marryat's best-known
novel. While not quite a *deus ex machina*, the Intendant, who had
been a friend to Cromwell, proves more sympathetic than the
latter's more fanatical followers, and will ultimately become a
saviour of the Arnwood estate and Edward's father-in-law to boot.

The problem that confronted Marryat in the planning of the
story was the dozen years that passed between the burning of
Arnwood and the Restoration during which the children of the
New Forest all grow into twenty-year-olds, while the political
tensions more or less disappear. There is some sleight of hand in
the galloping history of those years, but the fiction is saved at
its final, Hollywood-style denouement, by what has sustained it
throughout: Marryat's success in the portrayal of his maturing
characters.

Commentary

Michael Sadleir, the bibliographer of Victorian novels, published
evidence that the publisher, Hurst, originally planned to issue
Children in parts at the start of a proposed 'Juvenile Library'
of Marryat's stories, but was probably defeated by the author's
difficulty in keeping up with the press because of his unreliable
health. Nevertheless, at the close of the second volume the 'Library'
was announced (along with glowing puffs from press reviews) and
gave as its purpose the promotion of Marryat's writing in view of

'the few works [that have] appeared calculated for the amusement and instruction of the Juvenile Classes'. A customary criticism follows: 'The attempts made have rarely been successful; either the works having been written in such a puerile style as not to be relished by children who have been released from the nursery; or failing on the other hand, by entering into the discussion of subjects as much above their comprehension as unsuited to their taste.'

The two-volume presentation was soon reduced to a single volume after which began a long succession of new, abridged, and foreign editions down to the present time. The first edition was illustrated with twelve etched plates by the author's son, Frank, and once out of copyright it was open season for illustrators. Of particular note are the plates by Val Biro for the post-war edition in Weidenfeld's 'Heritage Library' series.

The 'Juvenile Library' continued with *The Little Savage* (1848) which was not only illustrated by Frank but completed by him since Marryat died before the two volumes were finished.

-12-

THE KING OF THE GOLDEN RIVER OR
THE BLACK BROTHERS
BY JOHN RUSKIN (1851)

The Pierpont Morgan Library in New York (now glorified as a 'Museum & Library') holds among its treasures a small manuscript miscellany compiled, written, and illustrated by the ten year-old John Ruskin in 1829. He gave it the title of *The Puppet-Show or Amusing Characters for Children* and it consists of a page-by-page series of drawings, mostly copied from book illustrations with texts invented by the youthful author. Some fifteen of these texts are accompanied by drawings which are very creditable copies of the etchings that George Cruikshank made for the first English translation of the Grimm brothers' *German Popular*

Stories (1823-6). Later in life Ruskin would refer to these tales as 'my favourite old stories' and would estimate the etchings as 'unrivalled in masterfulness of touch since Rembrandt'.

That evidence should be sufficient to confirm his love of fantasy tales (as well as his gifts as a draughtsman) so that when, in 1840, a young lady of thirteen years besought him to talk to her about fairytales he forthwith decided to invent an example for her. She was Euphemia Gray, the Effie Gray whom he would disastrously marry eight years later, and he fulfilled his promise in 1841 while on a recuperative stay at a physician's house in Leamington Spa.

The King of the Golden River, or the Black Brothers, which was the outcome, carries the subtitle: 'a legend of Stiria'. That cod-origin refers to a mountainous part of eastern Austria which Ruskin seems never to have visited, and the topography of the story owes more to his delight in the French and Swiss Alps. By naming the three brothers who are the leading participants in the 'legend', Hans, Schwartz, and Gluck, Ruskin enhances the teutonic flavour, although the naming of characters is an infrequent practice in the tradition.

Untraditional too is the bi-partite structure of the story with calamity followed by redemption. The drama is initiated by a visit to the brothers' farm by the South-West Wind Esquire. They farm in the fruitful Treasure Valley whose fertility comes from the Golden River, so-called because of the way its upper falls catch the light of the setting sun. Unfortunately though, Hans and Schwartz are selfish and brutal characters and thanks to their maltreatment of their unknown guest they bring disaster upon themselves and devastation to their land.

Moving to a city on the other side of the mountains, they seek to restore their fortunes by turning goldsmiths (drinking up the profits as they go). This leads to Gluck's encounter with the King of the Golden River through whom the age-old motif of task-fulfilment is introduced. As tradition demands, the wicked are defeated by their own selfishness and Gluck the virtuous (*Glück* = fortunate, or lucky) succeeds and restores the Treasure Valley to its former glory.

We do not know what Effie thought of this story and it

remained as a manuscript for ten years up to the all-too-brief period before she fled to the arms of Ruskin's friend Millais. It was published for Christmas in 1850 (dated 1851) by George Smith, who was also in the process of publishing the five massive volumes of Ruskin's *Modern Painters* and getting going with the influential *Cornhill* magazine. He called upon the *Punch* caricaturist Richard Doyle to illustrate it, sloppily in some places but with particular success in his portrayals of the South-West Wind and the King himself. (A reprint was soon called for and these first two printings are notable for Doyle giving the South-West Wind a nose like a small post-horn. Whoever this may have offended, Doyle was prevailed upon to provide the gentleman with a regulation nose from 1859 onwards.)

In the canon of imaginative children's literature in Britain, *The King of the Golden River* has a notable status. For sure, Comtesse d'Aulnoy pioneered the making of original fairytales (however over-written) and the Grimms inspired similar ventures by such writers as Brentano and E. T. A. Hoffmann in Germany, who in turn played into Andersen's imagination, but there had been no equivalent attempt in English. Ruskin thus had to find a voice to tell Effie his story and he does this in a prose that is immediately readable and also, importantly, read-aloud-able. True, there are over-lush scenic descriptions ('far beyond, and far above all these, fainter than the morning cloud, but purer and changeless, slept, in the blue sky, the utmost peaks of the eternal snow') but the dramatic action holds attention, the characters are broad-brushed as tradition demands, and the verbal interchanges, especially with the crusty old gentleman who inundates the Treasure Valley and with the tetchy King himself, are vastly entertaining.

Commentary

The book's British publication in the nineteenth century passed from Smith to George Allen, set up in business by Ruskin himself to issue his writings. The Doyle illustrations remained as definitive, although other artists supplied pictures for US editions, such as J. C. Johansen for a Rand McNally publication (1909) which included notes on Ruskin's 'Companions of St George' with their eight point declaration. I first read the story in Volume 3 of my mother's set of the *Children's Encyclopaedia* (ca.1903), illustrated partly in two colours by S. B. Pearse and blithely announcing at the start that the story 'is not quite all given here, but the little left out does not make any difference'. Several editions, dressed as either story books or picture books, have appeared in both Britain and the US since the war, the most notable being that from Edmund Ward (London, 1958) with fine line drawings by Charles Stewart. It also has a two-page glossary explaining some Victorian phrasing: pertinacious = obstinate; recruited his hardy frame = gave him fresh strength, etc. As this book goes to press, a further new edition appears, suggested and executed with drawings in full colour by Sir Quentin Blake. His interpretation of both characters and landscape have the indefinite suggestiveness necessary to the quasi-folktale and although he abjures Doyle's trumpet nose for the South West Wind Esquire he gives him a wonderful hat.

-13-

THE LITTLE DUKE
BY CHARLOTTE YONGE (1854)

'*The Codger*' would not really have done as the title for a magazine designed for young ladies of an Anglican (not to say High Anglican) persuasion in 1850, but it was how its designers used to joke about it among themselves. '*The Maiden's Manual*' wasn't much better, but when, on the first of January 1851 *The Monthly Packet* put in an appearance its acceptance was such that it lasted for the next forty-three years. It was left to a writer in the 1950s, John Rowe Townsend, to wonder whether the title was 'a bit unfortunate'.

The editor of this almost privately devised venture was the twenty-eight year-old Charlotte Mary Yonge, much under the influence of the eminent tractarian John Keble, who was incumbent at a parish near to her home at Otterbourne in Hampshire. Never to be married and devoted to forwarding church affairs, she had already had experience of the little Sunday magazines that were encountered by the village Sunday-school children whom she taught and she was right in thinking that there was no equivalent periodical for girls of the higher classes and indeed, *The Monthly Packet* can be seen as the first magazine to be edited for such a young person readership.

Lithographed frontispiece (100x130mm.) by Schenck & McFarlane, Edinburgh, after J[ane] B[lackburn] for *The Little Duke* London: John W. Parker, 1854.

Similarly, *The Little Duke* may be seen as the first in what was to be a long, long line of serial stories for children throughout the century which would usually graduate to book form, if at all, after establishing themselves through their magazine subscribers. It began publication in the very first number of the *Packet* and appeared as a printed book with lithographic illustrations after Jane Blackburn in 1854.

Family reading in history had brought Charlotte early to a love of the subject and it is encouraging to find that *The Little Duke*, her first solo in historical fiction, avoided what would become such hackneyed loci as Elizabethan England or the Civil War and was set among the Nordic adventurers who had only recently established their rule over territory in northern France. Her interest was probably piqued by the knowledge that the first invader to establish a leadership was the (probably Danish) Rollo who converted to Christianity at Rouen towards the end of the ninth century. He was the father of William Longsword, whose murder through treachery at the start of *The Little Duke* brought home to the Normans the fragility of their hold on their new land. His eight year-old son, Richard, may be a figure to inspire loyalty but hardly to mount any campaign of revenge.

The book has the structure of a novella, with the turning point being where King Louis of France claims the wardship of the orphan duke and carries him off to his court at Laon. Here the king's false bonhomie turns more severe, exacerbated by the intolerance of his bitchy queen, and it is only through the resourcefulness of the boy's Norman guardian that an escape is effected. Yonge is firm in her differentiations between the political antagonists while Richard's boyish impetuosity is shown in his care for the king's ailing younger son and opposition to the cruelties of his spoilt elder brother.

The escape engenders retaliation from the French and allied tribes which is foiled by aid from the Normans' ancestral comrades, the ruthless – and heathen – Danes. Their victory with the tables turned on the king, whose family now become hostages to the Normans, allow Yonge to develop a theme that has been present throughout the book: the power and virtue of Christian forgiveness as against historic barbarities. Richard did indeed become 'the Fearless' and his son 'the Good'. The breed reverted to type however in his great grandson: William the Conqueror.

Commentary:

The first edition of *The Little Duke* was published by John W. Parker & Son and illustrated with several powerful images in monochrome by Jane Blackburn (whose natural history drawings impressed Beatrix Potter). They were printed by the Edinburgh lithographers Schenck & McFarlane and were joined by some contrasting tinted drawings in 'the outline style'. The copyright later passed to Macmillan who reprinted the story many times with anonymous wood-engraved plates somewhat similar to those of Blackburn. A post-Second-World-War edition, illustrated by Jennifer Miles, was published by Oxford University Press in 1959 and a Macmillan edition was used for a paperback in the Jane Nissen reprint series in 2001.

Yonge's bestseller, beloved of adolescent girls (Jo is found weeping over it in *Little Women*), was *The Heir of Redclyffe,* which was written and published almost simultaneously with *The Little*

Duke. Two other shorter novels for children were *The Lances of Lynwood* (1852) set in the reign of Edward III, and *Countess Kate* (1862), a tale with a Victorian contemporary setting which was notably reissued in 1948 with illustrations by Gwen Raverat.

-14-

THE ROSE AND THE RING
BY WILLIAM MAKEPEACE THACKERAY (1855)

Hallowe'en is now seemingly the herald of the Christmas season and by the time you get to the evening of January 5th of the following year you are probably spent-up and partied-out. In earlier days, however, that Twelfth Night on the 5th was the culmination of less protracted and probably intenser merriment. Cakes could be made for the occasion through which a king and queen of the evening would be chosen and partying guests might imitate characters from pantomime or from comic picture-sheets: Alderman Gobble Guzzle, say, or Miss Tittle Tattle.

Thus it was that Thackeray, holidaying in Italy early in 1854, was prevailed upon 'to draw a set of Twelfth-Night characters for the amusement of our young people'. Their naming, though – King Valoroso, the Countess Gruffanuff etc – encouraged him to give them a more extended life and they coalesced into the larger cast of what he referred to as 'a nonsensical Fairy Tale with pictures'. He wrote it and designed its illustrations during February and March, 1854 ('It is wonderful how this folly trickles from the pen', he noted in his diary) and it was published for Christmas by George Smith – publisher also, as we have seen, of *The King of the Golden River* – as *The Rose and the Ring; or, the History of Prince Giglio and Prince Bulbo, a Fire-side Pantomime for Great and Small Children* and attributed to Mr M. A. Titchmarsh.

The conjunction of festivity and theatrical extravaganza that lie behind Thackeray's pleasure in writing his story resulted in the first literary farce in children's literature (although from medieval

times down to the productions of Grub Street and Seven Dials'
chapbooks there had been beguiling but by no means literary
delights on offer). The plot is triggered by the traditional device,
best known from '*The Sleeping Beauty*', of a grumpy godmother,
the Fairy Blackstick, wishing 'a little misfortune' at the christening
of the heirs to the kingdoms of Paflagonia and Crim Tartary.
Misfortune, though, was already lying in wait for them anyway by
her earlier gifts to their parents of a rose and a ring which were
endowed with the magic of making their possessors beautiful and
desirable to all who might behold them.

Betsinda meets Mrs Gruffanuff and the Princess Angelica with bun. Line block
by the author (70x85mm.) lower page 20 of *The Rose and the Ring,* London:
Smith, Elder, and Co. 1855.

The complexities of the misfortunes that do indeed ensue are
tumultuous beyond the powers of summary (several errors occur
in the first edition owing to the author himself not recognising
erroneous relationships). The two princes are matched against
two princesses, Angelica and Rosalba (AKA the foundling Betsina)
in realms that suffer from usurping monarchs; confusions arise
through rose and ring falling into unworthy hands; Rosalba, a
heroine throughout, is equal to bashing Bulbo with a warming-
pan and facing lions in Crim Tartary's arena. Fairy Blackstick is
never far off, however, and her magic assists the pantomime to a

just conclusion, not least through some larks with a door-knocker which are the best jape in the book.

Michael Angelo Titchmarsh plays his part however as master of ceremonies. He keeps his audience in mind with occasional comment ('I hope you do not think there was any impropriety with the Prince and Princess walking together in the palace garden …'); he draws attention to the spirited caricatures that he has drawn to accompany his text ('Would you not fancy from this picture, that Gruffanuff must have been a person of the highest birth?'); and he augments the text itself with rhymed running-heads at the top of each page-opening as an authorial commentary: 'Other girls, the author guesses, / Like to flirt besides princesses'. Such close integration of story and meta-fictional devices places *The Rose and the Ring* among those few children's books, such as Kipling's *Just So Stories,* that *sui generis,* lose flavour in any other version.

Commentary

The book had a notable history before ever it was published. The 'trickling from the pen' would seem to have taken place as a formal manuscript, accompanied by delightful pen and watercolour caricatures, undertaken for the pleasure of Thackeray's daughters, Annie and Minnie, who were with him in Italy. Present also was the daughter of his American friend, William Wetmore Story, who had been ill over the festive season and at whose bedside Thackeray read the book's episodes as they were written (see the account by BA and Felix de Marez Oyens in *Be Merry and Wise* pp. 248-255). The manuscript was revised and augmented for publication, when the running-heads were added, and the drawings reversed by Thackeray onto wood blocks for the engraver, inevitably losing the fluidity of the originals. The loose sheets of the manuscript, some of which had disappeared, were later bound up as an album and the whole beautiful object became another children's book treasure at the Pierpont Morgan Library in New York who produced a facsimile of it in 1947 with a detailed description by Gordon N. Ray. Many adaptations and abridgements appeared once the book came out of copyright, with America again responsible for the most elaborate version, that printed for the Limited Editions Club in New York for Christmas 1942. Thackeray's drawings were redrawn by Fritz Kredel and hand-coloured under his supervision; the running-heads were given as sepia-printed sidenotes.

-15-

THE HUGGERMUGGER STORIES
BY CHRISTOPHER PEARSE CRANCH (1855-6)

THE LAST OF THE HUGGERMUGGERS (1855)
KOBBOLTOZO (1856)

Anchored in the roads off Portland the good ship *Nancy Johnson* still awaits a signal to join the fleet of American children's classics. Such forerunners as Hawthorne's *The Golden Age* and *Tanglewood Tales* of 1852 and 1853 may have been among the first in the line, but they were merely arty retellings of classical stories. Before Little Jacket (alias Jackie Cable) went a-sailing no American contemporary had ventured into writing an original fantasy.

Little Jacket was ship's boy on a merchantman making for the East Indies, but after rounding the Cape she was caught in a storm and, like some memorable ships before her, was wrecked on an unknown island. This proved to be the homeland of a race of giants, the Huggermuggers, the last two members of which, childless, were living out the last of their days. Unaware of the kindly temperament of these huge creatures, the shipwrecked survivors took the chance to bring to an end what might have been a very short story by getting themselves providentially rescued by a passing vessel.

After landfall in Java, Little Jacket meets Mr Zebedee Nabbum who is on commission from Mr P. T. Barnum to collect animals and other exotica for his circus and a plan is hatched to return to the island and abduct the giants. On arrival, though, the hunters are disarmed by the affability of their prey and foresee a possibility that the Huggermuggers will make a voluntary trip with them back to Portland, New Hampshire. But all is frustrated by a dwarf shoemaker on the island, Kobboltozo, who, hating the giants, is able to activate a curse which brings about their deaths.

The tragedy (something of a surprise in the annals of fantasy) was delicately handled and prompted an immediate sequel. This was *Kobboltozo* in which Jackie and Zebedee return to the island a year or two later only to find its remaining dwarfish inhabitants also in a state of decline thanks to the dictatorial proclivities of the island's shoemaker. Much of the history is recounted to our heroes by Stitchkin the tailor, and, later, Hammawhaxo the carpenter, and it dwells on Kobboltozo's fruitless endeavour to gain the stature of the vanished giants while, in fact, dwindling away to nothing.

The author of these two engaging and original novellas was one Christopher Pearse Cranch, who confessedly 'had been born (and educated) with a diversity of talents, wooing too many mistresses'. He was the middle child in a family of thirteen (one of his sisters was to become T. S. Eliot's paternal grandmother) and early fell under the influence of Emerson. That detracted from his chances of being accepted as a Unitarian minister and he was drawn to both poetry and landscape painting. In both those capacities he resembled a lesser Edward Lear, turning out light verse and caricatures of genial freshness.

His two children's books stemmed from a lengthy stay in Europe, where he got to know the Brownings and Thackeray, and they originated as stories told to two of his own four children which gives them a natural storytelling timbre. Good humour abounds (Kobboltozo is but the best of his gift for inventing names), there is no attempt at a crashing moral lesson; and the pathos in depicting the passing of his kindly giants is truer than the factitious deaths so common in Victorian literature. It should also be noted that he is one of the first to replicate a distinctive American vernacular, especially in the ruminations of Mr Nabbum. (Here is Zebedee reflecting on a means to possibly pacify a captive giant by giving the critter *Rum*: ' "I guess he don't know nothin' of ardent sperits – [we can] obfuscate his wits – and get him reglar boozy …" ') Both books are also illustrated with Cranch's own excellent illustrations and pictorial initials, all of which he drew on the wood, the blocks being shipped home for the American engravers. He seems to have had a hope for publication in England since a footnote in the first book gives a definition of clams 'for the benefit of little English boys and girls, if it should chance that this story should find its way to their country'.

Alas, it did not.

Commentary

The Last of the Huggermuggers (but not *Kobboltozo*) gets only two lines as a 'border-line' case in Jacob Blanck's bibliography *Peter Parley to Penrod* (1938) and the claim that these kinds of fantasy stories were not encouraged by American publishers is borne out by the fact that there are but three entries for such things in Blanck before we get to *The Wizard of Oz* in 1900. The stories were reprinted on a few occasions but had only a short life and Cranch's poetry for children found place only in the pages of the periodical *St Nicholas*. A projected collection, '*Father Gander's Rhymes*' (a pre-echo of Denslow's *Father Goose*) never materialised. He did attempt to get one other story published, *The Legend of Dr Theophilus*, but that disappeared from view only to re-emerge in the 1980s. It was edited and published alongside its predecessors in a scholarly edition (which does no justice to Cranch's fine illustrations): *Three Children's Novels by Christopher Pearse Cranch.*[9]

9   Ed. Greta D. Little and Joel Myerson, Athens & London: University of Georgia Press, 1993.

–16–

TOM BROWN'S SCHOOL DAYS
BY 'AN OLD BOY' (I.E. THOMAS HUGHES) (1857)

The Tally-ho coach from Islington got to Rugby round about page ninety-six of this saga that was to instigate a literary genre that has lasted down to the present time. Certainly it was not the first 'school story' by any means (Robert Kirkpatrick, the bibliographer of the genre, has traced at least sixty predecessors, an early example of which appears above at item 5) but the *School Days* – later *Schooldays* – of Tom Brown had an impact not only as a more extensive narrative but as a document of some social and educational import.

The time taken for Tom to get to Rugby is devoted to laying the groundwork to show his early years as the 'robust and combative' son of Squire Brown in the Vale of the White Horse (a chalk monument whose scouring would form the subject of a novel by Hughes in 1859). It is an almost Kiplingesque paean to the history and local gods of this Berkshire landscape and derives, as do the two parts of the schooldays, from Hughes's own experience and his affection for the story he has to tell.

Rugby School itself, as portrayed round about the year 1833 when Hughes first went there, possessed a degree of *laissez-faire* barbarity which, far from being glossed in the story, forms one of its necessary elements. The reader is shown Tom arriving at an institution where much of the governance is undertaken by the pupils themselves through systems of customized hierarchy with the sixth form prefects, or praeposters, in charge, waited upon by younger boys, or 'fags', and wedded to a pre-Darwinian philosophy of the survival of the fittest. Not a teacher is to be found in the events of Tom's first day at the school, when he is at once befriended by a semi-relative, East, with whom he is to share a study, is involved in a sixty-a-side football match, cooks sausages for tea, acquits himself well in singing a solo in the common-room, is tossed in a blanket, and finally gets to bed.

From this point on the story proceeds in episodic form, singling

Tom's first exploit at football. Unsigned wood
engraving (155x95mm.) after Arthur Hughes from a
1902 Macmillan ed. of *Tom Brown's Schooldays*.

out for the most part japes and pranks and sporting endeavours,
as well as the famous scene in which the bully Flashman and
his gang roast Tom over the common-room fire. All the time,
though, it builds on an awareness of the presence of The Doctor
as a controlling influence: Dr Arnold, the headmaster of five years
standing, who was bringing a measure of humane conduct into
the traditions and whom history now adjudges the great reformer
of the public schools, most of which, in Tom's day were sorely
in need of a like authority. Arnold, indeed, is the only adult to

play any part in the teaching process (entirely devoted, to the mystification of today's young readers, to construing Greek and Latin classic texts). It is, though, Arnold who perceives Tom's cheerful irresponsibility and, through the second part of the book, is instrumental – through placing him in charge of a delicate new boy, George Arthur – in bringing out his natural strength of character.

Commentary:

Robert Kirkpatrick in his *Encyclopaedia of Boys' School Stories* (2000), noted above, also points out that the importance of Hughes's book lies in its being 'first to consolidate the foundations of the public school story, and second to popularise the genre as a whole'. (Nor does he neglect to note the further boost given by Farrar's *Eric; or Little by Little* which appeared the year after *Tom Brown* and, despite its 'overwrought sentimentality', had almost as long a publishing history.) An American edition of *Tom*, as *School Days at Rugby*, was published in the same year as the English one by Ticknor & Fields of Boston, and the first illustrated edition with wood engravings by J. D. Cooper after Arthur Hughes (no relation) and Sydney Prior Hall came from Macmillan in 1869.

–17–

THE WATER-BABIES: A FAIRY TALE
FOR A LAND-BABY
BY CHARLES KINGSLEY (1863)

Chimney-sweeps, eh? Isn't it all about sending boys up chimneys to sweep the soot down? Didn't they change the law because of it?

Well … not exactly. For sure Kingsley hated the practice, but his climbing-boy first came to mind when he was visiting the uplands of Airedale and saw all the dark lichen growing down Gordale Scar; 'Why,' says he, 'it's just as if a chimney sweep had slid down there on his backside'. So when, a bit later, Mrs Kingsley remarked that he had not yet written a story for his youngest child (his three older ones had had *The Heroes*) he remembered the slide down the Scar and straight off sent Tom and his master, Grimes, to sweep the chimneys of Harthover Place at four o'clock in the morning.

But that was not the start of a social tract. Kingsley the Realist gives us a Tom who takes hunger and beatings as 'the way of the world' and looks forward to 'the fine times coming' when he too will be a master, sitting in a pub and knocking his own apprentices about. It is Kingsley the Parson who is troubled. For Tom had never been taught to say his prayers. And, when the boy takes a wrong turning among Harthover's maze of chimneys and ends up in the pretty white bedroom of Ellie, the daughter of the house, he cannot identify the sad picture there of a man nailed to a cross: 'some kinsman of hers perhaps who had been murdered by savages'.

Knocking over the fire-irons in his confusion, Tom wakes the household and must needs make off through the bedroom window, down a tree, and away across Harthover Fell, under pursuit. As he speeds across the Pennine moors and, eventually, down Lewthwaite (i.e. Gordale) Crag to the secluded valley of Vendale[10], so Story turns into what Kingsley designates Fairy Tale.

10   Opinion veers as to where Kingsley had in mind, with Arndale, off Wharfedale, a good contender. William Mayne, a lover of the book, set several of his *Earthfasts* series and other books in a Vendale that was mostly Swaledale.

Realist and Parson join forces to produce what is a wild, self-indulgent, satirical, serio-comic fantasy unique in the annals of children's literature.

A narrative axis does exist. Exhausted by his escape, Tom bathes in the Vendale stream, drowns, and is transformed into a water-baby. As such, he travels down-river to the sea where, with many fellows, he plays under the seemingly benign rule of the sisters Mrs Bedonebyasyoudid and Mrs Doasyouwouldbedoneby. But Tom is a recidivist misbehaver and is eventually persuaded that he must purge himself of his ill-nature by travelling to the Other-End-of-Nowhere: going where he does not like, doing what he does not like and helping someone whom he does not like. The tutoress who encourages him to this decision is none other than the little girl Ellie from Harthover who has herself died in a seaside fall while arguing the toss about the existence of water-babies with a professorial companion (probably a caricature of Thomas Henry Huxley).

For her sake Tom makes his journey – she thus becoming a further aspect in the book of the presiding 'Eternal Feminine', Goethe's '*ewig weibliche*' – the Irish woman, the undersea Dames, and Mother Carey, 'making things make themselves'. As Tom suspected, he is brought to confront and share in the release of his former master who has been imprisoned in a chimney-pot by the vengeful fairies. He is sent off to keep the crater sides of Etna properly swept and Tom is united with Ellie with the prospect of leaving water-babydom and becoming a great man of science.

Such a plot-line looks factitious (or even barmy) but exerts a consistent fascination through Kingsley's use of it to parade a gallimaufry of his loves and prejudices. Before Tom ever gets to Harthover we have divagations on limestone springs and the topsy-turvy architecture of ancient family seats. With his flight across the fells we have a paean on the beauty of the high hills and before we get to the backstairs that lead to the end of the story we enjoy the author's ragbag opinions (learned, satirical, comical) on anything from salmon rivers and Irish gillies to an assault on rote-learning that is still relevant today.

Without doubt the book's eccentric structure owes much to

Kingsley's liking for Rabelais with his digressions and piled-up lists (among the multiple evils that fly out of Pandora's Box are Popes, Unpaid Bills and Tight Stays). At the same time this natural history of water-babies is shot through with references to Darwinian disputes – Kingsley's admiration for the *Origin* is noted in the second edition of that book, where his awe is credited to 'an eminent author and divine'. So much diversity and obscurity hardly make for a coherent read – and certainly not for the five year-old 'little man' who is its addressee. But it is all held together by the rolling periods of the author's rhetoric. What Queenie Leavis (no less) called the 'rich brew of words' of this secular sermon carry a winning conviction and Edward Lear, thanking Kingsley for the story, said as much when he assured him that he believed every one of them as true.

Commentary

A first version of the story was serialised in *Macmillan's Magazine* between August 1862 and March 1863 and its conversion into book form later that year saw substantial revision taking place, most significantly perhaps in the introduction of 'the Irish woman' who is a further manifestation of 'the Eternal Feminine'. The first edition was of small quarto format whose green cloth binding was decorated with a gilt image based on a design by Kingsley himself and book-collectors will know too that an *Envoi* leaf at the start of the book was cancelled during its printing, giving rise to an 'issue-point'. The second edition followed rapidly but was reduced to an octavo format with the binding decoration changed to a gilt pictorial oval. This was much to the taste of Charles Dodgson, whose *Alice* was in production via Macmillan at this time and he copied the design feature in that book.

The early editions were embellished with two rather dull lithographic plates by Noel Paton but also with six very attractive historiated chapter initials by Robert Dudley. A fully illustrated edition with a hundred drawings by Robert Samber became standard for the publisher and was used over and over again over many years and in several formats. When the text came out of copyright dozens of artists attempted to illustrate its eccentric subjects, the only ones to achieve a measure of success being William Heath Robinson in 1915 and Harold Jones in 1961. There were a number of American editions but the book looks to have been deeply unfathomable to both its illustrators and readers in that country.

-18-

ALICE'S ADVENTURES IN WONDERLAND
by 'Lewis Carroll'
(i.e. the Rev. Charles Lutwidge Dodgson)
(1862-1865)

'Oh dear,' said Alice, 'Why can't they leave me alone? Ever since that nice Mr Dodgson told about my falling down a rabbit-hole I've been harried by everyone. To hear some of them talk with all their theories you'd think I was married to Peter Pan.'

'Just look at it! Mr Barrie's play was such a jolly romp and so different from what people expected and the children loved it. And he didn't let on for years what the actual words were in the play and then along came people called Theorists, grinding the story between the upper and the nether millstones of their own fanciful ideas. It's easy to sympathise with poor old Peter.'

'So look at me! None of you can ever know what happened on that picnic trip, just as you don't know what happened on Mr Barrie's Black Lake Island where he got some ideas about pirates and the like. (Why, they're still arguing about the weather on the day we set out on that boating trip from Oxford in 1862.) Even dear Mr Dodgson has kidded them on about our *rowing* the boat when we were really only trying to cox – and we weren't much good and the bowsprit *would* get mixed up with the rudder sometimes.

'It was certainly like a dream. Along we went with Mr Dodgson rowing in the front and trying to tell us a story at the same time and old Mr Duckworth at stroke egging him on and wobbling with the oars for laughing out loud. And then there was the picnic when Mr Dodgson wasn't exerting himself so much, except with the kettle. (That was when poor Bill the lizard got kicked up the chimney and we all fell about over Mr D's attempt at an Irish accent.) He may have been a bit exhausted on the way home jumbling through that stuff about the caterpillar and the croquet and trying to sing a song about Beautiful Soup.

'Still, it was a wonderful afternoon and who can blame me for wanting him to write it all down for me? But that wasn't the same thing, was it? We rather missed Mr Duckworth even though he did turn up in the story as the Duck, down the hole swimming in my pool of tears with Edith and Lorina, but it wasn't so spontaneous despite those funny rhymes about the crocodile and Father William and that twisty mouse's tale.

Chapter-opening by the author (185x125mm.),
as designed for all four chapters, from p.40 of
the facsimile of *Alice's Adventures Under Ground*.
London: Macmillan and Co. 1886.

'It made a lovely book. He wrote it all out for me, doing the drawings himself, and we used to look at it a lot at home, remembering that happy afternoon. But it got shown around too (I wasn't quite sure why) and then, before long, he and Mr Tenniel destroyed everything. It stopped being our afternoon on the river and turned into the world's recreation ground for all those Theorists.

'Just look at it all now, a hundred and fifty years after the book came out for everyone to look at. Certainly he buffed up the messy bits towards the end by putting in things like the tea-party in the garden when he had us all living in a treacle-well, and the trial of the Jack of Hearts, and that sweet Cheshire cat, but it all got so clever. People began *using* it, quoting it in textbooks about money, say, or writing great big annotated explanations of what it all meant. (Well, why *is* a raven like a writing desk?) And once it came out of copyright all the artists wanted to show how superior they were to Mr Tenniel (look at that pretentious Mr Moser, or weird Mr Dali – but I *did* like funny old Harry Furniss's drawings). And don't let's talk about what happens on the teevee after nine o'clock in the evening or in the Google Swamps. Perhaps I will go to Black Lake Island and set up house there, away from it all, with Peter Pan.'

Commentary

The story of the making of *Alice's Adventures in Wonderland* has been told so often that it has become a bore but must needs be reiterated here. The tale began as a series of comic inventions told to Alice Liddell and her two sisters on a boating picnic down the Thames in 1862. The Rev Charles Dodgson, lecturer in mathematics at Christ Church, Oxford (where Alice's father was Dean) did write it out for her, as she requested, and the manuscript with his original drawings, now in the British Library[11], has become one of the most famous documents in the world.

11   In later life, married to a Mr Hargreaves and in some financial straits, Alice had it auctioned and it was sold to an American dealer. After some to-ing and fro-ing it was eventually bought by subscription in the United States and returned to Britain in gratitude for the stand against Nazism in the Second World War.

A year or so later, Dodgson asked to borrow the manuscript back so that he might convert it to a publishable book and, after much tribulation, especially over his choice of illustrator, the *Punch* artist, John Tenniel, the first edition came out in 1865. Its author was given as 'Lewis Carroll', a re-working of Dodgson's first two names: Charles Lutwidge, and it was published on commission by Messrs Macmillan – 'on commission' meaning that production was paid for by the author while the publisher merely had a share in the takings, if any. As it happened though, Tenniel objected to the printing of his commercially wood-engraved pictures by the Oxford University Press and the book was immediately withdrawn and a new issue was produced, printed by Richard Clay, dated 1866 but issued in time for Christmas 1865. A few copies of the earlier printing had escaped and are almost all now to be found in the Rare Books Departments of libraries. A purist intention to destroy the remaining copies was changed and the sheets were, frugally, sold to Messrs Appleton of New York for an American edition. Needless to say, the takings eventually were, and continue to be, substantial.

Study of the illustrative and textual changes made between the original 'picnic' version of the story and that smartened up for public consumption was facilitated by Dodgson when he published a near facsimile of the manuscript as *Alice's Adventures Underground* in 1886.

-19-

JESSICA'S FIRST PRAYER
BY HESBA STRETTON[12] (I.E. SARAH SMITH) (1866)

City life does not feature strongly in the canon of children's fiction. True it may be a site for family stories or tales of the fantastic, but until recently, few well-known books enter directly into the lives of children within an urban environment. The fame attendant upon, say, the episodic chapters of *The Children from One End Street* (1937) stems more from its unexpected appearance at that date than from a strong engagement with its urban theme.

A precedent may have been set by Kästner's *Emil and the Detectives* [see no.53 below] but to find substantial evidence of children directly involved in the life of a city one must turn back almost a hundred years before that to the shoals of tracts put out by concerned religious and other bodies in both Britain and the United States. The consequences of the industrial revolution had produced a vast expansion in the numbers of the urban poor and the more or less homeless to which the authorities were slow to react and it was left to 'non-government-associations' to do something about it. Their motives were often dictated by a religious purpose: and an 'inward mission' to bring the Gospel to the ignorant. This could not help but be associated with educative and social measures, especially the establishing of Sunday schools backed up by the publishing of, ultimately, millions of tracts which might both serve to preach understanding to the poor or rouse the consciences of their 'betters'.

The Religious Tract Society, founded in 1799 as a non-denominational publisher, would eventually become the most prolific producer of reading-matter for children in the nineteenth century. Its tract production was colossal, aided by its professional skills at distribution and from mid-century onwards the range of

12 The *nom de plume* was an invention drawing upon the initials of Sarah and her four siblings to make up H E S B A as forename and the family's neighbouring town of Church Stretton for the surname.

publications expanded from short tracts to tract-stories and novels, picture books (some of distinction in terms of production), and magazines, among which would later figure both the *Boys* and the *Girls' Own Papers.* Successes were legion, but few matched that of *Jessica's First Prayer,* which was serialised in the Society's family magazine, *Sunday at Home,* in 1866 and, soon after, published as a modest book. It was to become one of the century's bestsellers, clocking up sales of over two million copies, along with translations into at least fifteen languages. (Tsar Alexander II ordered copies to be placed in all Russian schools, an order rescinded by his successor when Stretton wrote a story critical of Russia's persecution of the Christian sect of the Stundists.)

The prayer in question, uttered by the street-waif Jessica when first she hears of God as a being who will listen to the appeals of the world is: 'Oh God I want to know about you. And please pay Mr Dan'el for all the warm coffee he's give me'. For Jessica, shoeless and 'in a tattered frock, scarcely held together by broken strings', has first appeared one morning at the coffee-stall run by Mr Daniel under the arch of a London railway bridge and he has become her benefactor to the extent of a mug of coffee and a bun on every Wednesday morning. By accident however, she has found him to be also caretaker and pew-opener of a chapel, a mysterious building where the gentry turn up on Sundays and where many strange words are spoken and where she is entranced by the 'sweet music' of an organ. It is irresistible to her and she regularly secretes herself behind a door to visit the services until she is discovered by the minister's two young daughters who become the instruments of her salvation.

There is a winning pathos in the portrait of the innocent waif (grown men were said to weep over her) but Stretton, who had experience of the city poor, has a double purpose. The tract story may be read by children as a sort of Evangelical *Goody Two-Shoes* even though Jessica is a far more passive victim than Margery, but the central point lies in Jessica's involuntary revelation to Daniel of his sinfulness as a hypocrite servant of the Lord, preoccupied with his own financial betterment. In a final crisis he is able to save and eventually adopt the wholly neglected child – a humble acceptance of true Christian principles. One wonders, however, what may be the thoughts and feelings of the top-hatted gentlemen and the ladies in their rustling silk dresses who flock to hear the minister in Daniel's pews.

Commentary

Jessica followed a rural tale, *Fern's Hollow*, as Stretton's second book and both gave promise of a writer with something to say and the capacity to do so with professional skill. Her direct experience of observing contemporary urban life and the neglect of city children inspired three immediate successors to *Jessica*: *Little Meg's Children* (1868), widely considered her finest book, *Alone in London* (1869), and *Pilgrim Street; a story of Manchester life* (1870), all illustrated with sympathetic wood engravings after the artist A. W. Bayes. Unmarried, Stretton lived a long life as a social campaigner (she was one of the founders of the National Society for the Care of Children) and died in 1911. A close study of her work by Elaine Lomax was published in 2009: *The Writings of Hesba Stretton; Reclaiming the Outcast*.

Jessica's First Prayer, with a companion waif-story, *Froggy's Little Brother*, by 'Brenda' (Mrs Castle-Smith) was edited by Elizabeth Thiel in Palgrave Macmillan's 'Classics of Children's Literature' series (2013). An exhibition on *The Religious Tract Society as a Publisher of Children's Books* had an extensive catalogue by BA and Pat Garrett (Hoddesdon: The Children's Books History Society 1999), which notes many variant editions of *Jessica*.

-20-

JOURNEY TO THE CENTRE OF THE EARTH
BY JULES VERNE (1867)

Whatever happened to the giant shepherd? He is encountered towards the end of this *voyage extraordinaire* at one of its most exciting moments, although much to astonish both participants and readers has already occurred.

The expedition began after Professor Lidenbrock of Hamburg discovered a runic manuscript by a fourteenth-century Icelandic

A forest of mushrooms . Full page wood engraving after Riou.

alchemist, Arne Saknussemm, reporting how he had descended to the centre of the earth. Eccentric, but of iron determination, the professor decides that he too will attempt the journey and – to the horror of Axel, his student nephew – will take the boy off as travelling companion. And it is to Axel that we owe the travelogue that follows.

Professor Lidenbrock is a 'learned egoist' and 'a selfish scholar' ('In Germany there are one or two professors like this' says his nephew, tongue-in-cheek) but as such he is a stickler for detail and it takes sixteen chapters of the book's forty-five (none of them long) to get the explorers to the extinct crater of Snaefells in Iceland, down which their descent must begin. En route they have hired Hans, a strong, silent Reykjavikian, who will prove to be a practical force upon whom the whole enterprise will depend.

On 28th June – for Axel is a scrupulous diarist – they go down the central chimney of Snaefells in 200 foot stages as their double rope allows, landing at the bottom 2800 feet down after ten-and-a half hours. From here they enter the first of an underground system of tunnels, created perhaps by lava flows, which, first of all seem to run horizontally rather than vertically, and second of all must be followed at junctions without certainty as to their continuance. Utter darkness prevails, provision against which the professor had brought along two Ruhmkorff lamps, a recent invention using a battery and an induction coil to produce light. (How the devil old Saknussemm got along is not explained.)

The big surprise occurs on 9th August when, after several dangers have been overcome, including water deprivation, the party discover a gigantic underground sea, lit from above through what is assumed to be an electrical origin 'like an aurora borealis'. It is here that most of the rest of the adventure takes place. The ever-capable Hans builds a raft from fossilised wood, the product of ancient, now sunken forests, and by erecting a sail, borrowed from a blanket, they make use of subterranean winds to explore the extent of the lake or sea. It turns out to be gigantic and also subject to maritime storms so that confusion surrounds Axel's record of their progress; a confusion enhanced by the appearance of living creatures in the sea recognisable to the professor as an icthyosaurus and a plesiosaurus, doing battle among the waves.

Nor is that all. In three chapters that were added to the 1864 first edition of the book in 1867, the adventurers make landfall not far from where they had originally sailed and explore the littoral. They cross a beach piled high and wide with the bones of many saurian creatures and then find first the preserved corpse of a man and then, in a forest beyond, a herd of grazing mastodon being guarded by a shepherd twelve feet tall. To a twenty-first century author that would be enough to provoke a whole new volume on the lines of Conan Doyle's *Lost World* of 1912. But Axel and the professor pass up the opportunity and sail in some terror further down the coast.

Here it is that they find again the initials of Saknussemm carved into a rock, pointing up a passage which may allow them to continue their long-interrupted descent. However, a rockfall has blocked the way and they decide to apply gunpowder to it from their stores. And that precipitates the final climax to the story resulting in our heroes being caught up themselves in a volcanic explosion which blasts them out of the crater of Stromboli, just off Sicily, and into the final pages of the story.

Commentary

The first of the *voyages extraordinaires* was *Five Weeks in a Balloon* (1863), soon followed by the present book which marks the sealing of Verne's collaboration with his publisher, Julius Hetzel. It was published as a book almost simultaneously with Hetzel's founding of his periodical, the *Magasin d'Éducation et Récréation* in which many of its successors would be serialized. Despite the implication that the journal was for children, Verne's 'journeys' are reckoned to be as much for adult readers as for children, a view of scholars who do not care to see themselves engaged with anything puerile and foreclosing on the idea that the young will find the adventures 'educational and recreational' in a highly beneficial way. (One must concur though with a common opinion among the cognoscenti, that, while science often plays an active part in the plot-making, the *Voyages* are in no sense forerunners of works of science fiction.)

The book was rapidly translated into English, although that and several later efforts have been deplored for mistakes and omissions. Robert Baldick's 1965 version appeared as a Puffin Classic and William Butcher's of 1992 was in the fully introduced and annotated form of Oxford's 'World's Classics' series. The French edition of 1867 included fifty-two, often very dramatic, wood engraved plates and a headpiece after Edouard Riou.

As befits a fantasy which, with its dependence on the facilities of a nineteenth-century world and the developing ideas about prehistory, there is a great imaginative appeal to the *Journey*, even though it took the travellers nowhere near the centre of the earth. At the same time, it will not do to question too closely coincidences allowed by the author or the provisioning of an expedition undertaken with no knowledge of the terrain or the supplies that may be needed. Above all, it would be nice to know, as the final explosion released the waters of the sea into an underground chasm, what became of the shepherd and his flock of mastodons.

-21-

LITTLE WOMEN [PART ONE]
BY LOUISA MAY ALCOTT (1868)

We meet them at the start in conversation about their plans for Christmas. They are Margaret, customarily Meg, Josephine, customarily Jo, Elizabeth, customarily Beth, and Amy, who is just Amy. The burden of their exchanges is how to manage the festive season with Father away, a pastor among the armies of the Civil War, with Marmee hard-pressed to run the household and the girls with barely a dollar apiece in their savings. The ensuing dialogue brings out the differing characters and mannerisms of the sisters, whose ages descend from Meg's fifteen to Amy's twelve.

Privations of the time are a constant through much of the book as the author's observation pulls back to show the different ways in which they acquit themselves through the year following that Christmas, at the end of which Father returns from the war. To begin with, insights into their character are framed by a reference to Christian's adventures in one of their favourite books, *The Pilgrim's Progress* – the impulsive Jo, for instance, besting Apollyon as she succeeds in conquering a righteous anger (one of the few occasions when the focus on domestic relations is intruded upon by sermonising). Following the establishment of good relations with the wealthy Mr Laurence in the house next door, social events begin to loom. His orphaned grandson Laurie, met at a dance, becomes a regular visitor; he and his tutor, Mr Brooke, organise a boating party, Jo has a story published and, towards the end, Meg is involved in a love affair with Mr Brooke which will end happily but inspires the wrath of rich Aunt March.

These and many other domestic incidents are portrayed with a directness and a zest which was wholly new in the century's tales of family life, although a forerunner might be seen in the graphic, but moralising, little sagas by Maria Edgeworth. The freshness of plotting and dialogue owes much to the fact that they derived from the 'queer plays and experiences' of Alcott and her sisters in their own very fraught childhoods. Furthermore, although it was not known at the time, her career as a writer was not as slender as it may have seemed for it included a substantial oeuvre of lurid romances written for the dime-novel trade under the name of A. M. Barnard.

On publication by Roberts Brothers of Boston under the perceptive editorship of A. M. Niles, who knew Bronson Alcott, Louisa's much-loved but feckless father, *Little Women* had an instant success. It was greeted as something new among stories written for girls, with Jo the tom-boy an early emblem for the feminist movement. Niles was keen to ride the wave of demands for a sequel and as a result, Alcott drew further on the resources that were behind the first book and within a year *Little Women, Part Second* appeared to like acclaim. (The success was replicated in Britain where the work was taken on by Sampson Low and it was they who designated the second part *Good Wives*). Their edition of the next volume in the series, *Little Men* (1871), came out two months before the Boston one to try to pre-empt competition in view of the lack of copyright agreements; *Jo's Boys*, the final sequel, regarded by Alcott as 'not a child's book' followed in 1886.

Commentary

The first part of *Little Women* was illustrated by Alcott's sister May, but the drawings were much disparaged for their amateurishness and the second part was undertaken by the professional Hammat Billings although he was not there acknowledged. The book and its successors proved a model for a succession of 'imitations', mostly with their heroines starting life as orphans. Niles led the way soon after *Little Women* was published with Sarah Chauncy Woolsey writing *What Katy Did* under the name of Susan Coolidge. (It was a book that seems to have been more popular in Britain than in North America.) Other examples are noted below in the entry on *Anne of Green Gables* [no.41] below.

-22-

THE RUNAWAY
BY ELIZABETH ANNA HART (1872)

Clarice Clavering, fifteen years old, is walking ruminatively in the garden of her substantial country home on the edge of London. Her mother is dead, her father is 'something in the City', whence he travels each day by train, and her chief companion is her governess, a pleasant enough lady but 'of few original ideas, no fancies, a reserved manner, and a well regulated mind'.

As an ardent maiden when we meet her, excited by Walter Scott's *Woodstock*, Clarice is dissatisfied with her genteel life. 'If only anything would happen' she thinks and, instantly on cue, there is a rustling in the shrubbery and something does happen as a beautiful, if tangled, little Olga emerges on the path:

> ' 'My goodness', cried Clarice. 'What is it?'
> 'It's me', said the girl, naturally ungrammatical at such
> a moment.
> 'Oh do hide me; you will won't you? Oh, please do' '.

Thus begins Clarice's longed-for adventure, as she smuggles Olga into her bedroom and becomes complicit in her plan to escape to Scotland. It seems that her parents live in India, where her father is a colonel in a Highland regiment and, rather than stay with her grandmother, who lives in a castle in Scotland, she had been sent to a boarding school in Yorkshire. It was not quite Dotheboys Hall for girls but she hated it and had run away, although, being a scatterbrain, she had got on the wrong train and had ended up hiding in the garden of Clarice's suburban home down south.

Scatterbrain does not fully summarize thirteen year-old Olga's intrepid but provocative determination to do things her way and this story of her secret stay in the Clavering household amounts to a succession of crazy escapades – pretending to be a ghost, disguising herself as a schoolmarm, climbing on the roof – that put at risk Clarice's comradely efforts to hide her. At the same time, Clarice's trust in Olga's tale is compromised when she learns that an agony column in *The Times* is advertising a reward for the apprehension of a servant girl who has absconded with money and jewels from a school in Yorkshire, thieveries which may correspond to similar possessions in a bag that Olga is carrying. How can Clarice remain loyal to the girl for whom she has conceived a great affection while avoiding telling lies or denouncing her as a thief?

Irrepressible and violently rejecting her reputed dishonesty, Olga persists in madcap exploits ('Of course I ought not to have done it' she remarks after one episode 'one never ought to do fun – but it was delicious'). The reader comes to wonder at the ingenuity of her various contrivances and how Clarice's dilemma may be resolved until, in a tremendous climax, which involves the almost simultaneous arrival of police ('This here go – though an uncommon rum go – is of no manner of use …'), a magistrate, and, in timely mode, Olga's Papa. Wrapping it all up, a telegraph boy brings news of the apprehension of the other runaway, the Yorkshire servant girl, for whom Olga has been mistaken.

There are perhaps few readers today who have come upon *The Runaway* or know anything of its author, Mrs Elizabeth Anna Hart. It was first published by Messrs Macmillan in the year that they also published *Through the Looking-Glass and What Alice Found There* (1872) and, as I hope may be seen by the above brief synopsis, it shares with that book a lightheartedness and an inventive delight in, as Olga puts it, 'doing fun' which is wholly at odds with the reputation of Victorian writers for children as dealers in evangelism and doom. (An unworthy thought strikes that Mrs Hart may have been couching a lance against Charlotte Yonge, who nevertheless, as we noted in the introduction, approved of the book).

The craftsmanship of the story, its pacing, its convincing household scenes, the credibility and differentiation of its characters are such that one may also wonder why it fell from grace. Indeed, it may still be entirely forgotten had it not been for the intervention of that great artist, Gwen Raverat, who had loved the book as a child and who was responsible for persuading Macmillan to bring out a new (very slightly altered) edition in 1936. This she illustrated herself with a plethora of superb wood engravings which place the book in the top rank of illustrated stories for children. Macmillan relinquished rights to it in 1953 when Duckworth were able to issue a new edition and Persephone brought it into the twenty-first century in 2002.

Commentary

The first edition was published as 'by the author of "Mrs Jerningham's Journal" ' which was a novel in verse, the same authorial designation being given to several other novels by Mrs Hart. (This one begins with an almost Olga-like Mrs J lamenting her too early marriage to a rather stuffy gentleman. Her rather brazen flirting with a guards officer comes to be much reprobated, causing Mr J to flee abroad, but all is finally resolved and, like Trollope's Lady Laura the she embraces respectability.)

Raverat's editing of the original text (which is the likely form now in which the book may be encountered) was not damaging and hardly seems to have been necessary. She shortens Clarice's ruminations on the romantic past (mentioning Harrison Ainsworth's Boscobel ("Have all girls read that quaint and enchanting volume?") which had only come out in 1871) and there is a crack about Papa's 'mysterious avocations ... from which the City article in *The Times* results'. The cutting of the third stanza of the poem on page 76 is no loss.

Raverat also illustrated several noted books for children, two with colour wood engravings: *Tales by Hans Christian Andersen* (the first four of the canon, 1933) and H. A. Wedgewood's *Bird Talisman* (1939). Fine wood engravings were also cut for Kenneth Grahame's *Cambridge Book of Poetry for Children* (1932) and pen and ink drawings for Eleanor Farjeon's *Over the Garden Wall,* Virginia Pye's *Red-Letter Day* (1940) and Charlotte Yonge's *Countess Kate* (1948).

–23–

THE PRINCESS AND THE GOBLIN
BY GEORGE MACDONALD (1872)

The three great pioneers of fantasy stories for children, not only arrived on the scene within a year or two of each other but the third, George MacDonald, was closely associated with his two fellow-writers. 'Uncle Dodgson', as well as photographing the family several times, gave the children the manuscript of *Alice* to read just after he had finished it; Charles Kingsley was a contributor to the magazine *Good Words for the Young* which MacDonald edited from 1870 up to its closure in 1872.

It was in that monthly periodical that four of his own fictions were serialised, *The Princess and the Goblin* being the third and coming out as a book on its conclusion. As a fantasy it differs markedly from *The Water-Babies* and *Alice*, which are pretty crazy examples of the genre, for MacDonald was much influenced by the German *Kunstmärchen*, of such as Novalis and Hoffmann and he owned up to de la Motte Fouqué's *Undine* as being his favourite. These were by no means crazy but might be seen as extensions of traditional wonder tales and might subsist as allegories or as an author's invention of 'a little world of his own' albeit one abiding by its own consistent laws. (You won't find such in *Alice* or among Tom's jumbled adventures.)

The venue for the story is a countryside among mountains where the motherless Princess Irene is cared for by her nurse, Lootie, while her King-Papa is away caring for events in his realm. Alongside their castle and its parkland, there are mines worked for their precious ores but also inhabited by a race of goblins whose generations-long existence in darkness has led to distortions of their once-human form and that of the beasts who live with them. The drama lies in their plans to undermine the royal house, extirpate its residents and carry off Irene to be a goblin princess.

It is a plot which will be frustrated at two levels, one through the diligence of a miner's son, Curdie, and the other through the spells of a wise-woman or house-spirit who claims to be Irene's great-

great-great-grandmother and who dwells in a magical solitude in the uninhabited passages at the top of the house.

In terms of story, the book is signal for its importing into English children's literature the accoutrements of the Romantic German writers (a more extended working than that of *The King of the Golden River*). As such it will prove a model for later writers in the nineteenth century and Narnia in the twentieth ('I regard him as my master' said Lewis.) But in his creation of the presiding spirit of the grandmother after whom Irene has been named (*eiren* = peace) MacDonald is drawing upon a myth of his own – he the controlling guardian of events. She is a figure found elsewhere in MacDonald's stories, most notably in the first of his *Good Words for the Young* fantasies: *At the Back of the North Wind*, where she has all the characteristics of Robert Graves's White Goddess.

There is correspondence too in the two sites of action: the palace, under threat from the goblins, and the mines where Curdie discovers the plot but is himself discovered and walled up near the goblins' council chamber. The conjunction arrives when the princess, thanks to a near invisible thread given to her by her grandmother, is able to seek out Curdie through the underground tunnels and rescue him before the assault on the palace begins. There is a grand battle with much stamping on goblin toes, their most vulnerable point, and in a final resolution their survivors are reformed: their skulls became softer as well as their hearts and, in a phrase that reflects both MacDonald's northern influences as well as one of the constant themes of fairytale, 'they grew milder in character, and indeed became very much like the Scotch Brownies'.

Commentary

Published from November 1870 to June 1871 in *Good Words for the Young,* the story was there illustrated with wood engravings by the Dalziels after Arthur Hughes. The designs were promiscuously jammed in to the magazine printings and came most fully to life when reissued in the book edition of 1871 (dated 1872). Hughes, whose collaboration with MacDonald has been seen as one of the most fruitful in children's literature, is first found accompanying the fantasy stories of *Dealings with the Fairies* (Strahan, 1867) and he also collaborated on the *Good Words* serializations of *At the Back of the North Wind* and *Ranald Bannerman's Boyhood*. By the time that MacDonald completed a sequel to the present book. *The Princess and Curdie* in 1877 the magazine had been replaced by a successor, *Good Things; a picturesque magazine for boys and girls* and the story was illustrated with stock blocks. It was though a strange farrago, whose pessimistic conclusion may have been occasioned by MacDonald's depressive streak and it did not appear as a book until Chatto published it in 1882 (dated 1883) with unsatisfactory illustrations by James Allen.

-24-

LOB LIE-BY-THE-FIRE; OR THE LUCK
OF LINGBOROUGH
BY JULIANA HORATIA EWING (1873)

The folktale of the little people – elves? dwarves? goblins? Scotch Brownies? – who come overnight to help humans, but leave when they are rewarded is found in many languages and forms. Mrs Ewing had used it in her story of 'The Brownies' (which indirectly led to that name being given to pre-Girl Guides) and she returned to it in *Lob*. She also gives warrant from Milton's 'L'Allegro' where he writes...

> ...when in one night, ere glimpse of morn,
> His shadowy flail hath threshed the corn
> That ten day-labourers could not end,
> Then lies him down the Lubber-fiend,
> And stretched out all the chimney's length,
> Basks at the fire his hairy strength.

The tale is a simple one:
  – that two spinsters are the chatelaines of Lingborough Hall up

by the sea in the Border country;

– that, walking home from a dinner-party one summer evening, they find a baby asleep in a hedge;

– that, despite the advice of their lawyer, they take the child in and have him baptised as John Broom;

– that, as predicted by their lawyer, he proves not so much a bad as a gaily unpredictable lot;

– that he runs away to sea, all the way to Australia and back again;

– that he is ashamed to return to Lingborough, until he is told to go back by a dying soldier who has befriended him and who was also a runaway;

– that he does so secretly and enacts the role of the 'lubber-fiend', bringing back luck to an estate that has fallen into sad decline.

The telling of the tale though is what matters, for Mrs Ewing is telling a realistic tale that not only contrasts with the comic and fantastic stories that have blossomed during the 1860s but does so with a craftsmanship not found in, and perhaps not applicable, to their wayward narratives. The portrayal of Lingborough society at the start suggests a tale set in the literary neighbourhood of Cranford, but once John Broom cuts loose, fleeing from the just dudgeon of the ladies' Scottish bailiff, we enter more adventurous territory.

John Broom in the hedge. Relief block after Randolph Caldecott (70x100mm.) within the text. From an early edition printed in sepia throughout.

It is low key adventure though for Mrs Ewing has an indulgent eye for her characters. The voyage to the Antipodes and back has none of the terrors of most naval sagas and John Broom's lodgement in the army camp is told with the amused knowledge of what goes on in such places, for Mrs Ewing was an army wife. What gives the story its depth, alongside its charm, is John Broom's emotional education in service to the Highland warrior and his return to Lingborough to do good by stealth. As a child, lying by the housekeeper's hearth, embracing the sheepdog, he had listened to her country tales, including that of the secret helpers. On his return, he plays the part and is only discovered to have done so by the parson who had originally picked him out of the hedge that had been his cradle and who finds him, at the end, 'basking his hairy strength' at that same hearth alongside the very same dog.

Commentary

The story was originally published with two others in a volume illustrated by George Cruikshank. In 1885, though, it joined the uniform run of Ewing's works that was being edited by the SPCK – the Society for the Promotion of Christian Knowledge – which had been inspired to a more secular policy in making books for children perhaps by its more prolific (and more ecumenical) rival, the Religious Tract Society. The books were all produced in a foolscap quarto format ($8\frac{1}{2}$ x $6\frac{3}{4}$ inches), which gave scope for the variant placing of illustrations within the page and this was to be the third occasion when Mrs Ewing worked with Randolph Caldecott. There is a wonderful insight into their friendly collaboration through the preserved correspondence on its making[13], the completion of which Mrs Ewing never saw since she died before the finished manuscript was printed.

13   Michael Hutchins ed. *Yours Pictorially: Illustrated Letters of Randolph Caldecott*. (Frederick Warne, 1976 pp.75-136).

-25-

THE ADVENTURES OF TOM SAWYER
BY MARK TWAIN
(I.E. SAMUEL LANGHORNE CLEMENS) (1876)

I'm inclined to think that the midnight killing of Dr Robinson in the St Petersburg graveyard, on the banks of the Mississippi River, is a revolutionary moment in the making of children's literature.

For one thing it is told with an unusually graphic directness: 'All at once the doctor flung himself free, seized the heavy headboard of [the] grave and felled Potter to the earth with it; and in the same instant the half-breed saw his chance, and drove the knife to the hilt in the young man's breast. He reeled and fell partly upon Potter, flooding him with his blood …' And for another thing it is so entirely unexpected. There, near to the grave, are Tom Sawyer and his comrade, Huckleberry Finn, with a dead cat (a vital element in their recipe for getting rid of warts) and the reader, who is expecting another comic episode, gets horror instead.

Furthermore the event, erupting about a third of the way into the story, converts what was becoming a sort of fictionalised memoir into a more focused drama. 'Most of the adventures in this book really occurred' says the author at the start of things ('but with some stretchers' adds Huck Finn on a later memorable occasion) and what many people remember about it are some of the famous pranks: whitewashing the fence, or the three boys camping out on an island, but believed drowned, and turning up to their own funeral service. But the malign figure of Injun Joe, the 'half-breed', once introduced, stays present as a threat which you know will sooner or later assume a dominant role.

The tension that is carried by this *fil rouge* in the story reaches a climax as it is twinned with the picnic outing to McDougal's Caves (a St Petersburg *actualité*). Injun Joe may here offer only a momentary danger compared to the labyrinthine caverns, where Tom and his sweetheart Becky nearly die, but the incident ends with Joe's own ghastly death after the local Health and Safety team wall up the cave's entrance with boiler iron. (When I read the book as a child I was utterly moved – on Joe's behalf – by the description of his pitiful attempts to cut an exit for himself.)

To say that the murder and the (accidental) walling up of Joe are revolutionary events in children's literature may be seen as an overstatement in so far as violence and disaster have long been present in the folktales, chapbooks and dime novels that are often children's favourite reading, even though rarely exploited in this manner before 1876. And Twain may also be exonerated from accusations of terrorising youth because – unlike our contemporary practitioners of the provocative, like Melvin Burgess – he does not seem to have thought, at the time of writing, that *Tom Sawyer* was a children's book anyway.

Its publishing history tends to confirm this. It has been said that the final draft of the story was among the first texts to be composed on a typewriter and, whatever the truth of that, there is no doubt that two copies of the original were completed. One of these was read by Twain's friend, William Dean Howells and it was he who saw it as 'a book for boys and girls' and edited it as such. With the collaboration of another friend, that version was brought to London where an unillustrated edition was published by Chatto & Windus in July 1876. The first American edition, based on the other, unedited typescript and illustrated by the little-known True W. Williams, only got into print at the end of the year and electros were shipped to Britain for a second edition, now with pictures.

Whether initially intended for children or not, *Tom Sawyer* remains a landmark book if only for its authentic portrayal of *ante bellum* village life in a riverside settlement in Missouri (St Petersburg = Hannibal where Twain himself was brought up). As such it records with the exactitude of lived experience something of the folkways and the vernacular speech of its community – altogether too vulgar for some of its early reviewers who weren't used to that sort of thing. It is also the first lasting contribution to that genre of children's literature that deals in stories about naughty or over-adventurous boys from *Penrod* and *Bevis* to the glories of *Just – William* and the feeble idiocies of Horrid Henry.

Commentary

A similar pattern of precedence in the English and American editions of *Tom Sawyer* occurred with its sequel, *The Adventures of Huckleberry Finn* with the English edition dated 1884 and the American 1885. Tom and Huck also feature in the largely burlesque sequels *Tom Sawyer Abroad* (1894) and *Tom Sawyer, Detective* (1896).

–26–

BLACK BEAUTY: THE AUTOBIOGRAPHY OF A HORSE
BY ANNA SEWELL (1877)

' "Come Ann," said Mamma, "let us take a walk in the green fields; the sun will soon set, but the air is now fresh and warm …" ' And thus they do, day by day over some sixty-four pages, with Mamma discoursing equably on the scenes about them or on such exotica as whales, sharks and ostriches, which last being one of the few words to defy her ordinance that the modest events of these promenades be recorded in words of one syllable only. And at the start of the sixth story they go to see a horse, newly bought by Ann's aunt: ' "See how still he stands in the stall to eat his corn and hay; while James, the boy–groom, rubs him down, and combs out his mane and tail" ' for it is needful for his owner to see ' "that he is well fed and kept nice and clean; and it is a sad thing when men or boys vex or hurt him …" '

If that visit did take place, what a harbinger it proved. For in these *Walks with Mamma; or Stories in Words of One Syllable*, Mamma is none other than Mrs Mary Sewell who, in one of her family's several financial crises, had sent off the manuscript to Mr John Harris at his shop at the top of Ludgate Hill, and he had kindly bought it from her for three pounds ('a little fortune to me then', she said) and published it in 1824[14] Little Ann, or Anna, or,

14   The book has a bibliographical interest in being one of the earliest ever to be bound for publication in cloth.

later, Nannie would have been about four years old at the time, walking the semi-rural highways round Dalston, north of the City of London, after having been carried thither from her birthplace at Great Yarmouth.

Such trailings about, always with wolves never too far from the door, were a feature of the Sewells' life, although they were a close-knit family, abiding by the humanitarian ideals of an inherited Quakerism. Both Anna and her brother Philip sound to have been bright children, despite the eccentricities of English education in the 1820s (Philip would eventually become a civil engineer with a pronounced social conscience), but it was during Anna's brief spell of schooling in her early teens that the calamity of her life occurred. Running home one wet afternoon, she slipped and fell, so damaging her ankles that, what with incompetent medical treatment, and perhaps an incipient tubercular disposition, she was to become a lifelong invalid.

Her disability did not quell her spirits however. Family removals continued – she even spent some time at a spa in Germany – and with walking now always a difficulty she undertook carriage-driving (partly from the need for someone regularly to take her father to Shoreditch station) and this was to develop not only her instinctive understanding of, and care for, horses (dating back perhaps to the visit to the stable with Mamma?) but also her awareness of the widespread abuse to which they were subjected.

Black Beauty was to stem from that experience. Anna and Mamma had always been more like loving sisters than mother and child and throughout much of her adulthood Anna was to act as 'critic and counsellor' in the editing of Mary Sewell's poetic effusions. These took the form of 'homely ballads' penned for children or for the lower orders, and achieved great, if brief, popularity. (*Mother's Last Words* of 1860 sold over a million copies.) As products though of 'a writing life' they could not help but accustom Anna to the paramountcy of print in everyday communication and it was to print that she thought to turn in what amounted to a campaigning novel on behalf of horses.

A central impulse was her hatred of 'the bearing rein', a fashionable but cruel device designed to keep horses' heads proudly in the air despite the damage it caused to their muscular system. She did not make the assault direct however, but chose first to cast her critique in the form of a novel and second – a brilliant inspiration – to make it indeed a tale from the horse's mouth: the autobiography of a horse, translated from the original 'equine'. (It was by no means the first animal story to adopt such a ploy – the earliest perhaps being Dorothy Kilner's popular *Life and Perambulation of a Mouse* of 1783 – but it was, initially, intended to be for all readers, its didacticism operating in a wider and more fully delineated social context than occurred in the children's stories.)

The presumed author goes about his purpose with great skill. His life as a colt is told in near-idyllic terms, the breaking-in and early training being accomplished under caring and knowledgeable folk in comfortable, rural circumstances. But even for readers who know his story well a certain *frisson* is inescapable from the start. This cannot be a picaresque tale whose hero may willy-nilly come through his adventures triumphant, but rather an account of one who is at all stages at the mercy of decisions beyond his control. There are premonitions of an uncaring world out there. A horse, eventually known to be Black Beauty's brother, is killed with his rider while hunting 'all for one little hare'. A stablemate, Ginger, tells of hard times that he endured before his present berth. Discussions occur in the field over tail-docking, and the foolish use of blinkers, and, inevitably, the torment of the bearing rein.

Forewarnings all, these prepare both Black Beauty and the reader for the descent into the abyss as human circumstances direct the lives of horses, with Black Beauty making it plain that almost perpetually the horse (still a major element in the conduct of life at this time) is disregarded as a sentient being but is just a piece of property to be worked for whatever benefits its masters may gain from it and then to be cast aside. The bearing rein proves to be only one example of the trials to which working-horses may be subject and as Black Beauty is brought down through no fault of his own from carriage-horse to job-horse, to cab-horse his autobiography becomes a record of human weakness and, over much of its final third, of the horrors endured among the

London cabbies. The suffering and death of his old friend Ginger, encountered among the cab-ranks, is the emotional heart of the book: 'Oh!' says Black Beauty, 'if men were more merciful, they would shoot us before we come to such misery'.

As an inexperienced writer, Black Beauty found for himself an almost ideal way to tell his story, casting it in no fewer than forty-nine chapters, but each well-judged in the way he both recounts each incident, and uses each to move the narrative on. His translator has given him a most winning voice, an aspect of her technique criticised by some because it brings the horse into the realm of human discourse when a third person narrative would be truer to the story's grim reality. To do so however, without turning the whole affair into a tract would demand skills surely beyond those of Miss Sewell, while her incursion direct into the horse's imagined consciousness brings a verisimilitude to all the varied crises thrust upon him and overlays them with a moving recognition of the beast's almost selfless endurance of his lot. We know that he must survive ill-treatment and indignity for, after all, it is he who is telling the story, and the manner in which he tells of that survival makes for a perfect adagio conclusion.

Commentary

Anna Sewell laboured for some six years at her 'translation' through bouts of illness in which she dictated episodes to her mother or pencilled them on to scraps of paper for Mamma to transcribe. The finished manuscript went to Mary's main publisher, Messrs Jarrolds of Norwich and London, who, in the manner of John Harris and *Walks with Mamma,* bought it outright for forty pounds. It was published in November 1877 to an acclaim which eventually carried it round the world – much, presumably, to the satisfaction of the company. Anna knew little of either its success or of the indignity perpetrated on her by the mercenary Jarrolds, for, five months after *Black Beauty* entered the world, his creator left it.

-27-

BEVIS: THE STORY OF A BOY
BY RICHARD JEFFERIES (1882)

Mister Mudie and his circulating library are to be execrated rather than thanked for imposing upon Victorian authors, publishers and readers the uniform dress of the three-volume novel. Such things may have been hardly relevant where children's books are concerned, but in 1882 there appeared in full figuration, *Bevis; the Story of a Boy* by Richard Jefferies. (The boy had, in fact, appeared the year before as central figure in a two-volume fantasy, *Wood Magic*, rich in sentimental whimsy, which at least apprises us of the rural locus for its wholly realistic successor.)

Such scale and dignity of production have thus given this magnificent study of boyhood an ambiguity of purpose from the start. Was it really 'for children'? For sure they had rejoiced in long books before, but here they are confronted by 875 pages where not much happens rather slowly and that makes for something of a challenge.

When we first meet Bevis (he's about twelve, much older than he was in *Wood Magic*) he is a wayward, impulsive, domineering child and his story takes place alongside his friend Mark on his father's Wiltshire small-holding through an almost cloudless summer holiday. The 'people' in the place, rather like Kenneth Grahame's Olympians in *The Golden Age*, are preoccupied with their quotidian routines and the boys and their long-suffering spaniel, Pan (one of the great dogs in children's literature), are left to engage in a climactic sequence of activities with a barely inhibited freedom which will provoke incredulity among the cotton-wool childminders of today.

Exploration is at the heart of things. In the early stages there is much attention paid to the nearby lake (actually a reservoir), a part of the landscape that they have known all their lives but which is transformed by their imagination into The New Sea. Its shores and islands – Serendib (from the *Arabian Nights)* and New Formosa – are mapped and after Bevis's governor has assured himself that they can swim they are given a boat whose fitting-out and whose management we see them undertake themselves.

In a central episode when tropical adventurism is abandoned in favour of classical warfare, the great battle of Pharsalia is organised with a group of boys from the local hamlet (Caesar Bevis against Pompey Ted) and its dramatic conclusion, when Bevis almost falls into a quarry, opens the way for the book's remarkable second half. Unbeknownst to their people Bevis and Mark plot an expedition to the island of New Formosa where they succeed in looking after themselves for eleven days. They had initially worked out how to design and build a matchlock gun (we watch them do it) and that provides a source for food. Then with their new-found sailing prowess, and with the building first of a hut and then of a raft they contrive an absorbed Crusoe-esque island life. (There is even a girl Friday in an episode where play comes to clash with the realities of rural life in the 1880s.)

The linear structure with no sub-plots, makes of this – the first 'holiday adventure story' – a four-month *Bildungsroman*. The point is made in the text, when Mark's older sister, Frances, realises when he returns from the island that he is no longer 'the boy she ordered to and fro'. (The presence of Frances and the briefer episodes involving Loo, the girl Friday, and another peasant girl, introduce a perhaps unintended sexual tremor into their encounters with our two pre-pubescent adventurers.)

Of more moment is Jefferies's intense feeling for the ambience of his story. The farm and the Longpond are closely modelled on his father's (not very successful) small-holding while his own, almost mystical, apprehension of the natural world give a sustained intimacy to his treatment of all the life within his text. I'm sure it's true, as Peter Hunt says in his introduction to the World's Classics edition of the book (1989), that the falling-off of the last few chapters is due to the need to fill the three-decker's third volume, but that must surely be forgiven when Bevis, Mark and Frances make their winter ride through the ice-floes of The New Sea in the final stunning paragraphs.

The presentation of the text after 1882 has often entailed much butchery (the Puffin had some disgraceful excisions) although a complete one-volume edition, with a good map of the theatre of action, came out in 1902 and had a superb successor from Jonathan Cape in 1932 with forty-three line drawings by Ernest Shepard. (Cape of course was the publisher of Arthur Ransome, who had a great love of *Bevis*.) Hacking down the wordage which looks so easy is liable to damage Jefferies's insights into the character of the children and the 'people' of his book as well as his clear-eyed reverence for both the beauties and the rough edges of a world now lost to us. You may indeed see The New Sea as you speed a few hundred yards south of it on the M4, but no naked boys will be bathing there now under the looming towers of Swindon, and streetlights everywhere forbid the ecstasy that Bevis found lying on New Formosa and watching the rising of Orion.

Bevis, Mark and Pan on the raft. Pen drawing by E.H.Shepard (65x90mm.) across centre of page 400 of the 1932 edition (Cape).

Commentary

Richard Jefferies had a rather disturbed childhood and adolescence. Coate Farm, the setting for *Bevis,* was not large enough to be profitable and between the ages of four and nine he was boarded out with an aunt in Sydenham, coming home only for the summer holidays. (The farm was sold in 1878.) His later schooling was in Swindon and in 1866 he began work as a reporter on local papers. He had an almost preternatural understanding and love of the natural world and established a name for himself as a writer on country matters, his journalism being converted into such books as *The Gamekeeper at Home* (1878). *Wood Magic* and *Bevis* were written after a move to the south-east and at the start

of years of increasingly bad health. He died in 1887, leaving a wife
and two (of three) children. 'The governer' died in 1896.

-28-

HEIDI
BY JOHANNA SPYRI (1884)

'Take up thy bed and walk'. Wheelchair stories with miraculous
cures make a dependable theme for authors seeking access to
popularity (see especially *The Secret Garden*). And if you top them
up with Fauntleroy stuff – young innocence melting the hearts of
the curmudgeonly old – then classic status is assured.

It is unlikely, though, that such mercenary thoughts ever crossed
the mind of Johanna Spyri as she composed the text of *Heidis
Lehr-und-Wanderjahre* which was published in Gotha in 1880.
(The German title is important, for this is to be a *Bildungsroman* –
a story about the maturing of a character – and it echoes the terms
of the ancient trade-practice of apprenticeship and journeying
found also in Goethe's two volumes about Wilhelm Meister: his
Lehrjahre and his *Wanderschaft* – two of Spyri's favourite books.)

She was fifty-three when it was published and already the
author of several of the books 'for children and those who love
children' which in part celebrated her Swiss homeland (an English
translation of some of these came out in 1888 as *Swiss Stories*)
and also partook of her earnest Protestant assurance that through
all vicissitudes we are in God's hands and can trust in Him. *Heidi*
would be generated by motives implicit there rather than by
anything so crudely commercial as the likely publisher's balance-
sheet.

Nevertheless the recipe had an instant appeal. There is Heidi at
the start, 'about five years old', cheerfully tackling a two-hour trail
up a mountain where she is to be deposited on her reclusive and
unsociable grandfather and his two goats. She relishes the climb

once she has got rid of a mass of garments and her stay among the upper pastures becomes a celebration of a freedom and joy not often the lot of little girls in Victorian children's books. It's no wonder that granpa-on-the Alp is soon on the way to becoming a reformed character.

A necessary crisis in this idyllic life obtrudes itself when Heidi is carted off to Frankfurt to be a (very young) companion to Clara, the wheelchaired invalid daughter of a wealthy businessman. This brings into play the contrast between the rural and the urban and also that between Granpa's comradeship and the domineering rule of Clara's governess, the dreaded Fräulein Rottenmeier. Despite much kindness from everyone else, including Clara's Papa and Grandmama (who teaches her to read), a debilitating homesickness supervenes and she is returned to the rocks and firtrees and sunsets of 'home'.

There it would seem the apprentice's journeyings are at an end, and even Granpa, through the words of that other journeyman, the Prodigal Son, is reconciled to his village neighbours. But Spyri did not choose to leave the story there and in the following year she published a second volume showing the apprentice's fulfilment: '*Heidi Makes Use of What she has Learnt*'. After reconnoitering the topography, Clara's Grandmama organises the great shipment of the invalid – wheelchair and all – up the mountain to the alp where, by dint of some very superior goats milk and the health-giving mountain air, the girl is persuaded to walk. (This is brought about not by any set plan but fortuitously, since Peter the Goat-boy, in a fit of jealousy, has chucked the wheelchair down the mountain.) All ends with the cast in a grand finale when Papa and the Frankfurt doctor also ascend to the Alp and bring about a measure of happiness and security to all.

With an interweave of sub-plots which serve to deepen Heidi's experience of both rural and urban life, it is easy to see how the two unified stories caught the taste and the imagination of their first readers. There was a clear affinity with the girls' stories that were popular in the United States and the first translation into English by Louise Brookes was published there in 1884; that land has seen more editions and abridgments than have occurred in

Britain, to say nothing of the famous movie featuring Shirley Temple in 1938. In typical fashion, sequels were also called for since Spyri did not see her story as needing any further Alcottish or Montgomery-esque continuations. Thus it occurred that *Heidi Grows Up* and *Heidi's Children* – sometimes thought to be by Spyri – were cobbled up by Charles Tritten who had been responsible for *Heidi's* translation into French.

The lame girl being carried up the mountain. Framed full-page drawing by Tomi Ungerer, printed in four colours (140x126mm.) from *Heidi kann brauchen, was es gelernt hat*. Zürich: Diogenes. 1978. p.101.

Commentary

Great affection has been generated for Heidi and her life-affirming story – as witness Eva Ibbotson, one of whose last pieces of writing was an encomium for the story in the Puffin edition of 2009. Hence it was generally regarded as sacrilege when critics schooled in modern modes began to complain about the book ignoring the realities of child-life in pursuit of a fairytale idyll. Everybody except the crudely caricatured Rottenmeier is seen as really too good to be true, while the pervasive insistence on God as a trustworthy arbiter of human affairs is hardly attuned to contemporary metaphysics. (The great illustrator, Tomi Ungerer, famed for his ferocious cartoons of modern life and indeed some interesting pornographic studies, was impugned for devoting his art to the sentimentalities of *Heidi* in a fine two-volume German 1978 edition.)

Such criticisms neglect the hold which fairytale idylls can exert on the imagination (is it necessary, for instance, that we explain Clara's seemingly impossible cure to the likely cause of her illness being purely psychosomatic – and, if so, why?). Ibbotson – who would probably have deplored the sequel mania as dragging the story too far into a spurious 'reality' – notes how 'it doesn't shut like a trap, but allows you to go on dreaming and speculating and wondering'. With Belloc she would also surely have deplored 'men who lose their fairylands'.

-29-

KIDNAPPED
BY ROBERT LOUIS STEVENSON (1887)

Scotland and the Scots as a presence in children's literature are not so widely remarked as they deserve. The ballad tradition, their colossal production of chapbooks and folktales (a pity that no one made any *Kunstmärchen* from Ossian), the towering influence of Walter Scott, and their indigenous publishing activities all need more fully charting. For us though, Robert Louis Stevenson must stand exemplar for the greatness of their contribution.

Treasure Island (1883) is the children's book that comes immediately to mind when he is mentioned but that, in its setting and its writing, is more an English than a Scottish book. *Kidnapped*, which followed it a few years later (both being initially serialised in *Young Folks* magazine) is Scottish to the core.

That cliché is an apt one; just look at the geography. The story almost amounts to a circular tour of the country in a kind of race-game punctuated by episodes of fierce danger. There is no let-up in the pace of the (often literal) plotting from David Balfour's initial encounter with his heinous Uncle Ebenezer at the House of Shaws to his triumphant return there at the finish. The kidnapping takes place on board the brig '*Covenant*' in the Firth of Forth; she is wrecked amid the Western Isles; and David makes an eventful journey back through the Highlands and the Highland Line to Edinburgh.

Just look at the history. The adventure takes place in 1751, six years after Bonnie Prince Charlie's failed march upon the Southron folk. Divisions between the neighbouring countries are overlaid by those between religious factions, between Highland and Lowland, and not least between the Highland clans themselves. The potential for drama upon drama is served up to the novelist on a platter.

And just look at the people. At every stage of David's journey Stevenson has him record with a fine precision both his own callow and stockish youthfulness and the succession of characters he encounters – every one living, as it were, in his (and rarely her) own skin. All are imbued with attitudes and philosophies that derive from their Scottish or their Gaelic upbringing – most of all the famous Alan Breck of the Highland Stewarts, liegeman to the King Over the Water and thus, through his companionship with David, bringing peril to both of them as they are hunted across the landscape by redcoats and Campbells alike.

All these attributes give a striking authenticity to the book whose central quality is surely the register of its storytelling and the music of its varied dialogues, giving it a dramatic strength beyond the different splendours of *Treasure Island*. But that is also its self-imposed limitation. For, amongst those classes and communities who demand a swift apprehension of what printed stories are saying, an author is bound to be suspect who asks them to have some notion of eighteenth century political quarrels; and when that author adds to their difficulties by regularly proffering sentences like 'Ay, man, ye shall taigle many a weary foot, or we get clear!' he runs the risk of contumely. (Stevenson occasionally gives a footnote translation such as 'gleg' = 'brisk', but the excellent World's Classics combined edition of *Kidnapped* and *Catriona* supplies a glossary that runs to fourteen columns.)

Kidnapped thus becomes not just a classic but one that measures both readerly skills and readerly willingness to trust the author. A child commentator recently named it as a favourite book, which encourages high hopes that Stevenson's art has overcome what may be a deterrent. But it's possible that the enjoyment may have come from some sanitised edition which deprives you of all that is essential, or even 'told in pictures' from a children's comic colourfully illustrated by Dudley Watkins.

These misgivings are redoubled when one turns to *Catriona,* the sequel to *Kidnapped* and Stevenson's last completed novel. This too was serialised – in the girls' magazine *Atalanta* (1892–3) – a fact which strengthens a case that might be made for *Kidnapped* to be labelled a yarn for boys, while *Catriona* is a teenage romance. It is, to my mind, a far richer book than its predecessor, in part because, for the first time in his career, the author gave living breath not just to one female character – the eponymous heroine – but to two, the second being the wonderfully self-possessed eldest daughter of Scotland's Lord Advocate (an historical figure) who plays matchmaker, while herself having feelings too for Mr Balfour of Shaws.

Approachable though these relationships are, the components of the book's plot are more complex. The story had its origins in Stevenson's desire to complete the story of Alan Breck's escape and to tie up other loose ends left dangling at the end of *Kidnapped*. But these matters begin by demanding a sympathetic understanding of the Caledonian legal and political toils in which David finds himself – elements which the author handles with much subtlety – and they end with David's journeying to Holland where he meets with what for his strait-laced contemporaries would be a position full of compromise in his relationship with Catriona. The matter would be solved in an instant by an historian today and the couple would blithely have jumped into bed together (an event of which, one suspects, Alan Breck would have wholly approved). But the tension that arises through the several stigmas attaching to so easy a solution lends a strength to the emotional currents of the book that is now denied to our liberated authors.

Catriona has never had the reputation of its forebear, exchanging that book's simple, picaresque form for what turns out to be a study from various angles of the devious and the true. But both books are cut from the same deeply-plaited Scottish cloth and are a gift not often matched by Sassenach looms.

Commentary

One must wonder what James Henderson, the editor of *Young Folks'* Paper made of 'Captain George North' whose story 'The Sea Cook' he began to serialise in his paper under the title of 'Treasure Island' with a single paltry illustration. It can't have been long though before he perceived that he had a genius on his hands and when he serialised two successor stories he gave them much more prominence in the paper: the first, 'The Black Arrow' with each episode being given an illustrated headpiece whose images summarised the events of that number, and the second, 'Kidnapped', with a full-scale pictorial headpiece. Only the map would be given in the first book edition of *Kidnapped*, but the plates by William Hole greatly pleased the author who was also chosen to do *Catriona*. That had been first published, unillustrated in *Atalanta* – largely aimed at a female readership – but Stevenson had died before the volume came out. There was some confusion over the British and American titling. The London editions first came out as *Kidnapped* and *Catriona*, although a uniform reissue in 1895 was entitled *The Adventures of David Balfour*. In the United States the two books were always *David Balfour* Parts 1 and 2.

-30-

THE FIFTH FORM AT ST. DOMINIC'S:
A SCHOOL STORY
BY TALBOT BAINES REED (1887)

Unlike Tom Brown's belated going to Rugby, we arrive at St Dominic's on page one with afternoon school just finishing and a chance to meet some of leading characters of its fifth form. There are the two friends, Wraysford and Oliver Greenfield, Tom Senior, the headmaster's eldest son, Braddy the bully, and Anthony Pembury, lame but waggishly clever and about to start *The Dominican*, a fifth form journal. Beyond the classroom and with never a schoolmaster in sight, are the warring factions of the junior school, the Tadpoles and Guinea-Pigs, the 'fagging' personnel, traditionally detailed off to skivvy for the seniors, and here, the source of much of the book's comedy.

As an introduction the chapter at once reveals the distance school story fiction has travelled after the linear, near-biographical, narrative of *Tom Brown*. These characters are to be the performers in a complex set of events devised for the entertainment, rather than enlightenment, of its readers although it shares with its progenitor the close focus of being enacted, for the most part, on the enclosed stage of the boarding school. It has become a truism of the genre that its appeal to many young readers lay in the opportunity it gave them to live within the confines of this imagined space.

The drama gets under weigh in the second chapter when Oliver Greenfield's younger brother, Stephen, joins the school as a new boy (later elected a Guinea-Pig). He faces a farcical 'entrance exam', set by Pembury as a joke, and is appointed 'fag' to the ambiguous figure of the prefect, Loman. Before long the latter enters dubious negotiations with a townee, the loutish publican at The Cockchafer and this generates a plaited plot with Greenfield senior being wrongly accused of cheating and Loman (who did try to cheat) driven to a near-suicidal despair.

The story was first published in 1881-2 as a serial in the *Boys' Own Paper*, to whose first number in 1879 Reed had contributed the opening story. (This famous and long-lived magazine came from the Religious Tract Society under the tactful imprint of 'The Leisure Hour Office' and was to serialise almost all of Reed's fictions and to whom he made over his copyrights.) It took five years for it to arrive as a printed book in 1887, since when it has hardly ever been out of print and was indeed referred to as a 'classic' by T. S. Eliot in his essay on the subject.

Because of its originating impulse it occasionally diverged into brief sermonising but that does not detract from the momentum of the story. In such books as this and later works like *The Willoughby Captains* (1887) or *The Cock-House at Fellsgarth* (1894) Reed's handling of several strands of plot is enhanced by his gift for varied and natural characterisation. It was charged in 1971 by the publisher Frank Eyre in his enjoyable *British Children's Books of the Twentieth Century* with having 'brought the school story to a perfection of unreality which later writers could only copy' but, given its date, it showed the dramatic potential of the school setting as an attraction to readers and it was the hundreds of school stories that followed it that demonstrated varieties of truth, reality and life-enhancement from Kipling's *Stalky and Co* to the ineffable Bunter and Molesworth.

Commentary

Fifty years after the events at Rugby, the influence of Dr Arnold would seem to have had its effect and while the pupils' lives still function with seeming independence from Authority, the traditional routines are altogether more orderly and the teachers, especially the housemasters, more cognisant of the lives of their pupils. The popularity of *St Dominic's* may be gauged by the many variant editions of the story (rarely abridged) and it was a favourite book of mine, bought new round about 1937. Several anonymous illustrators (or illustrators to be guessed at from their monograms) were commissioned and the book is one of a number that exemplify a frugal publishing practice. Round about 1903 it gained a place in an extensive RTS series of children's classics: *The Golden Library*, where it had a frontispiece and five plates in three-colour half-tone. These were probably produced in a substantial quantity for stock so that later cheap editions could draw upon single plates for use only as a frontispiece.

-31-

THE WONDER CLOCK, OR FOUR AND TWENTY MARVELLOUS TALES
BY HOWARD AND KATHLEEN PYLE (1888)

Howard Pyle's name first appeared on a printed book in 1881 when he illustrated *Yankee Doodle: an old song. 1775.* There was no political purpose to it and no story, just a series of rather dim, clumsily-rhymed jokes drawn from the original ballad. But they revealed first, Pyle's close knowledge of such things as the costuming and equipment of the revolutionary period and second, a graphic influence from Randolph Caldecott whose toy books had been captivating both the English and American markets since they had begun to appear in 1879.

At this time Pyle had just returned to his home at Wilmington, Delaware after several years writing and illustrating for journals, mostly for children, in New York. Although now twenty-eight he had been unable to decide whether he should concentrate on working as an author or an illustrator and a couple of years later he showed a capacity for combining the two professions when he published to general acclaim his *Merry Adventures of Robin Hood* [briefly discussed at no.44 below]. The book's twenty-three full-page line drawings and its headpieces, all with hand-drawn 'antique' lettering, marked it as an early example of the Arts and Crafts Movement in America and its success inspired Pyle to a dozen further volumes (including four on King Arthur) which followed similar principles of design.

The first of these was *Pepper and Salt; or, Seasoning for Young Folks* (1886) which drew upon material that he had published in periodicals. This was followed by *The Wonder Clock,* whose twenty-four stories were notionally based on little puppet-plays performed every hour of the day at the striking of the clock. Although it is nowhere stated, these stories are mostly Pyle's re-workings of wonder tales that come from the European tradition, whose classics, especially Grimm and Andersen, were a childhood delight, read to him by his mother. (She also introduced him to

Robin Hood through Ritson's notable edition.)

The twenty-four stories offer varied evidence of Pyle's methods as an adaptor. 'How One turned his Trouble to Account' has an opening sentence lifted straight from Andersen but then links to the trickster motif of passing on an unwanted trouble to somebody else. Or 'How Two Went into Partnership' expands on the Grimm tale of the cat and mouse in partnership (to the mouse's misfortune) but with Uncle Bear and a Great Red Fox as protagonists. Success is variable, for expansion or augmentation do not easily suit traditional tales, but Pyle has perceived that an adjunct to the tale is the manner of its telling and his voice points to the oral quality of 'the fireside tale'. There is an echo of 'Puss in Boots' in the opening of 'Peterkin and the Little Grey Hare' but it has an authentic phrasing which is Pyle's own:

> 'There was a man who died and left behind three
> sons, and nothing but two pennies to each. So, as there
> was little to be gained by scraping the dish at home,
> off they packed to the king's house where they might
> find better faring ...'

In the same way, he interpolates his own verbal comments: 'Dear, dear! If one could but have been there ...'.

In its presentation *The Wonder Clock* is of near-revolutionary design. Measuring round about 9½ x 7 inches it is in British terms roughly a small quarto and is a *tour de force* in its integration of graphic design and typography. There is an elaborate title-page faced by a pictorial frontispiece, the prelims have decorated headpieces and each story has its own decorated title-page with verses by Pyle's sister Katharine, taking us through the twenty-four hours portrayed in the life of a country house. Thus, at seven o'clock in the evening we have:

> The Work is over for the Day;
> The Sky is pale and far away
> The Village Children shout at play.
> Now from his Hole the Toad comes out,

And blinks his Eyes and hops about,
And likes the pleasant Air no doubt.

And then follow the illustrations with their antique lettering. It is surely outstanding among the American children's books of the nineteenth century.

Commentary

After settling for good at Wilmington in 1879, Pyle's creative work was later augmented by a comparatively brief, but notable career as a teacher of illustration. That occurred first with classes at the Drexel Institute in Philadelphia, but then in more specialised work with smaller groups, first near his summer home at Chadd's Ford, Pennsylvania, then at designed premises by his home at Wilmington. He took few pupils but engaged in intensive training with them and so became a 'father' to a new generation of distinguished American illustrators which included N. C. Wyeth. Maxfield Parrish, and Jessie Willcox Smith. The adage 'Brandywine School' may have been added later (after the Delaware district so named) but it celebrates what was clearly a joyous venture which ended too soon with Pyle's death after only some ten years of its existence.

–32–

PINOCCHIO
BY CARLO COLLODI (1892)

Just as *The Wizard of Oz* [no.35 below] achieved world-wide currency after Hollywood got hold of it, so did *Pinocchio* after Disney chose it to be the successor to *Snow White* in 1939. But the circumstances weren't quite the same.

La Storia di un Burattino began life as a serial in a weekly children's paper: *Il Giornale per i Bambini* in 1881. It finished at the point where the puppet is hanged, but an enthusiastic readership demanded to know what happened next, and the second half ran to the beginning of 1883 under the title *Le Avventure di Pinocchio* which became the title of the book in the same year. Success in Italy was instantaneous and the *Avventure* soon spread widely in translation. The first English edition appeared in 1892 but (as with *The Wizard of Oz*) the wealth of our native literature seems to have precluded a prominent reputation. In Germany though (where 'Pinocchio' = 'Pine Kernel' = 'Zapfel-Kern') it quickly became a favourite book, and there, and in the more receptive United States its popularity led to many abridgements and sequels from other hands. Disney was tapping into a ready-made public.

The literary purists (especially in the U.S. library profession) did not much care for Disneyfication. Unmoved by the virtuoso handling of the cartoons, they bemoaned, with some justice, the sentimentalisation and the de-naturing of Collodi's hero. For the *Avventure* are full of violence and irony. It may be a saga of redemption, with the puppet winning through to a live boyhood by virtue of his 'kind heart' (itself a sentimental and moralised conclusion) but on the way his selfishness and impulsiveness, and the rogueries of those whom he encounters, give the story its energy and its sustained comedy. There's a lot of ruthlessness, from the murder of the cricket to the humiliation of Candlewick, and this is in no way mitigated by the author's ironical conversations with his readers.

Carlo Lorenzini was born in Florence in 1826, a man of many parts and much diverse experience. He was involved with, and fought in, the wars of Italian independence. He was both civil servant and the bane of such people, a journalist. He wrote plays and novels, and he came to his masterpiece through an accidental commission to translate Perrault's fairytales into Italian. As a token of affection for his mother's village, where he had spent much of his boyhood, he adopted the pseudonym Carlo Collodi which had overtaken all the fame of Lorenzini before his death, unmarried, in 1890.

The vagaries of his story's progress as a serial largely account for *Pinocchio*'s loose and rambling structure. Collodi seems to have written it on the hop from week to week, bringing in incidents on the spur of the moment. What matters, though, is his handling of such incidents as the stay with the puppet troupe, the attempted hanging, the visit to the Land of Toys, the recurrent meetings with Fox and Cat, over which Collodi exercises firm control. His personality as master of ceremonies persuades us that this wild admixture of living puppets moving through a landscape at once real and fantastic – men and creatures sharing adventures – might really happen.

Commentary

The first English edition of *Pinocchio* translated by Mary Murray was a worthy piece of work. She happily caught the comic/sardonic flavour of the original and the publisher, Fisher Unwin, sensibly used the Italian line drawings by Enrico Mazzanti. Although they sometimes make our hero look like a decrepit bank clerk, they have plenty of verve and they may be found again in the new authoritative translation for OUP's 'World's Classics' series by Ann Lawson Lucas (1996). Sheets of the English printing were shipped to America for issue by the New York branch of Cassell which almost immediately suffered extinction through managerial embezzlement. The text and illustrations were then pirated by a Boston publisher, disguising their nefarious deed by changing the title to *Pinocchio's Adventures in Wonderland* (1898).

The book's American career was, as noted, far more extensive than in Britain with many new translations, abridgments and invented sequels. Of especial interest was the New York edition of 1925 which incorporated some four hundred illustrations by Atillio Mussino, first published in Italy in 1911. Praise for that work, along with the popularity of other versions must have influenced Disney's selection of the title for his cartoon – a decision whose result was strongly defended by Maurice Sendak in an article reprobating the original as 'a cruel and frightening tale'.[15]

15   Reprinted in *Caldecott & Co.* (New York: Farrar, Straus; London: The Bodley Head, 1988) pp.111–117.

–33–

MOONFLEET
by John Meade Falkner (1898)

Tears flowed apace some time ago in the fourth-year classroom of
a south London girls' comprehensive. Even the school librarian,
reading aloud the shipwreck of John Trenchard and Elzevir Block
on Moonfleet Beach, broke down and wept.

Such lacrimosity may be hard for the youth of our more
cynical times to credit, but it betokens a continuing resilience in
John Meade Falkner's *Moonfleet* over the decades since its first
publication in 1898. After all, for many years it existed chiefly
as a drab-looking 'class reader' (with its mild cuss-words toned
down so as not to offend sensitive teachers) and even in that
unprepossessing form it enjoyed an eager readership.

'Historical romance' is the category into which the book is
thrust by pigeon-holers, but, like all great fiction, it has the quality
of being simply itself. Certainly it is historic in its mid-eighteenth
century setting; certainly it is a romance in its adoption of such
conventional elements as rumours of ghosts in churchyards, secret
passages for smugglers, coded messages of the whereabouts of
the Mohune diamond, miserly squires and bonny publicans, and
betrayals and sacrifices.

But the craftsmanship is something else. Falkner may take
some of his materials from the stock box, but the articulation of
these into a felt narrative is the work of a master storyteller. He
gives the story's voice to an ageing John Trenchard, reflecting on
the dramatic events of his youth, and formulating descriptions
and explanations without marring the steady pace of the story.
As incident follows incident with increasing tension so one finds
them to be cunningly dovetailed into each other and matters
seemingly irrelevant emerge as vital components in the drama.

The characters too want for nothing – even John's girl Grace,
who has been called 'a stick' and might be thought present for
reasons of inclusivity if such a bright idea had existed in 1898.
Rather she, along with the schoolmaster, the Rev Glennie, fills a

necessary role in counterbalancing the dubious morality of almost everyone else: her own villainous father, Ratsey the smuggling sexton and Elzevir Block, the true hero of the tale.

The precision of John Trenchard's first-person address does much to reinforce the immediacy of the story. There is a graphic quality to his descriptions (the 'lattice of folds' in the paper carrying clues to the hidden treasure, the 'swealing of the parchment under the hot wax' at the end of the auction-by-candle) and such things give life to what might have been tired conventions. Through this, the reader is implicated. You know that calamities are bound to follow that auction, or the botched landing of contraband under Hoar Head, or the getting of Blackbeard's diamond and the naïve attempt to sell it ('evilly come by and bringing evil with it'). But how can you climb into the book to give due warning?

The graphic quality is present too in *Moonfleet's* topography. The village itself is an imaginative extension of the actual Fleet which lies above Chesil Beach to the west of Weymouth, and the whole area from there to the Isle of Purbeck is so portrayed as to endorse the truth of the action – most completely in the climax with that gulp-provoking scene on the lee shore of Moonfleet. These places were well-known to Falkner whose boyhood had been spent in Dorset where he acquired a profound sense of the history within the landscape.

How come then that he wrote so little else? For although he lived for thirty-five years after *Moonfleet* appeared, dying in 1932 at the age of seventy-four, he published only one other work of fiction, a fine novel, *The Nebuly Coat* (1903 – a rather obsessive ghost story, *The Lost Stradivarius* had preceded it in 1895). The slightly astonishing explanation is that, soon after graduating from Oxford in 1882, Falkner had become tutor to the children of Andrew Noble of the Newcastle armaments firm of Armstrong Mitchell (later Whitworth). From this modest position he moved into the company and eventually became its chairman during the crisis-ridden time of the Great War. Strange fate for a sensitive novelist, and strange too that he ended his days as Honorary Librarian to Durham Cathedral (beside which he had his home) and as a fabled collector of medieval manuscripts.

Commentary

The first edition of *Moonfleet* is now a rare book (as opposed to all those school editions). Its earliest appearance in the United States came belatedly in 1951 from Little, Brown of Boston, when, perhaps to make it more attractive to its new-found audience, it was given some handsome illustrations by Fritz Kredel. Only in 1955 did Arnold publish an illustrated edition in England, with drawings by Geoffrey Fletcher. BA edited the story for the 'World's Classics' series published by Oxford University Press in 1993, an edition now vanished beneath the tides.

-34-

THE STORY OF THE TREASURE SEEKERS; BEING THE ADVENTURES OF THE BASTABLE CHILDREN IN SEARCH OF A FORTUNE
BY E. NESBIT (1899)

It took a long time for these records of a quest for riches to get themselves into a book. Edith Nesbit, the recorder (Daisy to her childhood friends), was certainly not lacking in experience for such work. Having herself fallen on precarious times after her marriage in 1880 she developed connections with various magazines and publishers and by 1899 had written or edited about fifty books and placed dozens if not hundreds of stories, articles and poems in periodicals.

Precarious times had in fact characterised most of her life, her father, quite a notable teacher, dying when she was three and a half and plunging her into a turbulent and unanchored childhood. It was through this, as well as later troubles, that she developed the idea in 1894 of portraying a family of children, whose mother is dead and whose father is having financial troubles, seeking to amend their fallen fortunes. The first glimmer came with her submitting a brief story in which the Bastable children set up a scheme for editing a newspaper.

This was the first episode of a serial whose two later parts were separated by a year each for they appeared under the title of 'The Play Times' in a *Holiday Annual* published by the firm of Nister.

Stimulated by the potential of the idea and by a suggestion that she might write about her own childhood, which resulted in a twelve-part recollection of 'My School-Days' in the *Girl's' Own Paper* from October 1896 to September 1897[16], she began to publish more Bastable stories in two magazines with a largely adult circulation, *Pall Mall* and the *Windsor Magazine*. By the autumn of 1899 what would become the complete run of sixteen chapters for *The Treasure Seekers* had been published and what was needed was their organisation into a connected whole that would be a coherent story. Opening sentences for one story or references within it would relate back to previous events so that the reader comes to live with the children and observe their endeavours as recounted by themselves.

They were having a strange time of it, these six: Dora the eldest at thirteen, then Oswald, Dicky, the twins, Alice and Noel, and H.O., the youngest (he is really Horace Octavius but it got jokingly shortened after they had seen an advertisement saying 'Eat Hornby's Oatmeal'). Circumstances have brought them close together for their father isn't able to afford school fees at the moment and our recognition of their community as a family is enhanced by Nesbit's ingenious idea to tell their adventures through one of themselves. This, from the start, is Oswald but his attempts to disguise the fact is one of the running-jokes of the book.

The schemes that they draw up for reviving their fortunes mostly involve adults from whom money may be obtained by ploys of variable ingenuity: selling their newspaper, which never gets beyond one issue, selling copy (Noel's poems) to a Fleet Street editor, planning to borrow money from a money-lender in order to invest £100 buying a 'partnership in a lucrative

16   The articles were collected in a volume published by Ronald Whiting & Wheaton in 1966: *Long Ago When I Was Young*, with an introduction by Noel Streatfeild and illustrations by Edward Ardizzone.

business'. Their innocence in such stunts and the way it can yield small but unexpected rewards, even when, as usually happens, the plans go awry, makes up the narrative substance of the stories. (Their characters are beautifully differentiated, which leaves one wondering how their father's misfortune should be so great as for him not to recognise more readily how his straitened circumstances affect them. Much sympathy comes from Albert-next-door's uncle who devises ploys for alleviating matters in a small way, muttering the while 'Poor little beggars'.)

For historians the dependence of the stories on the details of the everyday life of the period are also illuminating. The children, or at least Oswald, cannot help referring to a myriad things that characterise this London suburb on the edge of Greenwich Park: shops and houses, clothes, food and drink and getting around. As the fictional children of the author, the Bastables are also a bookish crowd and hardly a chapter goes by without pertinent references to their shared reading. Kipling and the Jungle Books are plugged in 'Good Hunting' (*Just So* and the Puck stories had not yet been published) and you could almost do a bibliography of 'references from the well-read child of the time: Maria Edgeworth, *Sherlock Holmes*, *Dick Turpin*, *The Children of the New Forest,* summoned up by Oswald to persuade his siblings that tough mutton is really venison. And today, *The Treasure Seekers,* along with much else in Nesbit's oeuvre, also stands as a classic reference point.

Commentary

In the recent Palgrave Macmillan edition of *The Treasure Seekers* Claudia Nelson of Texas A&M University has given useful notes on the textual changes that took place between the magazine and volume printings of the story although saying nothing of the illustrations by Lewis Baumer and (mostly) by Gordon Browne taken from the periodical blocks. She combined her account with a like treatment of the book's immediate successor in 1901: *The Wouldbegoods; being the further adventures of the treasure seekers.* The two volumes mark the point at which Nesbit 'found her voice, 'as a storyteller and created the run of fictions on both 'realistic' and fantastic themes that have brought her a continuing affectionate regard. The definitive biography, *A Woman of Passion* by Julia Briggs (1987) includes a full chronological bibliography of her large corpus of work, compiled by Dr Selwyn Goodacre.

-35-

THE WONDERFUL WIZARD OF OZ
BY FRANK BAUM (1900)

It was hardly wonderful that when Oz's Wizard first received a welcome from the British public he was accompanied by Judy Garland; the date was 1939 but he had been a favourite with American readers since 1900 and it needed the wizardry of Hollywood to give him purchase on the eastern side of the Atlantic.

Denslow's use of the page from a facsimile of the first edition of *The Wonderful Wizard of Oz* (Chicago: Geo. M. Hill Co. 1900), London: Pavilion Books Ltd., 1987.

Hodder and Stoughton had made an effort in 1906 at the start of their joint-venture in children's book publishing with Oxford University Press but had little success. Hutchinson had a go in 1926, but the assumption must be that a forty-year tradition of home-bred fantasy obscured the succession of 'wonder tales' that Frank Baum had instigated in Chicago at the beginning of the century.

His original story, with never a rainbow or bluebird in sight, was indeed a rather reach-me-down affair. Little Dorothy and her dog Toto are swept up in their house on the Kansas prairie by a cyclone (*recte* a tornado) and crash down in the land of Oz. Their landing has served to obliterate Oz's Wicked Witch of the East, much to the satisfaction of her subjects, the Munchkins, and winning for Dorothy a magic kiss from the Good Witch of the North and the silver (not carmine) slippers of the squashed tyrant. Thus fettled up she needs to find a way of getting back to Kansas.

A magic message, coming from we know not where, advises Dorothy to go to the Emerald City where the Great and Terrible Wizard may be able to help her and she sets off with Toto along the yellow brick road that leads there. The journey takes eight chapters within which she is joined by the three characters who will accompany her through the rest of the book: the Scarecrow, who is in search of a brain, the Tin Woodman, who wants a heart, and the Cowardly Lion, seeking courage. After several random adventures, they arrive at the City (where it is *de rigueur* to wear green spectacles) and are taken to be interviewed by the Wizard.

This proves fruitless in so far that the Wizard will only help them if they cross a local wasteland and kill the Wicked Witch of the West, a great enemy of the Wizard. That takes four more chapters, the Witch being easily destroyed when Dorothy chucks a bucket of water over her, and then, back in the City, they seek out their reward. However, just as the City is emerald by virtue of the green spectacles that everyone must wear, so the Wizard himself proves a fraud, he being a little man from Omaha who ended up in Oz when a balloon trip went wrong. He is however able to prove that, through their adventuring, the Scarecrow, the Woodman, and the Lion have achieved their desires by their own efforts, and he offers to fly Dorothy and Toto back to Kansas in his balloon.

Alas, with Toto chasing a kitten at the last minute, the balloon takes off without Dorothy and six more chapters of travel are needed to get her to Glinda, the Good Witch of the South, who reveals that the silver shoes can have the magic power of transporting her home after all. Although that might have happened at the start of things had she known their properties, the journeyings have allowed Mr

Baum to fulfil a purpose stated in his Introduction of creating 'a modernised fairytale, in which the wonderment and joys (of historic fairytales) are retained and the heartaches and nightmares are left out'. It is a specious claim, backed up by an erroneous understanding of the nature of 'old-time fairytales'. Dorothy's delightful travelling companions, the daft revelations of 'the Wizard', and some of the episodes entirely justify claims that *The Wizard of Oz* was a landmark in American fantasy for children, but Baum's fear of frightening his young readers caused him to strip the salt out of the mixture.

In one respect however, *The Wizard of Oz* was a unique book for its time and that was in its illustration by Baum's then associate: W.W. Denslow (they had collaborated on a *Mother Goose in Prose* in 1899). Denslow brings a verve to his illustrative methods unlike anything attempted before on either side of the Atlantic. The twenty-four colour-plates are conventional enough, but give us perfect images for the three fantasy protagonists (Dorothy is a dumpy maiden, but Toto a delectable Cairn terrier); for the rest of the book Denslow offers colour-tinted line drawings – the colours varying for each episode and the drawings spread through the pages in happy, disorganised abandon bringing a needful dynamic to Baum's workaday narrative.

Commentary

The success of *The Wizard* impelled Baum to write a successor, *The Marvellous Land of Oz,* with Denslow being replaced by John R. Neill as illustrator (1904) and, willy-nilly, he finally found himself producing before he died a further twelve *Oz* titles, all illustrated by Neill. These were much reprobated by institutional buyers but formed a passionate hunting-ground for collectors, further stimulated by posthumous continuations mostly from Ruth Plumly Thompson who also worked with Neill[17]. Even so, the enthusiasm has not spread beyond American shores and in Britain, even after 1939, few publishers engaged with either the original work or the

---

17   The bibliography is complex and hence a joy to book-dealers who are offered a great array of distinguishing 'points' in the varying editions. A recent (2017) catalogue lists a variant of the second state of *The Wizard* at $35,000.

many sequels. The first book's status as a classic is largely through
its featuring as one of the many out-of-copyright 'favourites' that
are selected by publishers to give their illustrators a canter although
none of them can equal Denslow.

-36-

PETER PAN
BY J. M. BARRIE (1902–1928)

Author:

James Matthew Barrie b. Kirriemuir 1860, d. London
1937; created baronet 1913, OM 1922; founder/captain of the
Allahakbarries cricket team, novelist etc. but not otherwise
implicated in children's literature.

Genre:

A multivalent dreamscape.

Evolution:

1902 – *The Little White Bird:* a fragmented novel, whose chapters
13–18 are later published separately (see below).

1903 – *Peter Pan:* a kind of scripted pantomime first produced at
the Duke of York's Theatre, but no text then published.

1906 – *Peter Pan in Kensington Gardens:* separate publication of
the White Bird chapters, garnished with illustrations by Arthur
Rackham. A *succès d'estime*.

1906 – The *Peter Pan Keepsake:* a prose version of the play edited
by Daniel O'Connor 'with Mr Barrie's kind assent, to enable
children to revive their memories' of the story. A slightly amended
version appeared in 1907 as *The Peter Pan Picture Book* (illustrated
by Alice B. Woodward) and this text remained in print for over
sixty years.

1911 – *Peter and Wendy:* Barrie's own novelization of the play,
including much material that also later appeared in its elaborate

stage directions and explanations.

1928 - *Peter Pan*: the eventual publication of the play-text, with a twenty-six page Dedication 'to the Five' who inspired it. This deserves to be seen as the 'true' *Peter Pan* and was republished in a Folio Society edition in 1992 with rebarbative illustrations by Paula Rego.

In 1929 Barrie gave rights over all versions of *Peter Pan* to the Great Ormond Street Hospital for Sick Children. In 1987 the legal term of copyright expired and Lord Callaghan succeeded with a Bill in the Lords to restore the Hospital's continuing right to royalties (but not its control over variant interpretations). Europe's 'harmonization' of copyright returned *Peter Pan* to full protection until 2007.

Right into the Jaws
of the Crocodile. Full
page 4-colour half-tone
under a captioned guard
(245x175mm.) after
Alice B. Woodward.
From the 14th ed. of
the *Peter Pan Picture
Book* by T. O'Connor
(Hodder, 1922)

So what's Peter's story? Resident in Kensington Gardens, as we find him in 1902, he is shown to already possess three attributes which will figure in his stage career: an initial capacity to fly (stemming from his new-born consciousness of pre-natal life as a bird); a consequent desertion of his mother in quest of liberty and 'fun' (hence his status as 'eternal child') and a bizarre knowledge that babies who fall out of their perambulators are rapt away by the fairies.

Peter's removal from W8 to the Neverland in the play engenders a multiplication of fantastic events, many deriving from Barrie's attachment to, and larks with, the five sons of Arthur and Sylvia Llewelyn Davies. Peter intrudes upon the Darling family while the nursemaid, a Newfoundland dog called Nana, is unfairly in disgrace. He shows them how to fly and they zoom off to the Neverland along with Peter's pugnacious coadjutrix, the fairy Tinker Bell. Here they meet Peter's tribe of Lost Boys who survive in a landscape of boyhood romance circa 1900: an underground house and a varied population of redskins, wolves, fairies, with a regular threat from pirates led by Captain James Hook. The antagonism between Peter and this Old Etonian scoundrel forms the theme of the most dramatic action, but it is underlain by the tensions between Wendy, as child-mother, and Peter, as amnesiac *Gauleiter*. Whether his cocky intransigence becomes tragic when the children return home is matter for debate. (The best-realised characters in the whole show are Nana and the Lost Boy, Tootles.)

Beerbohm got it right when he called the first production of the play 'a riot of inconsequence and exquisite futility'. While the *Kensington Gardens* story may be ridiculous, its rootedness in a known place and its controlled register of satiric whimsy give it a comic charm. But the play, and the narratives derived from it, present a farrago of happenings 'in such wise that one can conceive nothing that might not conceivably happen' (Beerbohm again).

Nevertheless, the play itself has always been able to overcome this deficiency through spectacular 'business' – just as Peter's fascist tendencies have been disguised by usually having him played by a Principal Girl. And, undeniably, the psychological dilemmas at the heart of the story – tortuously articulated by Jacqueline Rose in *The Case for Peter Pan* (2nd ed., Macmillan, 1992) – have an inexhaustible interest. Barrie's *Peter and Wendy* does plug some narrative holes in the play, experiments like Spielberg's movie *Hook* show a potential which Barrie did not exploit, but his homemade myth of the gains and losses of maturation and the fragility of child/adult relationships cannot help but endure.

Commentary

Jacqueline Rose was surely ill-advised to attempt to attach a theory about the 'impossibility' of children's literature from readings in so unstable a text. Better would have been to consider the themes and the various *obiter dicta* on childhood as a function of Barrie's biography and especially his relationship with the Llewelyn Davies children, but that had already been done in Andrew Birkin's powerful study of *J. M. Barrie and the Lost Boys* (1979). For a fully edited text of *Kensington Gardens and Peter and Wendy,* see the one-volume World Classics edition, *Peter Pan and Kensington,* edited by Peter Hollindale (1991).

-37-

THE TAILOR OF GLOUCESTER
BY BEATRIX POTTER (1902–3)

Christmas, 1901 'My dear Freda, Because you are fond of fairy-tales and have been ill, I have made you a story all for yourself – a new one that nobody has read before …'

No one had certainly done so then, but versions of the tale had gone the rounds by word of mouth in Gloucestershire where Helen Beatrix Potter had heard it from Caroline Hutton, a distant cousin, who lived near Stroud. What seems to have happened is that a Mr Prichard, a Gloucester tailor, had been hard-pressed for time and had left the making-up of a fancy waistcoat for the local mayor unfinished over a weekend. Coming back on the Monday though he found the whole job done except for a single button-hole to which was attached a note: 'no more twist'.

Delighted as he was by the discovery, Mr Prichard was mystified as to how it had occurred. Alert to its publicity value however, he put the garment in his window with a little notice: 'Come to Prichard where the waistcoats are made at night by the fairies'. (Only later was it revealed that the work had been done by two of his assistants who had snuck in over the weekend and done some unpaid overtime.)

Who could doubt that the tale with its mysterious denouement

Three-colour separation of Potter's watercolour frontispiece (50 x 70mm.) reproduced from the reprint of the original ms. of *The Tailor of Gloucester* (London: Frederick Warne, 1969).

would have had a great appeal to Miss Potter. She was a lover of fairytales and surely knew the Grimms' tale of the brownie shoemakers who worked secretly overnight for a cobbler. But when she came to work up the story in her Christmas letter to Freda Moore her imagination carried it beyond fairyland and into 'the time of swords and periwigs and full-skirted coats with flow'rd lappets' when it seems that the creatures of Gloucester had an enchanted life of their own.

For what Freda gets is an extended riff on the original anecdote in which the tailor – ailing – offends his dutiful housekeeper, the cat Simpkin, by depriving him of a cache of mice that he was saving up for his supper, and the mice, by way of gratitude, play the part of Mr Prichard's fairies. (The freeing of the mice, impounded under teacups and the like, occasions an unusual modification in Beatrix Potter's usually testing vocabulary. 'Was I wise to enfranchise those mice; undoubtedly the property of Simpkin?' asks the tailor querulously in Freda's manuscript – but 'let loose' comes to replace it in print.)

The manuscript is a substantial volume: eighty-five pages of text with twelve watercolour illustrations, all found in an exercise book bound in a moiré-grain cloth. ('There ought to be more pictures towards the end, and they would have been the best ones', writes the donor teasingly, 'only Miss Potter was tired of it! Which was lazy of Miss Potter'.) And the story went through a double transformation in its progress towards the 'little book' version which we have now. For at the time when Beatrix was composing it she was also involved in the private publication, at her own expense, of *The Tale of Peter Rabbit* – whose source, long before, had been a picture-letter to Freda's brother Noel. And such was the success of that private venture that the author-publisher was getting a taste for entrepreneurship and determined upon a like treatment for *The Tailor*. She borrowed back the exercise-book and set about editing its contents to make a companion volume to *Peter* but with more colour. (The 'private' *Peter* only had a colour frontispiece.)

Editing was something of a wrench. One of the characteristics of Freda's story was the author's joyous indulgence in reprinting a cacophony of carols and nursery rhymes as the cat Simpkin wanders the city streets on Christmas Eve. Beatrix loved these as much as she did fairytales and there are no fewer than twenty-three of them in the manuscript, including a complete performance of 'Kitty Alone' by some black rats carousing in a cellar. These were all too numerous for the ninety-six small, square pages (plus sixteen plates) of the first, privately printed, edition and Beatrix grievingly curtailed some and dispensed with others.

She probably realised too that the story sagged in the middle under the weight of these interpolations and when Frederick Warne welcomed the chance to bring the book out in a trade edition as a successor to *Peter Rabbit* she steeled herself to yet more cuts. Only six rhymes survived the slaughter and the drunken rats vanished utterly. 'For the life of me I could not see why Mr Warne insisted on cutting [them] out' she cheekily complained.

With diligence it is possible to compare the three versions of the story for a facsimile of the manuscript was published in 1968 and the text of the private edition is given in Leslie Linder's magnificent *History of the Writings of Beatrix Potter* of 1971. The author herself is on record as saying that the latter version was the favourite of all her books and although the rhymes are certainly *de trop* the narrative has a more natural flow than the somewhat tinkered-up trade volume that is with us now. And anyway she saw those early versions as a celebration of 'the old story that all the beasts can talk, in the night between Christmas Eve and Christmas Day in the morning' so we ought to be allowed to hear their

tuneful words as the bottles are emptied and the mice are stitching
away till they run out of cherry-coloured twist.

Commentary

The reduction of Beatrix Potter's stories into a uniform format
conceals the fact that there was considerable diversity in their
original appearance and that they varied more in length than
may be apparent. *Little Pig Robinson* (1930) and the farrago of
The Fairy Caravan (1929) were both first published in foolscap
octavo format, the latter only for sale in the United States. Her
attempt at a novelised folktale based on 'Bluebeard', *Sister Anne,*
was also published there and, fortunately for her reputation, never
in Britain.

-38-

THE ADVENTURES OF UNCLE LUBIN
BY WILLIAM HEATH ROBINSON (1903)

Sick with some childish ailment I was lent a book by a neighbour.
He knew my predilection for railways – the real ones, with steam
engines, and guards, and posh dining cars – and thought I might
enjoy a picture book celebrating the 1935 centenary of the old
Great Western.

He was lucky to get it back. For here were railway activities
from Madland, all the madder for taking themselves absolutely
seriously: the clerk sitting on the front of an engine with notebook
and a suspended alarm clock checking the entries for the first
timetable; a whole pageful of nineteen employees and char-ladies
cleaning all the parts of a dismembered locomotive – one later
finishing it off with a powder-puff. This was *Railway Ribaldry* by
the (unknown to me) W. Heath Robinson.

Ten years or so later, I discovered that this man, who had given an
adjectival phrase to the English language for his designs of fantastic

gadgets, had done many book illustrations before those were ever thought of. A favourite bookstall in Exeter's covered market charged me all of three shillings for a fat and slightly wobbly copy of *Hans Andersen's Fairy Tales,* printed, surprisingly, for Boots Pure Drug Company. This turns out to be, according to Geoffrey Beare's richly informative book on WHR's illustrations (1983), the sixth edition (1927) of a very stylish gift-book edition first published by Constable in 1913. (Andersen seems to have been a Robinson speciality. The very first book commission that he ever received was for an edition of the stories in 1897, followed by a more elaborate affair, done with his brothers, Thomas and Charles, in 1902 which went through some thirteen reprints.)

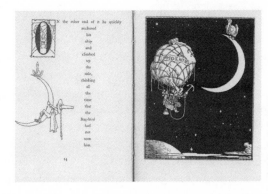

Double-page spread after drawings by the author (300x210mm.) from a New Edition of *The Adventures of Uncle Lubin.* London: Chatto & Windus, 1925.

By 1902, however, Robinson claimed that he was being trailed by an homunculus in a tall hat and a buttoned-up long coat whose story he was being prevailed upon to write and illustrate. So it was that in 1903 *The Adventures of Uncle Lubin* was published as Robinson's first authorial work and one of marked originality in a period by no means lacking in that quality. Uncle Lubin, now as a pictorial manifestation of Robinson's down-at-heel Good Genius, reaches us in Episode One, carelessly allowing his baby nephew Peter, to be stolen by a wicked Bag-bird and only after twelve adventures is a triumphant recovery effected. (That happens entirely by accident. Uncle Lubin has suffered a bombardment of coconuts from a very tall tree which it takes him two days and a night to ascend, but there at the top is Peter in the Bag-bird's nest among all the little Bag-chicks.)

It must be said that the book is inconsequential from beginning to end – as is a successor volume, *Bill the Minder* (1912). The reason may well be that, when young, WHR used to write stories Edgeworth-fashion on a school slate with the result that no story could exceed the scribal area of the slate. Brevity was needful and continuity difficult once the slate was filled so that progress occurred only through semi-connected passages. What mattered however was not the continuities (unfortunately the beady-eyed bird is almost entirely eased out of the story by Uncle Lubin's separate adventures) but the crazy events of his hunt and the brilliant graphic construction of their presentation.

Each story follows the same graphic pattern. There is a full-page chapter title lettered in red (blue in a later edition) with a single black and white drawing emblematic of the coming adventure. That adventure is then told in anything from seven to thirteen page-openings with the left-hand page given over to a red pictorial initial at the start of the monochrome text alongside a single drawing. (The story texts are very short and are amusingly arranged in different typographic shapes, often dwindling to a string of lines of one word each.) The page opposite consists of a full-page monochrome drawing (in three instances there are drawings across the spread) and each story then ends with a pictorial conclusion.

The random wanderings that Peter's enthusiastic but hapless uncle undertakes may be seen as essence of Heath Robinson. He constructs a balloon (filled from the domestic gas supply) and goes to the moon, which fortunately is in its crescent phase so he can hang his belongings on it; he visits mer-children in a home-made submarine (having cunningly despatched a sea-serpent in the previous story); he successfully melts a stalagmite with a candle but it falls on his head and knocks him over ... every drawing is not only full of comic detail but a wonder of graphic organisation on the page.

Commentary

Although there are hints throughout *Uncle Lubin* of incipient Heath Robinson contraptions, it was only after the book's publication that a man from the Lamson Paragon Company, concerned with commercial products, recognised in the illustrator the makings of an advertising draftsman and the way was opened for the inventiveness that was to produced *Railway Ribaldry* and so much else. Far from fading with the period in which his work was rooted, Heath Robinsonism has come to be increasingly revered and in recent years a HR Trust has been formed, through whose vigorous sponsorship a Heath Robinson Museum has now opened at Pinner, where he and his family lived for a few years after 1909.

–39–

A LITTLE PRINCESS; BEING THE WHOLE STORY OF SARA CREWE NOW TOLD FOR THE FIRST TIME BY FRANCES HODGSON BURNETT (1905)

My mother was a late Victorian child. When I asked her what had been her favourite reading at that time she named a book by Frances Hodgson Burnett called *Editha's Burglar*, pronouncing the name with a long 'i' as she must have done when first she read it.

But was it a book all on its own? The story, about a little girl who persuades a burglar to do his work *very quietly* so as not to disturb Mama, is quite short and was first published in that peerless American children's magazine, *St Nicholas* in 1880. There was hardly enough of it for an independent existence and when it did appear in 1888 as the book my mother read it was joined by a longer Hodgson Burnett story, also from *St Nicholas*: *Sara Crewe; or What Happened at Miss Minchin's*.

This dramatic tale (I'm surprised my mother didn't prefer it to *Editha*) brings Sara Crewe from India to London with her widowed father, who places her in Miss M's 'Select Seminary for Young Ladies' as a posh 'parlour boarder' before returning to the sub-continent where, alas, some time later, he is bilked by a friend and dies penniless. Thus Sara Crewe is removed from her comfortable suite and, from being star pupil, is reduced to maid-of-all-work, banished to the attic with its fireless grate and iron bedstead. Miss Minchin, who is perforce her guardian, for there is no one else, works her to the bone, although Sara, a child of much character, survives by persuading herself that she is a lost princess who will one day come into her own – and that indeed happens. Back in England, an invalid from India, with his Lascar servant (and a monkey), takes the house next door and proves (of course) to be Papa's old friend – recovered financially but racked by guilt over the latter's death and the disappearance of his daughter.

Burnett was good at this sort of drama, as witness *Little Lord Fauntleroy* and *The Secret Garden*. It's not surprising therefore to find that *Sara Crewe* came to be converted into a play, as *The Little Princess*, in 1903, running with acclaim in both New York and London. Both the author and her publisher thought this an opportunity too good to miss, and Burnett – a pro if ever there was one – set about reconstructing *Sara Crewe* as a full-dress fiction. It was published in superior style, begirt with colour plates, as *A Little Princess* in 1905.

'The story tells itself so well', she wrote to her son, speaking of the 'lightning rapidity' of its composition, that it proved no hack job, no mere bulking out of a superannuated text. In a chummy preface to her readers she expressed one of the great thrills of fiction, that 'between the lines of every story there is another story, and that is one that is never heard and can only be guessed at by those who are good at guessing'. With the conversion of *Sara Crewe* into a play she had discovered more about the goings-on in Miss M's seminary than she had formerly known and she felt it very blameworthy of the new characters who had appeared on the scene, such as spoiled Lottie and the half-starved scullery-maid, Becky, and grey-whiskered Mr Melchisedec (who lived behind the wainscot) for their 'slouching idle ways' in not presenting themselves to her earlier.

These narrative extensions effect radical changes to the nature of the story. For instance, Sara's traumatic reduction from riches to rags occurs only after some ninety pages in which her privileged status and her relationship with her admiring or jealous classmates is dwelt on with a degree of detail impossible in the five introductory pages of *Sara Crewe*, The same applies to her life in the garret through whose skylight begins her friendship with her neighbour's Lascar servant, which will lead to the happy conclusion. But this time, the gentleman's illness and its cause are revealed long before the denouement so that the reader (who may well have guessed it in the shorter book) is now constrained to watch how the storyteller will bring the two together over a longer timespan.

Such changes, to which may be added a rather less credible treatment of the transformation scene, where the Lascar secretly converts Sara's attic into what she at first believes to be a room in Fairyland, give a depth to the story which has held readers continuously from the time of its first publication.

" BECKY RAN TO HER AND CAUGHT HER HAND, AND HUGGED IT TO HER BREAST, KNEELING BESIDE HER "

'Becky ran to her ...' four-colour plate (image 150x100mm.) by Harold Piffard facing p.108 in *A Little Princess* (Frederick Warne, 1915).

(The Puffin edition, which dates back to 1961 is especially commendable for its sensitive line drawings by Margery Gill – or 'Hill' as a recent printing called this disgracefully forgotten illustrator). Nevertheless, there remains much to be said for the earlier *Sara Crewe*, whose comparative brevity sharpens the intensity of the tale.

Commentary

An excuse needs to be proffered to readers who expected to find *The Secret Garden* of 1910 as the knock-down choice for a story by Burnett. Both tales deal in a heroine who struggles against the odds and both verge on sentimentality in their drama, but I find the golden-hearted Yorkshire peasants of the later book less credible than the Lascar in the attic of the earlier one and am less satisfied with its conclusion where the emphasis shifts suddenly to the healed boy, leaving our heroine almost mute among the happy throng of admirers. For bibliographers and textual critics the transformations of the text of *A Little Princess* offer much scope for comparative criticism.

–40–

PUCK OF POOK'S HILL
BY RUDYARD KIPLING (1906)

'The train, the twelve o'clock to paradise ... ' is an invocation by Harold Monro, the founder of the Poetry Bookshop, round about 1920. The paradise was, as much as anywhere, in the county of Sussex where the train would take you for a weekend on the Downs or by the sea.

Poets, writers and artists would be among those in the carriages, but Kipling, who has claims to be hymnologist of the county, had no need to travel for he lived there, at Batemans, a seventeeth-century house in the Sussex Weald. Belloc wrote of Hanaker Mill down the road, Enid Bagnold, at Rottingdean, wrote of *Alice and Thomas and Jane's* exploits there (see no.51 below), Eleanor Farjeon walked the Down round Alfriston – on one occasion accompanied by D. H. Lawrence.

Pook's Hill, which stands above Bateman's was to inspire the stories that were stage-managed by Puck, 'the oldest Old Thing in England' and presented to the children, Dan and Una, in the splendour of an Edwardian summer, (their names stood for those of Kipling's own son and daughter, John and Elsie).

Rooted in the historic landscape they were to be, as Kipling said in a letter, '<u>not</u> a notion of history but of the time sense which is at the bottom of all knowledge of history[18]'and he stole a narrative device from Edith Nesbit's *The Phoenix and the Carpet* which he had been reading to 'Dan and Una'. Where Nesbit's children were conveyed hither and yon by the magic carpet, Kipling's history was brought to them on their own patch of Sussex turf.

Puck himself introduces the founding episode, a tale of the mystic figure of Wayland (later Wayland Smith of Wayland's Forge upon which the name of the neighbouring village of Willingford was putatively based). This serves to introduce Saxon Hugh who, in the second episode, encounters the Norman Sir Richard Dalyngridge, just victorious at Hastings, with their association marking the start of a fragile unity between conquered and conquerors. (The village of Dallington is just down the road from Bateman's.) Hugh and Richard and Pevensey Castle occupy three episodes before Puck takes his audience backwards to the closing years of the Roman occupation, significant for the book's purpose of showing how another invading army comes to find Britain as a home within the fragmenting empire. (The influence of these passages on Rosemary Sutcliff[19], who lived much of her later life in Sussex, are noted in our discussion of *Eagle of the Ninth* at no.71 below.)

Disruption of the time-frame occurs further in the final three episodes,

18   From a letter sent to Edward Bok in July 1905, quoted from Harry Ricketts, *The Unforgiving Minute* (Chatto, 1999) p. 289.
19   She wrote a brief account of his work in the Bodley Head Monograph series in 1960.

although links are sustained directly or by implication with Puck's Sussex regime. In the penultimate story he engages with Old Hobden, the local hedger, while he and the children are roasting potatoes on an oast-house fire. Hobden has been a recurring figure in the telling of the tales, an emblem of the 'time sense' in a family rooted in the Weald over countless generations (Puck knew his ninth great-great-grandfather).

Scattered though the themes may be, the presence of the sixteen poems, placed as intermediaries between the prose texts, have a unifying effect and enhance the narrative power. Some, such as 'Puck's Song' at the start, and 'A Tree Song' give the Sussex setting, while others, such as 'The Harp Song of the Dane Women' or the famous 'Smugglers' Song' are reflections on some part of the stories: 'Watch the wall, my darling, while the Gentlemen go by!'

One may wonder what Puck may make today of the need for the achieving of such a sense. At the time of writing, you may be frustrated in finding a twelve o'clock train to Sussex while the paradise when you get there may be somewhat modified by motorways, satellite villages and impending invasions from nations beyond those of Normandy or Rome.

Commentary

Somebody once said that the line of longitude in children's literature flows through Kipling, by which, presumably, they meant that he has written great examples of stories that cut across the lines of latitude of the genres: illustrated stories for telling to younger children, invented animal fables, school stories, a sea novel, an exotic adventure story and the explorations of history in *Puck of Pook's Hill* and its successor, *Rewards and Fairies* (1910).

The stories in *Puck*, as with much of Kipling's work, were first published separately through magazines, in this case *The Strand*, with illustrations by Claude Shepperson (and by different executants in the American journals). The verses were added when the printed book was published and the illustrations were done by H. R. Millar (the decision possibly influenced by Kipling's liking for his work for Nesbit). *Rewards and Fairies* was illustrated by C. E. Brock.

-41-

ANNE OF GREEN GABLES
BY LUCY MAUD MONTGOMERY (1908)

No pro in the inky trade likes to pass up a good idea for a story and by 1904 the Canadian, Lucy Maud Montgomery (Maud to those who knew her), was indeed quite a pro. Her first effusion, a thirty-nine stanza ballad, had been published in a local paper just before her sixteenth birthday in 1890 and from then on came forth a seemingly unstoppable flow of verses and stories for magazines, whose requirements she studied carefully. In 1901 she went to Halifax, Nova Scotia and spent a year there working as proof-reader and journalist for a sister paper of the Halifax *Chronicle*.

Instant inspiration thus followed her discovery of a news story which she noted as 'Elderly couple apply to orphan asylum for a boy. By mistake a girl is sent them'; she began developing the potential of that event, setting it on Prince Edward Island, Canada's smallest province. It was there that Maud had been born and brought up and it is generally acknowledged that something of her own childhood and much of her love for the place is celebrated in the book that finally emerged in 1908 as *Anne of Green Gables*.

You'd have to be an unenterprising pro not to have made the most of the small drama that engendered the book (and, in recognising that, it is proper to envisage the impact that the book's opening would have had on Maud's earliest readers. They lacked today's benefit of knowing 'what happened next' which now derives from Anne's worldwide fame as classic heroine. It is said that in Japan sales of the Avonlea series top twenty million copies). Suspense is engendered straightway as the curtain-twitching Mrs Rachel Lynde wonders why Matthew Cuthbert is taking the buggy into town dressed in his best suit of clothes when he ought to be sowing turnips. With his discovery of Anne, bereft on the station platform, suspense is further heightened over what her fate will be once he gets back home and has to reveal to his grim, spinster sister, Marilla, the mistake that has occurred.

The normally hen-pecked Matthew shows unprecedented steel

in nudging Marilla to an unwilling acceptance that Anne should stay at Green Gables and what follows becomes an extended justification of his faith in the child. On the ride home from the station he had been astonished (as perhaps are many readers too) by her loquaciousness and by her command of a vocabulary beyond any discourse to be found among Avonlea's citizens, and through this he perceives a resilience of spirit that demands sympathy and nurture. (I do not find the explanation of how she gained her intellectual capacities, as given in Budge Wilson's prequel *Before Green Gables* (2008) very convincing.)

And so the book evolves into that familiar form of *Bildungsroman* where, episode by episode over some five years, Anne proves herself to be capable of reform from a jabbering air-head to a mature and responsible young lady, winning a scholarship and all set to start training to become a teacher. She makes a notable place for herself in the activities of the small-town populous – such that one is occasionally reminded of life at Ambridge before sex was invented – and, willy-nilly, as the book concludes, Maud's enthusiastic audience is yelling for more. (She does not seem to have been as keen on the idea as her publishers and came to see the saga as a burden – and one which eventually led to a nine-year court-case over their unauthorised use of inferior copy.)

In a letter to a youthful Mary Baldwin – she who later married the Rt. Hon. Harold Wilson – Maud confessed to dissatisfaction with much of her own work and remarked that her own favourite among her books was not *Green Gables* but a yet more autobiographical sister-story, *Emily of New Moon*, published in 1923. She also implies that both books were not really conceived as 'for children' (and indeed the first publication of *Green Gables* as a Penguin saw it published by Kaye Webb in her 'Peacocks' – an early stab at a YA series – and the whole Avonlea 'chariot', at whose wheels Maud saw herself dragged, surely belongs with such bestselling middlebrow vehicles as the '*Whiteoaks*' collection by that other Canadian, Mazo de la Roche.)

What saves *Green Gables* from being just another tale of everyday country folk is not Anne's *Bildungsroman* at all, but that of Marilla. Anne's volatile character and her rather forced long-term antagonism towards he who will become the boyfriend are stuff of a hundred such narratives – carried along by Maud's often vivacious and sometimes satiric writing. But stern Marilla, unwilling to compromise on the entrenched proprieties of those in her station, is a character to be reckoned with. Her creator may occasionally give us authorial insights into her burgeoning recognition of Anne's qualities and her growing love for her as the daughter she could never have: 'dismayed at suddenly finding herself inclined to laugh', or, later, 'holding [Anne] tenderly to her heart, wishing she need never let her go', and it is this transformation in her character that powers the book beyond the ruck.

Commentary

Anne of Green Gables was in no way original as a tale of an outcast girl finding a way for herself in 'the wide, wide world'. Those very words belong to the title of one of the earliest manifestations of the genre (first published in New York in 1850): six hundred pages devoted to the tearful and prayerful adventurings of Eleanor (coincidence) Montgomery after she is sent to her gruesome Aunt Fortune when her feckless father and ailing mother head off for Europe. That book was a bestseller in both America and Britain (mocked by Kingsley in *The Water-Babies*) and was to be followed by others of the same kidney – mostly American: Martha Finley and *Elsie Dinsmore*, whose tribulations ran to thirty volumes; the still-honoured sequence involving the 'little women' whose father was away at the war; Katy and her doings; and the ineffable Pollyanna.

In relation to *Anne*, the most intriguing is Kate Douglas Wiggin's *Rebecca of Sunnybrook Farm*. First published in 1903, this bestseller treats of the exile of an all-too rumbustious member of an all-too large family to the chill care of two maiden aunts. (We first experience *her* garrulity, as we did Anne's, on the buggy-ride to her new quarters.) Like Anne she is irrepressible; like Anne she is shown maturing through several years in her adoptive town, winning everyone's esteem; and like Anne she thaws the icy disciplines of Aunt Miranda, a much less attractive personage than Marilla. Did Maud, I wonder, up in the Island, writing the first classic Canadian girlhood story, earlier encounter the work of Kate Douglas down in the States? Is Rebecca an influential New England relative of Anne?

-42-

THE WIND IN THE WILLOWS
BY KENNETH GRAHAME (1908)

Aunty Toothache came visiting. Four milk-teeth were extracted 'under gas' (fearful phrase to a seven year-old) so by way of consolation my mother bought me a book for recuperative reading: *The Wind in the Willows* by Kenneth Grahame.

It was an unimpressive affair (I have it before me as I write: its endpapers embellished with the blotchy results of an attempt to carve criss-cross lines on a school eraser to make a decorative rubber stamp.) The covers were of an unfetching brown sand-grain cloth, blocked with the drab series design of Methuen's Modern Classics (fifty-second edition) and its 192 pages were innocent of any pictures.

After two pages however such things were of no consequence. Mole had only to bowl over that elderly rabbit who tried to levy a sixpenny toll from him and then trot on his way crying 'Onion-sauce! Onion-sauce!' for one young reader to become his devoted companion for the 190 pages that remained.

As English pastoral, which is what some readers have called it, *The Wind in the Willows* is more country polka than idyll. Mole's escape to the River Bank is rapidly succeeded by his meeting with Water Rat (really Water Vole, as is frequently pointed out in conservation literature, but too assonant with 'mole' to be employable). The first of those feasts which gloriously punctuate the adventures is prepared; Mr Toad is momentarily spotted in his wager-boat – first glimpse of the great central narrative; and

Mole's impulsive, but unschooled, oarsmanship sets the tenor for his perfect liaison with the ever-practical Ratty.

30   *The Wind in the Willows*

Rounding a bend in the river, they came in sight of a handsome, dignified old house of mellowed red brick, with well-kept lawns reaching down to the water's edge.

'There's Toad Hall,' said the Rat; 'and that creek on the left, where the notice-board says, "Private. No landing allowed," leads to his boat-house, where we'll leave the boat. The stables are over there to the right. That's the banqueting-hall you're looking at now—very old, that is. Toad is rather rich, you know, and this is really

'"There's Toad Hall", said the Rat'. Centre-page pencil drawing by E.H. Shepard (185x125). Page 40 of *The Wind in the Willows* (38th ed. – the first illustrated by Shepard – 1931.) showing Rat at the sculls rather than Mole as the text requires.

Where such a train of events is not being expounded (Mole lost, say, amid the whistlings and patterings of the Wild Wood … Rat to the rescue … Badger and the eucatastrophe …) there may be equally appealing explorations of the character and relationship of these rural folk (Ratty's low-key, almost sentimental, setting-up of the party for the carol-singing field mice) and I still recall in that first encounter with the story how readily I came to trust my author. Confidence grew that, in another page or two, more jokes (Mr Toad before the Bench), or more word-play (the arming ceremony before battle: 'a-sword-for-the-Mole, a-sword-for-the-Rat, a-sword-for-the-Toad …') or more farce (especially the Toad's vainglorious follies) would sustain the pleasure of the reading.

The shared verve is not surprising since, as so often occurs with these classics, the story began with the author telling it aloud at bedtime to a child and then, over time, supplementing the oral version with continuations in letters. The chronology is not clear and the sources of inspiration are variegated (the idea probably came through Grahame's liking for fables; 'The River Bank', usually assumed to be that of the Thames, may well involve the Fowey River in Cornwall too) but what is carried over from the family tale to the printed book is Grahame's mastery of the language and the pacing of his narrative.

Except of course – yes, of course 'of course' – those two chapters that have so often roused critical grumblings: 'The Piper at the Gates of Dawn' and 'Wayfarers All'. Both are ruminative interpolations with no direct bearing on the rapidly developing drama of Toad's adventures, and have been seen as self-indulgence on Grahame's part. (Alas that there is not space here to pursue their relationship to his earlier writings: the *fin de siècle* essays of *Pagan Papers* (1893) and those story collections that foreshadow *The Wind in the Willows: The Golden Age* (1895) and *Dream Days* (1898)[20].

From those earlier examples and precedents it seems reasonable to argue that Grahame was willing to risk the charge of self-indulgence for the sake of bodying out and reconfiguring a larger purpose behind his epic fable. Whatever readers might find of comedy or allegory in the doings of these animals it was important for them to recognise behind the larks an all-embracing unity in the natural world and an unquenchable zest (fulfilled or not) to venture beyond the next horizon. Few years remained beyond 1908 when such Romantic idealism could have any validity, and it looks pretty threadbare now with the River Bank clogged up with people-carriers and beakers full of the warm South served up on £5 flights to Venice.

The illustrator Michael Foreman in a Note to his expansive,

20   Will someone please reissue those, preferably in the combined edition illustrated by Charles Keeping and published by The Bodley Head in 1962?

but overweight, illustrated edition of the story (Chrysalis, 2001) strongly commends these two 'difficult' chapters, but erroneously remarks that they are 'often omitted from modern editions'. So far as I can discover they are always included but are indeed noteworthy for offering illustrators little in the way of narrative purchase – thereby emphasising the dearth of action at points when the reader is most expecting it. (Attempts at Pan, including that by Ernest Shepard, should really be forbidden – although Foreman does better than most – and apart from him the artist is thrown back on variably successful boating scenes and pictures of the Seafaring Rat gesturing 'Go South, young man'.)

Such illustrative problems are not confined to those two chapters however and there is much to be said for having the story published in plain text as first occurred (apart from a soggily symbolic frontispiece by Grahame's friend Graham Robertson, along with a gilt-blocked Pan on the front board and Toad in motoring gear on the spine). Efforts to add illustrations in 1913, 1922 and 1927 were uniformly disastrous and it's no wonder that when E. H. Shepard (the publisher's illustrator-of-choice after his success with A. A. Milne) called on Grahame in 1930 to discuss a new edition the author plaintively cried 'I love these little people. Be kind to them'. (He was not kind enough in his picture of Mole and Rat rowing down the river as to give the sculls to Rat, who is 'settled comfortably in the stern' rather than to Mole.)

Peter Green in his perceptive biography of Grahame, first published in 1959, sums up exactly the arguments against illustrating the book. There is a 'fluidity of viewpoint' about the storytelling (most obvious in the shifts between animal and human behaviour in the characters). The inner eye of the reader – such is the genius of Grahame's exposition – 'sees no incongruity in these metamorphoses (and in fact hardly notices them) while visual representation at once pins down Grahame's imagination to a single static concept'. He accepts that Shepard 'came as near as possible' to finding a balance (now joined, in my view, by Patrick Benson who was given the book by HarperCollins after his work on William Horwood's first sequel *The Willows in Winter*). But that child in the big armchair, consoling himself with the drab little

'Modern Classic', assures me that he never felt need for someone to show him what was going on. Mr Grahame was sufficient.

Commentary

In 1944 Grahame's quaint and unreliable widow, Elspeth, published *The First Whisper of the Wind in the Willows* where she confirmed that the saga had begun with bedtime stories to his son Alastair and continued in letters written to him while they were apart. The latter ended up in the Bodleian Library and have been more formally published as *My Dearest Mouse* in a volume edited by Daniel Gooderson (1988). A recent brief volume on *The Making of The Wind in the Willows* by Peter Hunt also makes good use of Bodley's resources (it is published by the Library) and focuses, in a rather offended way, on several continuing mysteries about the book and its publishing history.

Elspeth also included in her little volume the text of a delightful Christmas tale which Grahame had written about a pig and two rabbits (Peter and Benjamin!) who had gone on a festive jaunt and had ended up by enjoying some of the contents of Mr Grahame's larder and drinking his champagne. This was made into a pretty book, *Bertie's Escapade,* in 1949 with illustrations, naturally from E. H. Shepard.

The Wind in the Willows also has several adjunct texts, most notably A. A. Milne's play *Toad of Toad Hall* (1929), but also such sequels as Horwood's *The Willows in Winter* (1993) and events as seen from the point of view of the crushed proletariat: *Wild Wood* by Jan Needle (1981).

-43-

THE THREE MULLA-MULGARS
BY WALTER DE LA MARE (1910)

For eighteen-and-a-half years Walter de la Mare had been in bondage as a clerk at the Anglo-American Oil Company in the City of London. It was a killing job from which he was rescued in the summer of 1908 by Henry Newbolt, who gained for him a Crown grant of £200 to pursue a burgeoning career as a writer.

The response was immediate, for within a week or two of his release he was writing 'the inane adventures of three monkeys' at a rate of one to two thousand words a day. (Before long that became every other day since he started to run it alongside a novel that was to become *The Return*.) In fact there was an oral origin for the 'inane' tale in that he had been telling it as a bedtime story to his children, but its formalisation as a written work demanded a disciplining of its wild imaginings and in 1910 its 312 pages were published (with some misgivings) by the firm of Gerald Duckworth, the half-brother and abuser of Virginia Woolf.

An absorbing mystery pervades the story from its opening in the Forest of Munza-mulga where we meet the old, grey fruit-monkey, Mutta-matutta and her sons Thumma, Thimbulla, and Ummanodda: 'and they called each other for short, Thumb, Thimble and Nod'. Their father, silent and moody Seelem, was a Mulgar of the Blood Royal, a Mulla-mulgar and brother to the Prince Assasimon of the Valleys of Tishnar, but he had left his brother's palace to go adventuring. Now he longs to return and leaves his family, promising to come back 'with slaves and scarlet and food-baskets, and Zeverras' to collect them.

He does not come and Mutta-matutta pines and dies, distributing among her sons what little of Seelem's riches she had stored, including the Wonderstone which she gives to Nod, for he is a Nizza-neela and has magic in him. Soon after, for all that they dwell in a great jungle, a bitter winter, with ice and snow, comes upon them and they determine to follow their father to the Valleys of Tishnar beyond the Mountains of Arakkaboa. They knew nothing of the route, seeming like dogs 'to smell out their way' and for the rest of the book we follow their adventures.

Enough has been said to show that de la Mare is writing a book for which few precedents exist. He has always been fond of occultation (' "Is there anyone there?" said the traveller …') and what must be Africa is now seen in a distorting mirror with its winter snow, its zevveras, its ephelantos and the like while its population have varying languages. (In a cod preface, only found in the first edition, the author claims to be translating from Mulgar Royal, some parts of which he has had to leave in the original.) There is also a disquisition, transferred to an appendix after the first edition, on Mulgar lore in which is explained with typical de la Mare obliquity – 'chattering about what I do not understand'. 'Tishnar' is not so much a place as a condition of inexpressible peace, while there are the external shadows of Immanâla preying upon the living and Noomanala, which is death.

The presence of such mysteries in fact serves to strengthen the reader's sense of Otherness which is sustained with a compelling consistency. It is easy to believe – and I have proved it myself – that this long book makes for powerful storytelling. The characters of Thumb, Thimble, and Nod are endearing from the start and the episodes of danger and encounters with the exotic are inventive with a graphic originality very different from those met among, say, the traditionary travellers in *The Hobbit* (see below no. 57).

It is true that de la Mare, a voracious reader, was influenced by the seventeenth century farrago of *Purchas his Pilgrimage* (Nod's sojourn with the English sailor, Andy Battle, owes much to that) but the references are seamlessly internalised within the writer's own imaginative world.

Commentary

The Three Mulla-Mulgars sported a frontispiece and a single colour plate by E. A. Monsell in 1910 (acknowledged on an errata slip) and a handsome American edition, illustrated with twelve plates and many line drawings by Dorothy P. Lathrop came out in 1919. Eight years and two reprints later a new edition with illustrations by J. A. Shepherd was published by Faber & Gwyer with the title changed to *Three Royal Monkeys* and thus it has remained, with a new edition illustrated by Mildred E. Eldridge appearing in 1946. The gradual transfer of much of de la Mare's writing to Faber & Faber (as they became in 1929) owes much to the company's employment of his son Richard as a production manager and eventually director.

-44-

ROBIN HOOD AND THE MEN OF THE GREENWOOD
BY HENRY GILBERT (1912)

The good burghers of Nottingham did well to stake out a claim for Robin Hood as a hero of their Sherwood Forest, profitable as a bit of local publicity, but somewhat specious in terms of the sites of action. Nottingham may serve frequently as a place of japery around the figure of its hapless Sheriff, who in some tales gets killed by Robin, and the forest was as good a place as any for secret encampments, but lacking any exact evidence as to whether the outlaw really existed or is just a myth, he is arguably a Yorkshireman running his meinie in Barnsdale to the north of Sherwood in what became the West Riding. Sometimes Nottingham is brought about forty miles nearer to Barnsdale to allow for some easier travelling between the two.

It is in the ballads, some of great antiquity, that the outlaw's fame is primarily recorded. 'Rimes of Robin Hood' are mentioned in the manuscript of Pierce Plowman in the fourteenth century and the earliest and most celebrated of them to have survived was the *Gest of Robyn Hode* (printed round about 1500), which brought several episodes together to make a serial account of the hero's adventures. Thereafter he often features in single stories, but those closest to some kind of oral tradition find him in named places such as Wentbridge or the Sales, north of Doncaster.

Compulsive though the ballads were for children as listeners or readers, it was not until the early nineteenth century that adaptations were published specially for them such as a 240-page reprint of Joseph Ritson's major collection 'which could with propriety be put into the hands of young persons'. When his exploits are more directly edited for them, Robin comes to be garbed in prose. From the 1820s onward he was a natural participant in story books and picture books, often with slender content, and it was the American author/illustrator Howard Pyle who, in 1883, first put together a jumbled but sustained account of *The Merry Adventures of Robin Hood of Great Renown*. He added *in Nottinghamshire* to the title, thus substantially focusing attention on the southern county.

Pyle knew the ballads, probably from Ritson's volume, and incorporated features from them in all his stories but with a genial insistence on the 'merriment' of the whole proceeding and for more than half a century his book came to be highly regarded on both sides of the Atlantic. It was tricked out in an 'olde worlde' fashion, with side notes and elaborate illustrations and headpieces which enhanced its medieval feel. (The same can hardly be said of its cod Elizabethan prose, especially in conversational exchanges: 'I make my vow, Little John, my blood tickles my veins as it flows through them this gay morn. What sayst thou to our seeking adventures, each one upon his own account?'.)

Not much is known about Henry Green, who published his *Robin Hood* twenty-five years after Pyle but it can easily be seen as a corrective to the altogether lighter American work. Green was certainly also cognisant of the ballad sources, and benefited from the huge and authoritative collection published in Volume III of Francis James Child's *English and Scottish Popular Ballads* of 1888.

Much of the setting is in the Barnisdale Forest rather than Sherwood, which, as noted above, gains authority from the ballads, and the thread of the enmity between Robin and Guy of Gisborne – together with the less publicised Sir Isembras de Belame – gives a greater unity to the unavoidable progress of the regularly recurring skirmishes and pitched battles. (Guy has only a brief appearance in the penultimate chapter of Pyle.) He also admits to inventing elements of his own, not the least of which is his introduction of the 'little people'. Ket the Trow and Hob o' the Hill who are the reclusive forest-dwellers of ancient pre-Roman ancestry. The traditional ballad incidents, such as the meeting with Little John and Father Tuck, the wedding with Marian (a late arrival in the sources), the killing of the Sheriff, and the romantic death are all knitted into what is, in effect, a novelisation, making a more coherent and powerful story than standard retellings.

The impressive dress of the first edition as a large octavo with seventeen colour plates by Walter Crane was much reduced after the publisher, T. C. and E. C. Jack, sold out to Messrs Nelson. The format was reduced to that of the many volumes in their *Famous Books* series, 'ideal for School Prizes or the Home Library' and, while a single Crane colour plate was retained as a frontispiece, the sixteen other illustrations came from pen-drawings by H. M. Brock which were more fitting for the story than Crane's.

Commentary

One of the earliest prose versions of the stories for children was a thirty-two page paper-covered booklet, illustrated with four nice etchings and claiming to be 'a complete history of the notable and merry exploits performed by [Robin] and his men on many occasions, (1818). For Victorians, the earliest significant account of *Robin Hood and his Merry Foresters* was that by 'Stephen Percy' (in fact, Joseph Cundall, the man who published it in 1841). It appeared also in the United States and is said to be the source text known to Tom Sawyer, playing the adventures 'by the book' in Hannibal, Missouri.

In 1995 an immense exhibition: *Robin Hood; the Many Faces of That Celebrated English Outlaw* was organised by Kevin Carpenter at the University of Oldenburg, whose three-hundred page, partially bi-lingual catalogue reveals the many forms in which the hero has been presented.

–45–

THE MAGIC PUDDING; BEING THE ADVENTURES OF BUNYIP BLUEGUM AND HIS FRIENDS BILL BARNACLE AND SAM SAWNOFF
BY NORMAN LINDSAY (1916)

Oh who would be a puddin',

> A puddin' in a pot,
> A puddin' which is stood on
> A fire which is hot?
> O sad indeed the lot
> Of puddins in a pot.

The Puddin' owners with their charge. Pen and ink drawing by the author.

The chanter of this mournful ditty is the puddin' himself, Albert by name, possessed by the Society of Puddin' Owners, Bill Barnacle, a sailor and his friend Sam Sawnoff, a penguin bold. They are encountered at a lunch of steak-and-kidney pie by Bunyip Bluegum, a koala bear who has left his tree home on account of the discomfort of living with his Uncle Wattleberry whose whiskers take up too much room.

As a Gentleman of Leisure, possessed of only a walking-stick, Bunyip is getting hungry and at the insistence of the Puddin', a notably grumpy character, he is invited to join the others at their meal. There they reveal that Albert is a Magic Pudding, a cut-and-come-again pudding, who delights in being eaten and supplies slices to all who ask for them without growing any the less. Moreover he is able to supply on demand whatever kind of pudding may be required; you only had to whistle twice and turn the pot round (steak-and-kidney pie, boiled jam-roll, and apple-turnover are favourites).

Strolling along after their meal (Albert accompanies them, walking on little spindly legs) our three heroes run into two unsavoury characters round a bend in the road, a Possum and a Wombat, sharpening a carving-knife on a portable grindstone. These prove to be two notorious Puddin'Thieves who have tried to steal Albert on previous occasions and must be summarily dealt with through fisticuffs, Bunyip preventing the flighty puddin' from running away by upending the pot and sitting on it. Pleased by this collaboration, Bill and Sam invite Bunyip to join the Club and the First Slice of the book ends with them carrolling the Puddin' Owners Anthem:-

> Hurrah, we'll stick together,
> And always bear in mind
> To eat our puddin' gallantly
> Whenever we're inclined.

Appropriately the story is divided into four slices rather than chapters and the remaining portions mix in additional endeavours by the Possum and the Wombat to make off with the puddin'. The grand finale engages satirically with a court scene where Bunyip rescues the puddin' from the Bench, where he is being consumed accompanied by a bottle of port, by asservating under oath that he has been injected with poison. (Bunyip has throughout shown an intellectual distinction in devising means for foiling the Puddin'

Thieves rather than encouraging the snout-bending violence customary with Bill and Sam).

Escape from the court and from the town of Pooraloo is encouraged by Bill under the realisation that 'we are pretty close up to the end of the book and something must be done in a Tremendous Hurry or we'll be cut off short by the cover'. Enough pages are left however to allow them to build a tree-house with a Puddin' Paddock attached and there they may be found feasting on puddin' and coffee and singing the songs and ballads in which their story abounds. When night falls they protect themselves from Puddin' Thieves by just pulling up the ladder.

Commentary

Norman Lindsay was an Australian writer, draftsman, painter, etcher, sculptor, and cartoonist whose ninety energetic years led him to a prolific output. (A museum set up in his house at Faulconbridge, Victoria is devoted to his work, officially established by the Australian National Trust in 1970.) His eldest son, Jack, with whom he worked in Australia founding the Fanfrolico Press, brought the Press to England in 1928 where he settled for good. He too was a prolific writer and published several well-regarded stories for children. A second son, Philip, also lived in England where he was noted as an historical novelist.

-46-

THE TREASURE OF THE ISLE OF MIST
BY W. W. TARN (1919)

It was the yellow centipede who remarked on Hegel and the unity of opposites, for he was a philosopher. Fiona had gone to see him first thing in the morning to get some advice on how to get to Fairyland, for her small friend, the Urchin, had been rapt away by 'the little people' for throwing a stone at a shore-lark.

Fiona is the daughter of The Student who is writing a learned work (probably on Hellenistic civilisation) in their house on the Isle of Skye. He is the owner of the larger house nearby but lets it out and the Urchin is the son of the current tenant. He and Fiona had been making plans to hunt for the sunken treasure of a Venetian galleon that had been wrecked off their part of the coast in the course of the failed Armada. It seems it may have been unshipped and hidden in the west cave on the island of Scargill. (Much information, including that from an old whale and later that from the caterpillar is gained by Fiona, thanks to the gift of an ancient bracelet. She had recently received it from a travelling hawker from whom she had just bought some necessary buttons.)

When, in the depths of the cave the Urchin disappears, a complication arises. For the Urchin's uncle, a disreputable, self-seeking man from the City, has also discovered the location of the treasure and he has followed the children into the cave to wrest it from them (if they find it). But he meets with an accident when part of the cave wall falls onto him and is rowed back to the big house in a coma.

The upshot of all this is that Fiona, with her father's blessing, takes to the valley of Glenollisdal out of which she climbs and, after strange encounters, gains access to the island's Fairyland. Both the Urchin and the spirit of his knocked-out uncle are there to be tried before the Fairy Court for their transgressions (the King of the Fairies has a splendidly comic advocate, reflecting perhaps Tarn's one-time profession as a lawyer) and both are instantaneously freed, the one, with Fiona, back on the Glenollisdal hillside, the other, out of his bedridden coma. The book ends with Fiona and The Student taking their boat to the cave where they encounter again the hawker who is an earthly manifestation of the Fairy King and whom The Student had himself met as such in his youth. The bracelet is returned, Fiona thereby relinquishing her childhood and she is given the treasure which is the soul of the island upon which she lives.

The gift is given in a speech of poetic cadences which is a culmination of the tenor of all that has gone before. For what that crude and truncated synopsis of the story given above could not do was to illuminate the mastery of Tarn's composition. He has the directness, the wit and the irony of a great storyteller to which is added his consuming love for the ground and waters of his story's setting. Throughout the book there are small litanies in praise of the sea and its creatures, the landscape of the Glenollisdal valley and even of the island's ancient singers:

> Cuchulain and the forgotten heroes who fought before Cuchlain; Ossian and the forgotten bards who sang before Ossian; Columba and the forgotten saints who died before Columba …

The book speaks of a place, a wild life, and a community that was still existent when it was written but is now, a century later, irrecoverable.

Commentary

W. W. Tarn has been called 'a gentleman scholar' inheriting sufficient wealth and earning enough as a barrister to enable him to engage in scholarly pursuits (he was an authority on the Hellenistic age and Alexander the Great) without the onus of academic responsibilities. He was born in London but moved to Scotland for health reasons and his attachment to Skye came through his daughter Otta who lived there and became an authority on the island's history and culture. It was to her, as a child, that he told the first version of the *Isle of Mist* in 1913 and it was only published as a book in 1919. Although an American edition was published in

1934, illustrated with fine and varied drawings by Robert Lawson, the book made little headway in Britain until 1938 when a new edition was published by the London office of Oxford University Press, with a Preface by Tarn who gives much information on the Skye background, renaming the invented Glenollisdal as Brandersaig. (He also acknowledges help from 'Miss Allen' who would shortly become Mrs Hogarth, of later high reputation as an editor of children's books.) The new edition was illustrated with twenty four sepia-printed photographs which would have made a dramatic addition except they had such poor resolution. In 1950 Oxford brought out 'second edition' – really the fourth – with a delicate and expressive series of chapter headpieces and intra-text vignettes by Margery Gill.

–47–

JUST – WILLIAM
BY RICHMAL CROMPTON (1922)

Reminiscence: as an evacuee (of sorts) I have every reason to be grateful to William Brown – or perhaps rather to John Overton (where is he now?). I had been exported to Bristol – where there was as much likelihood of being bombed as in North London – and there I encountered Master Overton, who possessed what must have been a complete run of Richmal Crompton's 'William' books together with a generous disposition about lending them. (They still had their dust-jackets on and would be worth many sacks of Gooseberry Eyes on the market today.)

Day in, day out I read my way through the collection, most volumes having ten or more stories in them and most stories working ingenious variations on the simple theme of the best laid plans ganging all agley. I am pretty confident in saying that my gratitude for being allowed to participate in this feast had nothing to do with any distraction it might provide from hearing news of the horrors of war and everything to do with what John

Rowe Townsend has perfectly described as the young reader's 'happy blend of identification and condescension'. You joined the Outlaws in their optimistic endeavours (wishing that you could join them just down the street) and you simultaneously gaped at the certainty of coming disasters which they themselves were too preoccupied to perceive.

And they never learned. The first ever calamity occurred in the story 'Rice-Mould' (a name for a gruesome pudding foisted upon children in the 1920s – *cf* A. A. Milne's Mary Jane). 'The girl next door' hates the stuff and William gallantly assures her that he can abstract for her some cream blancmange from the party-fare that his family are preparing. It is an idle boast of a kind that he will be prone to repeat interminably, for in his panicky raid on the kitchen larder he ends up by stealing for her just another gollop of lookalike rice-mould.

That was in February 1919 when the story was printed in the journal *Home Magazine* in response to a request for a story about children for its female readers. It must have been well-thought-of by the editors for the March issue carried a second one, 'The Outlaws', and from then up to 1922 thirty-nine more stories appeared. In that year though the publisher, George Newnes Ltd, started a new monthly for family reading, the *Happy Mag,* and William took up residence there until May 1940, having an adventure printed in 204 of the intervening 230 months. Back in 1922, however, his popularity had become something of a by-word beyond the readership of a magazine for genteel ladies and Newnes had the good sense to gather up twelve of the published stories to make the first William book: *Just – William.* Eventually the tally of William stories would reach beyond three hundred (more being published in other magazines after 1940) and these were gathered into a run of thirty-eight volumes, including a full-length story, the last being *William the Lawless* in 1970. Only one story was never transferred from periodical to book: 'William on the Trail', in which our hero encounters a young girl who fools him with the sort of scandalous tales that he was himself inclined to foist on other people.

Almost from the start, Thomas Henry accompanied William

as his inseparable portraitist in books and magazines alike and for most readers his illustrations are an essential part of the saga (oddly though, he only met Crompton on a single occasion, at a Nottingham book festival in 1958, almost forty years after their first collaboration). It took him a book or two to perfect a rendering of the boy which would endure, with minor modifications, as far as *William and the Witch* in 1962, when Henry died after completing only two drawings. The preliminary stages of his visualisations can be seen in the pre-1950 editions of the first three books which he then re-illustrated to bring them into conformity with all the rest.

Owen Dudley Edwards in a monstrous tome on *British Children's Fiction in the Second World War*, makes a number of perceptive assessments of Crompton's work, for William is one of the heroes of his book. In the course of these he notes first that no William book ever got close to consideration for a Carnegie Medal and second that none was reviewed in the *TLS* (in the days when they *did* regularly review children's books). From this we may derive a further implication that like another author on whose work he has much to say – Enid Blyton – Crompton was regarded as a sort of story machine, cranking out undemanding narratives to a single pattern to keep the customers happy.

The accusation has some justice. After all, there is something unnatural about a leading character who remains stuck at eleven years old from 1919 to 1970 and has to have political, social and linguistic affairs updated around him ('clots', 'shambles', 'drug-pushers' turn up towards the end). And, however the dates are manipulated, the topography of William's village and the foibles of its local characters remain the same so that similarities and repetitions of plotlines can hardly be avoided. But what needs to be emphasised is the skill with which Crompton surmounts such limitations. The stories may be seen as the equivalent of eighteenth century harlequinades. Everyone knows that the scope for action of Harlequin, Pantaloon, Columbine and so on (*cf.* William, Hubert Lane, Violet Elizabeth Bott, etc.) is fixed, the genius lies in manipulating those actions with a continuing freshness so that even the predictable comes as a surprise.

Moreover within the set-pieces there is space for variation

whether of unexpected walk-on characters or of Crompton's not-always-noticed satiric intent. It is also instructive to see how she manages what might be called her double-plots. While many stories (such as 'Rice-Mould') progress simply from starting idea to denouement, others cunningly merge separate strands. Thus in the early 'The Show', from *Just – William*, we find the Browns plagued by a house-guest from hell: Aunt Emily. William however is preoccupied with trying to raise five shillings for a bow-and-arrow and arranges a (farcical) exhibition in his bedroom with local children as paying visitors. The plots merge when he hears Aunt Emily snoring during her siesta in the next room and includes her in the exhibition as 'Fat Wild Woman Torkin Natif Langwidge'. She awakes affronted and instantly packs her bags and leaves, with the result that William's normally sardonic father gives his son a handsome tip.

And that, of course, exemplifies Crompton's foremost characteristic: her stories are, and remain, *funny*. A couple of years ago I had occasion to read 'William Holds the Stage' (from *William the Pirate*) to a party of American librarians, (Crompton is not known in the States) and a question had come up about William's equivalence to Booth Tarkington's very similar hero, Penrod (not known to Crompton.) The story concerns William's tussle with authorial and textual problems in *Hamlet* and the reading could hardly be completed since both audience and reader were exhausted with laughing. With the books of how many Carnegie winners could that occur?

Commentary

The mass popularity of some writers for children – Frank Richards of 'Billy Bunter' fame and other writers for boys' story-papers, Mary Tourtel and 'Rupert', 'The School at the Chalet' and many other girls' school stories, etc. – has engendered fanclubs and the like in which collectors have gone to almost metaphysical lengths to establish bibliographical points and priorities. William has had particularly fruitful attention paid to him, primarily by that great authority on popular literature of all kinds, Mary Cadogan. She has written a biography of Richmal Crompton

(1986), a *William Companion* (1990), and an illustrated account of *Just – William through the Ages* (1994). The 2019 centenary of the first story has evoked much nostalgia, including memories of the telling of the stories on radio by Martin Jarvis.

-48-

POOR CECCO
BY MARGERY WILLIAMS BIANCO (1925)

The Velveteen Rabbit by Margery Williams was first published by Heinemann in 1922 and became a vastly popular story, especially in the United States, where in 2015 it was included in the exhibition of *One Hundred Books Famous in Children's Literature*. To my (some think unbalanced) mind, though, it is a meretricious exercise in ontology, making sentimental play with a dud concept of Reality as applied to nursery toys. It is undeserving of any classic status other than in its role, since coming out of copyright, as a commercial con trick.

But see here: three years later, in 1925, that same Margery Williams (who had married Francesco Bianco in London as early as 1904) turned to another account of life among the nursery toys. With *Poor Cecco,* named after her eldest son, she created a masterpiece. Certainly it had a distinctly commercial send-off, being serialised in *Good Housekeeping* in the United States where much was made of its illustrations by Arthur Rackham. But it did not last (and indeed *The Velveteen Rabbit* was also little regarded until after the Second World War) and a biographer of Rackham, writing in 1990, spoke of his drawings as having 'sunk with their text'.

That text, though, sees the sogginess of the Rabbit book turned into narrative strength, a point best made by differentiating the characterisation of the participants. The human agents who forward the action around the colourless Boy in the first book are his nurse, who dumps the rabbit on him in the first place (he has shown no care for it before) and the doctor who demands its destruction at the end as carrying 'a mass of scarlet fever germs', while the rabbit himself is shown as obsessed with a desire to become Real, an outcome that is brought about by the intervention of 'quite the loveliest fairy in the whole world ... the nursery magic Fairy'. In *Poor Cecco* however the action lies almost entirely with the inhabitants of the toy cupboard – no fairies there – whose depiction gives the book its winning combination of drama and comedy.

Frontispiece by Antony Maitland depicting and naming the nursery characters (223x180mm.). New ed. of *Poor Cecco* (London: André Deutsch, 1973).

Murrum the cat and a community of rats are the only living creatures of consequence in the story. We meet the first at the start, pursuing a nightly campaign against the toys whose regular post-midnight prancing, singing and partying interfere with Murrum's mouse-catching activities. He remains an ominous presence till triggering the final denouement, but, aside from him and the rats, who also feature at that point, there are only walk-on parts for sundry small animals (so treated that one wonders if Russell Hoban had encountered them before he wrote *The Mouse and His Child* [no.79 below]). Only a blind man and his deliciously portrayed black dog, an anonymous automobile driver, and what I take to be a postman, play tiny parts *ex machina*. Of the owner of the toys and the residents of the house in which they live not a word is said.

Margery Bianco finds in these toys a storyteller's dream. Whether (as is averred) or not they originated in the toy cupboard of her own family, they are a wonderfully miscellaneous bunch acquired from who-knows-where: Bulka and Tubby, battered toy puppies whose marriage will make a climax to the story; a wooden lion who is in love with a lamb on wheels; an Andersenian Money-Pig; two rather sniffy dolls; a Harlequin, much given to saying 'Hey Presto'; and an engine and an Express Cart, useful for transport. They are all too busy being themselves to bother with any Reality-making twaddle and they are seen in the light of an amused affection for their shortcomings and precarious existence. Their leader is the ever-versatile Poor Cecco, a jointed wooden dog, who outwits Murrum on his midnight prowl and whose picaresque adventure with Bulka forms the centrepiece of the tale.

'We are going for a walk', says he to Bulka, first thing in the morning after his tail got broken after an attempt to use it as a lever. (He fears that when the others wake up they will want to play at hospitals, which he cannot stand.) Blithely the two of them set off into a world of which they know nothing where the danger of random incident feeds into a purposive mission through their meeting with Jensina, a wooden doll who has made a home for herself in an ash-dump where she is having trouble from some neighbouring rats. Despite her staunch independence, she sees the wisdom of her returning with the others to the safety of their toy cupboard and, although trailed by rat policemen, they devise a scheme to post themselves back home where Jensina, and indeed the policemen, assist in the final frustration of Murrum.

Tribute must be paid to Bianco's skill in turning this nonsensical plot into a convincing entertainment. She does so through her discriminating management of her large cast of toys, each sustained with its own comic foibles, and through a voicing of events which brings them to life in the reader's, or perhaps listener's, imagination. (It has been said that the episodic plot owes its shape to bed-time storytelling sessions.) Paramount though that must be, the book also demanded illustrations and Rackham supplied seven full-page colour-plates for its first edition, as well as a succession of often-repeated line vignettes. Although the plates share the imaginative vision of the author they also shared the publishing custom of the time, by being separated from the text behind their own title leaves which announce their subject on one side and give a descriptive quote on the other.

How much more satisfying therefore was the unheralded re-publication of the book in 1973 after almost half a century of oblivion. Joining the distinguished list that Pamela Royds, following Philippa Pearce, was fashioning for André Deutsch it had a sympathetic introduction by Margery Fisher and a sequence of pen-drawings by Antony Maitland. Varying between chapter-heads, full-page drawings and drawings placed within the flow of the story (and with built-in, hand-written captions, rather than Rackham's separated ones) these were perfect examples of narrative illustration. It is a puzzle how public taste has been led to favour its cheap velveteen predecessor over our honest-to-goodness timber dog – with or without a snapped-off tail.

Commentary

Born Margery Williams in London in 1881, she moved to the United States after the death of her father in 1888 and she was schooled there. She returned to England in 1901 where, in 1904, she married an Italian citizen who was managing a London bookshop. After travels and the disruption of the First World War, when her husband served in the Italian army, the family moved to America which remained her home for the rest of her life. It was there, under the literary influence of Walter de la Mare, that her writing career took off with *The Velveteen Rabbit* being published in 1922, illustrated by the great English painter and graphic artist William Nicholson.

Bianco published many further children's books and novels, some in collaboration with her daughter Pamela who became a painter and illustrator. De la Mare supplied 'illustrative poems' for Pamela's book of childhood pictures *Flora* (1919).

-49-

WINNIE-THE-POOH
BY A. A. MILNE (1926)

There was a sound of revelry by night. Nothing to do with Waterloo – although it did occur on the sports ground of the Honourable Artillery Company. Rather it was members of the Garrick Club, in their jolly ties, enjoying a little smackerel of something by way of celebration.

Tra-la-la, tra-la-la,
Tra-la-la, tra-la-la,
Rum-tum-tiddle-um-tum.
Tiddle-iddle, tiddle-iddle,
Tiddle-iddle, tiddle-iddle,
Rum-tum-tum-tiddle-um.

'"Tra-la-la; tra-la-la"'Pen drawing (105x85mm.) by Ernest Shepard from p.21 of *Winnie-the-Pooh* (London: Methuen, 1926).

The immediate sponsor of the jollifications was the Walt Disney Corporation who had recently handed over many millions of pounds to the Club, as also to the Royal Literary Fund and to Westminster School. The true founder of the feast though was A. A. Milne, whose happy legatees, which had also included his son, Christopher Robin, were here receiving a modest competence for the sale of some merchandising rights.

And that meant Pooh. It meant other things as well, of course, but the origin of the wealth lay in Milne's four famous books and Winnie-the-Pooh is the outstanding emblem of their presence. In fact, he made an appearance, as Mr Edward Bear, in a Bellocian ballad, in the first of them, *When We Were Very Young* (1924), and since he was clearly a notable resident in the Milne nursery it is unsurprising to find him becoming the hero of a bedtime story as well.

Winnie-the-Pooh: a new story for children was printed as a Christmas Eve treat in the *Evening News* in 1925, and next day figured among the festive wireless programmes. It was the tale of the bear and the bees, cast in the awkward narrative frame of a dialogue between teller and listener that was retained for the first chapter of the book 'in which we are introduced ...' Although no further instalments were envisaged, the success of that story (as concept and in its execution) inspired Milne to sequels, seven of which were printed in the *Royal Magazine* before the book itself was published in October 1926. Its ten tales were followed by the ten of *The House at Pooh Corner* in 1928 and the total amounts to the Pooh Bear Canon.

His name has been the subject of near-metaphysical debate, not greatly helped by the author's Introduction to the first book (the second one, on advice from Owl, had a 'Contradiction'). Apparently 'Winnie' comes from a brown bear deposited at the London Zoo during the First World War by a Canadian soldier who had called it after his home-state, Winnipeg. As for 'Pooh', said implausibly to have been borrowed from a swan, that's anyone's guess, although cloacal explanations are barred as anachronistic. Christopher Robin himself insisted on the masculinity of the name: *recte* Winnie-*ther*-Pooh. 'You know what "ther" means?'

His adventures have also been the subject of critical debate, most memorably by Dorothy Parker, as 'Constant Reader' in the *New Yorker*: 'it is that word "hummy", my darlings, that marks the first place at which Tonstant Weader thwows up'. Any assessment more objective than that runs serious risk of being idiotic – as demonstrated in Frederick Crews's *Pooh Perplex* of 1963 which used the text to guy the language and critical dispositions of contemporary academics. (Alas, it came too soon to deal with Deconstruction, Post-modernism, Post-colonialism, and Gender Studies. Useless to hazard a female support-group for single-parent Kanga, or a full clarification of the relationship between Pooh and Piglet, or a transfer of the whole shebang to Finsbury Park.)

The only Rissolution for critical doubts lies in an assertion of the Absolute Integrity of the texts as originally published by Messrs Methuen. Those chaste octavos make no extravagant claims for themselves. Take the authorial voice or leave it as you choose, but accept (even without the help of Alan Bennett) that this urbane storytelling is not subject to modification. The word-play, the self-reflexiveness, the jokes that fly over the heads of a nursery audience are (*pace* Tonstant Weader) a necessary defence against an incipient banality. Furthermore, you find in those early printings the one, true, authentic manifestation of the work of Pooh's other creator: E. H. Shepard. The perfection of his visualisations and of their sequencing through the text stand among the triumphs of English book illustration.

Which is to bewail the merchandisers. Like Peter Rabbit and Babar and other nursery heroes, Winnie-the-Pooh early fell victim to the exploiters of his popularity, and the integrity of those early printings has been compromised more damagingly than most. Shepard himself was responsible for colouring-up the drawings, thus obliterating much of their expressive line, and the publishers have compounded matters with their tumult of excerpts, adaptations, novelties, and fatuous cookbooks, workout books, etc. Disney accelerated the bandwagon over thirty years ago, sullying what was left of the Enchanted Places, and on the evidence of such exercises as 'character marketing' the welcome 'Special Facsimile Editions' of the original books are hopelessly outweighed by the kitsch. But the Garrick chaps did have a sportive evening on the dodgems.

Commentary

The publication of Ann Thwaite's prize-winning biography of A. A. Milne in 1990 gave much revelatory evidence about the life of a prolific and honoured author whose work (and the life of his son) had been swamped by the worldwide fame of four children's books. It led to a couple of heavily illustrated spin-off compendia which detailed primarily the impact that the two Pooh books had had on the popular market: Ann Thwaite's own *Brilliant Career of Winnie-the* [not ther]-*Pooh* (1992) and Brian Sibley's *Three Cheers for Pooh* (2001). Now, the arrival of Frank Cottrel Boyce's movie '*Goodbye Christopher Robin*' and an associated exhibition '*Winnie the Pooh; Exploring a Classic*' have triggered renewed interest. Ann Thwaite has drawn upon her huge biography to make an approachable survey, titled after the film and the V&A's exhibition catalogue, while preserving and augmenting many illustrations of exhibits, manages in between them an authoritative commentary by its organisers, Annemarie Bilclough and Emma Laws. The latter's chapter, which draws upon the Museum's holding of Shepard's multiple designs, (mostly in pencil) for his illustrations marks not only a description (previously engaged in by Brian Sibley as long ago as 1984 in his *Pooh Sketchbook*) but a fully articulated discussion of the nature of book illustration itself.

Ann Thwaite's biography, *A. A. Milne: His Life*, is still in print but not her lively study of *The Brilliant Career of Winnie-the-Pooh* (Methuen, 1992) nor yet Brian Sibley's account of Shepard's drawings in *The Pooh Sketchbook* (Methuen, 1982).

-50-

THE MIDNIGHT FOLK
BY JOHN MASEFIELD (1927)

'A great book'. Thus proclaimed nine year-old Naomi emerging from her encounter with Kay Harker of Seekings House and the friends who helped him to the recovery of the treasures of Santa Barbara: Nibbins the cat, Mr Rollicum Bitem Lightfoot the fox, and many another, including bats, otters, mermaids, and Rat the cellarman who 'does a bit in the dustbin and comes a bit close to a old bone now and then'.

You will not find Seekings in Pevsner although it can't be far away from the Priory in Ledbury where John Masefield spent idyllic years in his later boyhood. Nor is the local town of Condicote on any map, although its setting may owe something to his later love of Cotswold country. And as for Santa Barbara, that is one of the fictional 'sugar states' of South America that are the setting for several of Masefield's novels, beginning with one about an ancestor of Kay's: *Sard Harker* (1924). The dust jacket of a successor, *Odtaa* (1926), provides a chart of those romantic and dangerous places.

Seeking the treasure of Santa Barbara may provide the central purpose of the adventures chronicled in *The Midnight Folk* but its fate was a puzzle to all concerned and one of the glories of the book is the uncoordinated tumble of adventures through which Kay Harker unravels the story of how the treasure was stolen from his great-grandfather's ship, the *Plunderer*, so long ago. (And there is a side-serving of events through which he also unearths old Sir Hassle Gassle's grandfather's gold repeater, purloined long years before by Benjamin the highwayman.)

First hints of nefarious goings-on are disclosed to Kay when he and Nibbins venture out to a witches' coven on broomsticks (a besom and a broom-broom). Thereafter bits and pieces of the story come to be fitted together by equally unlikely means: a night-flight on a horse to Yorkshire to interview the centenarian Miss Susan Pricker, sitting up in bed, 'reading a sprightly story' and drinking champagne; a swift voyage to the Caribbean on a mimic *Plunderer* crewed by water-mice; an involuntary journey on a black stick with a crooky handle to hear the revelations of a Talking Head; vital help from liege-men from King Arthur's Camp...

Phantasmagoria rather than fantasy it may be. You climb into the book rather as Kay climbed into the portrait of his great-grandfather and find what might be the imaginings of a child all strung promiscuously together. But the seemingly casual succession of scenes and the arrival on cue of requisite magic (a phial of Invisible Mixture, a pair of one-league shoes) are held together and controlled by a painterly precision of detail and a perfection of discourse. Whether he deals in 'real' things: the countryside setting – flowers, birds, buildings – for instance, or the accoutrements of magic – those brooms – Masefield makes them live on the page, while phrase after phrase and conversation after conversation flies free of the dead weight of conventional children's-book-storytelling. *Exempli gratia*: 'What I'm for' (said Pimply Whatto) 'is to bang them black and blue with my knoppy blackthorn' or 'Ellen's uncle had fallen at the Tuttocks and broken his huckle-bone.'

In truth, when it first appeared in 1927, *The Midnight Folk* did not look much like a book for children: 328 pages of solid type, no illustrations, and a jacket of not very fetching dark green and blue, where might blackly be discerned Nibbins the cat. Within four years, however, illustrations were called for and Rowland Hilder supplied both line drawings and colour plates for a handsome gift-book edition, the black-and-whites subsequently being incorporated into what became the standard trade edition (1957). (Curiously, the one concession to graphic statement in the first edition – a reproduction of Sir Piney Trigger's last words, scratched on the metal casing of a lantern – got accidentally omitted from the gift-book edition and thus also from most subsequent trade printings.) Since that time Faith Jaques has illustrated an unforgivably abridged edition, and Quentin Blake – commissioned by Messrs Mondadori to provide colour plates for an Italian translation – has had his work incorporated into a (sloppily proofed) English edition (1990).

Inexplicable the waywardness of fashion. If that unsatisfactory, not to say perverse, publishing history betokens anything it is surely a neglectful carelessness on the part of our publishers and our arbiters of taste. For *The Midnight Folk* is indeed 'a great book' – to my mind, one of the greatest of all children's books – and yet for much of its life its virtues have been buried as obscurely as Sir Hassle Gassle's repeater.

Commentary

Masefield's contribution to children's literature is not as widely recognised as it deserves to be. His first book in the genre was *A Book of Discoveries* (1910) in which two 'roving youths who liked adventure' come to find out about the depths and history of their own countryside in company (an old dodge) with a learned local resident. This was followed by two historical adventure stories: *Martin Hyde, the Duke's Messenger* (1910) and *Jim Davis* (1911), a tale of smuggling, which had success as a Puffin Story Book fifty years later. The rather severe entry of *The Midnight Folk* into the lists was mitigated in 1920 with the fine 'gift edition' noted above. The book's perhaps more famous 1935 sequel, *The Box of Delights* (which was one of the great successes among the 1930's Children's Hour serials on the BBC) was illustrated with niggly pictures by the author's daughter. It is a wonderful book but, as Graham Greene remarked, ruined by its ending that shows all to have been a dream.

A 906-page bibliography: *John Masefield; the 'Great Auk' of English Literature* by Philip W Errington was published by the British Library in 2004.

-51-

ALICE AND THOMAS AND JANE
BY ENID BAGNOLD (1930)

'He thought of cannibals, who eat explorers. And of Chinese, who eat dogs. And he made up his mind that a boy was not a man unless he could eat snails …'This master Thomas, aged eight, attempts to do even though, not long before, he had consumed two jugs of chocolate, along with two little jugs of milk, some dry biscuits, and some white crusty bread (such as they didn't get at home) with iced butter and honey. Predictably, he is 'as sick as sick could be' and 'glad to think that he hadn't got a snail in his inside, but glad too that he could do it'.

What had happened was that his two sisters were confined at home with whooping cough and Thomas, the usual instigator of their joint adventures, had allowed his feet to take him solus to Newhaven and then accidentally(?) on to the Dieppe ferry which will take him to his first encounter with French gastronomy. He has also bought three tortoises in a Dieppe shop and some pretty shell ornaments to take home as presents before Mother, coming across on the midnight ferry, rescues him.

This episode is announced at its start as the last one that the author is recounting to her own three children and they 'hardly breathed' in its telling. This makes for an interesting frame since the reader can never be sure how far Alice and Thomas and Jane are surrogates for the actual Jones children whose own childhood adventures are being subject to delectable embroidery. (Bagnold was married to Sir Roderick Jones, the head of Reuter's.) The setting is confessedly Rottingdean with all its (now vanished) connotations as a Sussex coastal village of the 1920s: the hierarchy of household and community (shopkeepers, servants, a governess), the local details of topography and environment (the green bus with no top, the cobble-cranes, the neighbours' 'Kipling House', which presumably was formerly Burne-Jones's where Bagnold and family now lived).

Of the three children, the imperious and inventive Thomas is

leader but wholeheartedly backed-up by seven year-old Jane and
Alice who is only five but 'might be as good as seven at times'.
Indeed, it is Alice who stows away on the flying machine up on
the Downs and it is she who undertakes the hazardous journey,
hanging on to the back of George Dumpling's boat, when she
discovers him to be smuggling dogs in from France to avoid
quarantine charges. The intrepidity of their often hair-raising
adventures is reinforced by their comradeship and by Bagnold's
genial stewardship of her cast, as indulgent as that of the children's
put-upon parents and nursery guardians.

'Mummy having a baby'. Pencil drawing with grey and pink wash
(83x149mm.) by Laurian Jones (the author's daughter) from p.9 of
Alice and Thomas and Jane (London: Heinemann, 1930).

Not to be neglected either is the integration of tinted illustrations
into the text undertaken by Bagnold and her six year-old daughter,
Laurian Jones, a photograph of whom stands as a frontispiece to
the book and who signs her efforts with a bold L. J. Despite the
difference in skills and in the spelling of the captions ('Ales and
thomas and Jane out-side there house with rwo vilig children')
there is a homogeneity in the freedom of the graphic style which
enhances the engaging tones of Bagnold's storytelling. The book
is surely the most joyous of those of the *entre deux guerres* – and
perhaps of most succeeding periods as well.

Commentary

Alice and Thomas and Jane was originally published in both Britain and the US in the squarish format of a foolscap quarto (8¼ x 6¾ inches) which had the attractive hint of a nursery book about it. The quest for economy common to all publishers led to the size being reduced to that of a common demy octavo (8¾ x 5½ inches) round about 1950. Rottingdean was also the site of Bagnold's bestseller *National Velvet* (1935) and of her adult novel *The Squire* (1938) which gives a kind of sideways glimpse of home life *chez* the Jones'es.

-52-

SWALLOWS AND AMAZONS
BY ARTHUR RANSOME (1930)

"It isn't worth it", said Captain Flint. "Never any of you start writing books. It isn't worth it".

But he was depressed at the time, for his cabin trunk had been stolen with *Mixed Moss* in it, – what he hoped would be his autobiographical masterpiece. When it was recovered though, on Cormorant Island by Able Seaman Titty and ship's boy Roger, he may have changed his mind. Why? We are told later that the work went through eight editions in a couple of years.

When those words were written Captain Flint was not to foresee such success for his book, nor yet Arthur Ransome, his *alter ego*, in the creation of the somewhat experimental tale in which the Captain appeared. The two of them shared an adventurous past that, for Ransome, makes a story of its own: flight from a nagging wife to Russia where he witnessed and reported on the Revolution, played chess with Lenin, and eventually ran off with Evgenia, Trotsky's secretary. A rolling stone perhaps, but he had always known that his home-ground was not that of a footloose wanderer or parrot-harbouring pirate, but of a born writer.

'Making the Ship's Papers'. (130x113mm.) by Clifford
Webb facing p.20 of *Swallows and Amazons*. (New ed.
London: Jonathan Cape, 1931)

At first, like many another, he had not known where to go, and
the less said about his early children's books, such as *Highways and
Byways in Fairyland* (1907) the better. But the escape to Russia
resulted in his finding a true voice for his *Old Peter's Russian Tales*
(1916) and a confidence that generated the memoir of his return
escape (with Evgenia) *Racundra's First Cruise* (1924).

Back home though and living near Lake Windermere, he took
up with a friendly family, Ernest Altounyan and his five children:
Taqui, Susan, Titty (so-called because of her fondness for *Mrs
Tittlemouse*), Roger, and Brigit. Through the summer of 1928 he
was much involved with them, he and their father encouraging
their sailing adventures in two small boats on Coniston Water. In
the autumn they must needs return to Syria, where their father
was a doctor, and before departing they presented Ransome with

a handsome pair of slippers, 'real Turks, bright scarlet, shaped like barges'.

And that's what started it. Despite temptations of secure work at the *Manchester Guardian*, Ransome had already determined to make his way as an independent writer, and his summer jauntings with the Altounyans inspired him with the idea of a sailing adventure story for children. He planned it carefully before commencing, but, once started, he suddenly found such formality redundant. As he reported to a friend, the Altounyans took over the typewriter and almost wrote the book themselves.

'Experimental' in 1930 was surely a just word for what emerged as *Swallows and Amazons*. Like the much earlier (and equally experimental) *Bevis*, by Richard Jefferies, first published as a three-decker in 1882 [our no.27], it was a long book, arriving on the market with its 350 pages unillustrated apart from endpaper maps and a chart-sketch of Wild Cat Island as a frontispiece. Nonetheless, the market responded enthusiastically and – sensing a long-term potential for the story – Jonathan Cape put out a second edition in 1931 with chapter tailpieces and twenty-eight plates by Clifford Webb inserted into the text-block. (The first US edition of that year had head- and tail-pieces by Helene Carter.) Only in 1938 was the book illustrated by its author, by which time it had reached its fourteenth edition, outrunning for sure *Mixed Moss*.

Its popularity hardly needs explaining. Not only (*Bevis* excepted) had any story about contemporary children depicted their adventures with such accuracy as to both character (including two Amazons) and setting, but rarely was childhood freedom-with-responsibility so winningly celebrated. The twin plots of the naval war between the opposing crews and then their joint assault on Captain Flint serve to give the narrative its energy but what makes the book a 'touchstone' classic is the alternative life within its pages that it offers the reader – and indeed within the pages of its eleven-and-a-half sequels.

Commentary

That life grows more and more a fictional dream as the years pass. Allowing a bit of latitude, suitably circumstanced children of the 1930s might well have experienced something of the same adventurous freedom of the Swallows and the Amazons. And indeed, in that decade's fiction the reader could join other holidaying families travelling in the Swallows' wake: the Hunterlys of *Far Distant Oxus* by the schoolgirls Eleanor Hull and Pamela Whitlock (commended to Cape by Ransome himself), or the Locketts of M. E. Atkinson, or Geoffrey Trease's *Mystery on the Moors* and *Detectives in the Dales.*

Such high-jinks are unlikely now in these crowded days under the eyes of Child Protectionists and Health and Safety officials, deterring duffers from drowning (and No Fires and No Camping says the National Trust on Wild Cat Island). Shall we eventually, I wonder, reach the dystopia of Elizabeth Mace's enigmatic and sunless *Ransome Revisited* where it is beyond all believing that children could ever have lived the life depicted in that forbidden, battered, but secretly treasured, *Swallowdale?*

–53–

EMIL AND THE DETECTIVES
BY ERIC KÄSTNER (1931)

Being published in Berlin in 1929 but dated 1930, *Emil und die Detektive* was, for its time, a remarkably cheerful comedy. What's more – and what is not always recognised – it was remarkably innovative as well.

The story is straightforward enough: Emil, whose father is dead, leaves his much-loved mother in the provincial town of Neustadt, where she is a hairdresser, for a holiday-visit to relatives in Berlin. Falling asleep on the train, he is robbed of his money (140 marks, translating then as seven pounds sterling) by a Man in a Bowler Hat. But by good fortune Emil spots him getting off the train at

a Berlin station just before the one he's heading for, so he follows
the culprit with some notion of getting him arrested (his tram fare
being paid en route by a friendly fellow-passenger).

His unfixed plan gains resolution through his meeting
Gustav with the Motor Horn, an instrument through which
Gustav rounds up the youth of the neighbourhood to help in
the apprehension of Bowler Hat. These, or at least the foremost
members of the crowd, set themselves up as the Detectives.
They sort out a communications system ('Password Emil'), send
reassuring messages to Emil's puzzled relatives, then follow the thief
to his hotel, to keep a watch on him overnight. Next morning,
accompanied by half the urchins of the city, they triumphantly
apprehend their quarry who is trying to deposit the stolen money
in his bank. He turns out to be a Wanted Man with a price on
his head so that Emil gains both a reward and hero status in the
national press.

If you think that that's all too easy and indeed rather crudely
far-fetched then you need to take into account the manner of
its presentation. This may not seem unusual to most readers of
English editions who start the story with Emil's mother, Mrs
Tischbein (= Table-leg) asking her son to bring in a jug of hot
water. In German editions however that event doesn't take place
until you get to page thirty-seven or thereabouts. For to begin
with you have a twelve-page Introduction under the heading 'The
Story's Not Beginning Just Yet' where Mr Kästner gives a farcical
account, with many digressions, of how he came to put his story
together. (It seems that he had writer's block with what sounds
like a batty tale of the South Seas and, seeking inspiration by lying
on the floor of his study, looking at the chair- and table-legs, he
was visited by the tale which the reader is soon to encounter.)

That's not all though. Before Emil is sent to fetch the hot water
we are also presented, in the German edition, with ten leaves of
drawings by Kästner's indispensable illustrator, Walter Trier. These
introduce us to some of the main places and persons whom we are
going to meet in the story, each accompanied by conversational
remarks from the author who stokes up interest but without
giving anything away. And even after the story has begun, we are

not free of him, for he is an easygoing omniscient author, enjoying the scenes as they unreel and willing, on occasions, to interject comments of his own. (A little masterstroke occurs when Emil is being interviewed by the press after his triumph and one of the journalists – none other than the man who paid his tram-fare – turns out to be a Herr Kästner.)

Emil and the Detectives has rightly been seen as a work of historic interest, one of the first children's books of the twentieth century to bring in credible city children, speaking an acceptable enough vernacular. But, so far as English editions are concerned, readers increasingly lose out on its additional interest as an experimental narrative. Thus, so far as I know, no attempt has been made to contrive a feasible translation of the Introduction, while the parade of pictures at the start has also been abandoned. The first translation (by the unacknowledged Cyrus Brooks) did a shuffle by putting in all of the plates, printed on a bright yellow background, with most of Kästner's remarks, but these were dispersed throughout the book along with what looks to be a freshly commissioned colour plate. Such a treatment at least retained something of the book's unusual character, but subsequent editions have increasingly denuded it of that, while a new translation by Eileen Hall, done for Puffin in 1959 was hardly an improvement on Brooks's.

Commentary

Such vagaries are part of the book's own chequered history. Kästner was no friend to the Nazis; his illustrator was Jewish as was his publisher, Edith Jacobsohn, who had established her firm as the Williams Verlag in 1924[21]. With the coming of the Third Reich in 1933, Trier and Jacobsohn left Germany, the latter dying in England in 1935, while Kästner saw out the war in Germany under many restrictions and confinements. Perhaps it was with a sort of pride that he saw his books, including *Emil*, dismembered and burnt on the

21   Kurt Maschler, in whose name the Maschler Prize enjoyed its brief but glorious career, with a statuette of Emil as part of the award, had bought the Williams Verlag in 1935, making it over to Cecilie Dressler who continued it through the War. He left Germany in 1937 and became agent for Kästner's literary affairs and was father of the energetic editor at Jonathan Cape, Tom Maschler.

streets where his innocent detectives had flourished – pride that he was a writer whose integrity warranted such extirpation.

Mein schöner Verlag: Williams & Co. by Frank Flechtmann (1997) is a substantial pamphlet giving a fascinating history of the Williams Press with a bibliography of its productions, which specialised in translations of English language children's books. These included most of Lofting's 'Doctor Dolittle' books, *Winnie-the-Pooh, Tom Sawyer,* and Disney's *Three Little Pigs.*

–54–

THE CAMELS ARE COMING
BY W. E. JOHNS (1932)

Ah, Mr Salway, how perceptive you were, way back in 1969. No one now knows much about *Children's Book News* which was at that time one of the few review journals for children's books, but it was there that you reviewed the final adventures of Captain (later Major) James Bigglesworth. The stories of *Biggles and the Little Green God* and also *The Noble Lord* took us a hundred volumes on from his earliest flights and were published just over a year after the death of their archivist, 'Captain' William Earle Johns (he was actually a Flying Officer).

'Biggles Breathes His Last' was the title of your piece and its perceptiveness lay in its recognition that, despite what you called the predictability and banality of the works under review, and despite the author's facts being 'often wrong and his geographical and anthropological errors frequently grotesque', his hero had 'given rise to a myth that is unlikely to disappear with time'.

The rightness of your forecast was very apparent in 2014 when publishers set off on the five-year trail of 'war memorial' books. Right at the start, Random House pounced on *The Camels are Coming* and, wing-tip to wing-tip alongside four further 'action-packed adventures', reprinted the seventeen short stories that marked Biggles's arrival in the world of very English derring-do – a classic by reputation rather than performance.

The action takes place in France during the battles of the First World War – 'Camels', as his first readers would have known, being 'single-seater biplane fighters with twin machine-guns synchronised to fire through the propellor'. (The Random House edition was furnished with many such useful explanatory notes both on English and German planes and on contemporary slang ['Buffs'] and technology ['Scarff rings'].) As to what happens, Johns excuses himself in his Foreword that 'it may seem improbable that only one man could have been in so many hazardous undertakings and yet survive', his Biggles being the sole recipient of many adventures that 'did actually occur and are true in their essential facts'.

Even so, the 'show' will seem pretty incredible to readers today. For one thing the character and performance of those Camels with their fabric cladding and their delicate struts, and with their liking for landing and taking off in farmers' fields rather than airfields has a primitive charm unlike that of the warplanes that we now know and love. For another thing, their unsophisticated modes of combat encourage an equally primitive romanticism. Biggles lands in a field to gather a spy's message stuffed down a rabbit-hole; Algie Lacey (later to be a long-term comrade) revenges himself on the Boche by bombing a bed of geraniums; dangerous assaults are made on a German observation balloon in competition for a case of pre-war whisky. It is so different from what was going on down below among the 'half a million men' in that 'intricate tracery of thin white lines that marked the trench system' that one thinks one is at a schoolboy rugger-match where coming down in flames (there were no parachutes) was a customary hazard.

An analogy with boys' school stories is not inappropriate to our first meeting with Biggles in 266 Squadron: 'a slight, fair-haired, good-looking lad, still in his teens'. As Acting Flight-Commander he is a prefect, perhaps soon to become Head Boy, with his Squadron C. O. as master-in-charge, and Colonel Raymond as shrewd Headmaster. There is much badinage and endless heroics amid the tracer bullets, and even an embarrassing *affaire de coeur*

[sic] with a female spy. Only later in the ensuing series would a more-or-less adult Biggles assault a changing nation's views on what should be the politically correct behaviour of its adventurers.

Commentary

First published in 1932, the book was among several others that Johns put out through the firm of John Hamilton who specialised in such works. His catalogue of 1935 lists over fifty, including boys' stories by George E. Rochester which could have competed with Biggles. But in that year Johns was induced to join the whacky Children's Division of the Oxford University Press in London, for which august imprint he became an unlikely bestseller. Such a time of international crisis offered a fruitful opportunity for flying to all points of the compass with patriotic zeal and Biggles was to feature in two books every year up to 1942. At that time reforms set in at Oxford's London home at Amen House and our hero moved on to the runways of Hodder & Stoughton where what Lance Salway called his 'sinister and poisonous opinions' found a more comfortable lodgment in company with those coadjutors Gimlet the commando and Worrals of the WAAF.

-55-

LITTLE HOUSE IN THE BIG WOODS
BY LAURA INGALLS WILDER (1932)

By the time we get to page seven, two deer have been shot and hung up on a tree before being smoked. A lot of fish have been caught in a net on Lake Pepin and the hog is being killed. Little Laura did not like to hear it squeal. As I'm sure the RSPCA would not, but then the RSPCA were not living among the big woods of Wisconsin a hundred years ago. And anyway, smoked venison is delicious when the snow is all around and after the pig is slaughtered you can make a balloon out of its bladder while roasting its tail which is great fun and tasty too.

Little Laura, big sister Mary, little sister Carrie and Pa and Ma have made a home for themselves in the big woods and this is a story of a year of their lives there. It's not much of a story so far as exciting events go, although danger from bears and wolves and forest panthers are present enough, but for readers today, or when it was first published in 1932, it brings alive a world and a way of life that are deeply exotic. Smoking the venison is but one example of several descriptions of the family's almost total dependence on what they can do for themselves: Pa makes bullets for his gun, Ma makes butter and cheese (one of Uncle Henry's calves has to be killed to get the rennet), Laura and Mary work in the garden or gather nuts to store for winter.

And there are entertainments too apart from on Sundays when the day must be spent peacefully, looking at pictures in *The Wonders of the Animal World* or in the Bible from which Ma might read. There's a party at Grandpa's to which they must ride through the woods. There's a day when Laura and Mary are first taken to town with all its surprising houses and the big store where Pa can trade furs from his trapping for coloured prints and calicoes that Ma can use for dressmaking. This recollected childhood comes alive again for the reader, not least at home, after work, when Pa plays his fiddle, popping the fiddle-string as he sang:

All around the cobbler's bench
The monkey chased the weasel,
The preacher kissed the cobbler's wife –
Pop! Goes the weasel

But the recollection has been shaped into a fiction and its publication in 1932, when Laura Ingalls Wilder was sixty-five seemingly arose from the rejection of an actual autobiography that she wrote under the title of *Pioneer Girl* (an annotated edition was published in 2014). This, and her known biography, bear witness to the way in which 'life' has been adjusted to allow Laura's growth through childhood, adolescence, and marriage to make an American *Bildungsroman*. Furthermore, the decision both to write

Pioneer Girl and then convert it into the first of the children's books was encouraged by Wilder's daughter, Rose Wilder Lane, who was herself a writer and a credible case has been made for some kind of joint authorship. Nevertheless, the seven-book saga has been much loved (and much re-worked in other media) and in 1954 the Children's division of the American Library Association named her as the first recipient of a Medal for 'lifetime achievement' named after herself.

Commentary

The autobiographical sequence reflected in the 'Little House' books continued with *Little House on the Prairie* (1935), *On the Banks of Plum Creek* (1937), *By the Shores of Silver Lake* (1939), *The Long Winter* (1940), *The Little Town on the Prairie* (1941) and *These Happy Golden Years* (1943). A second book, *Farmer Boy* (1933) dealt with the childhood of Wilder's husband, Almanzo Wilder. The whole series was illustrated by Helen Sewell, one of the finest illustrators of her generation, later assisted by Mildred Boyle. In 1953 however Garth Williams was brought in to begin a re-illustration which he undertook after spending time visiting the sites where the adventures had originally occurred. They are now seen as definitive and their presence eventually, in 1953, brought the series to Britain for the first time. Williams was the son of two British artists who had moved to America but returned to London with their son in 1912 and he later attended the Westminster School of Art, whence he gained a four-year scholarship to the Royal College. He married in Britain but returned to the United States with his wife and daughter in 1943 and his first illustrations commission was suggested by E. B. White for *Stuart Little*. Later, amid much prolific, but graceful, work he would illustrate *Charlotte's Web*, using his daughter as a model for Fern. [See no.68 below].

Critical rumblings about the role of Rose in the books' authorship have recently been augmented by the more radical objection that the books reflect 'dated cultural addenda' (ie. making serial theft of Native American territory). Mrs Wilder's life and work seem not to have been an achievement after all and the Medal, for what it's worth, may still acknowledge her presence as a writer for children but is now, less glamorously, the Children's Literature Legacy Award.

-56-

BALLET SHOES: THE STORY OF THREE
CHILDREN ON THE STAGE
BY NOEL STREATFEILD (1936)

Great-Uncle-Matthew (no relation to the Uncle Matthew in *The Pursuit of Love*) collected babies. There was Pauline, saved from a shipwreck, and Petrova, orphaned after her parents fled from the Russian revolution, and Posy, adopted from a widowed dancer and sent along with a pair of ballet shoes. She was delivered to the house in Cromwell Road by a district messenger since the Gum, as he came to be called, did not dare face his housekeeper and ran away on a yacht to collect fossils in some distant quarter of the globe.

Taking the name of Fossil, the three little women were thus brought up not my a Marmee but by the Gum's great-niece, Sylvia, who teams up with her old nanny, and between them they create a happy but 'very ordinary' nursery life for their disparate family. However, the eccentric, professorial Gum has been rather lax in the matter of financial provision and the story takes off when the older girls must be withdrawn from school and their education falls into the hands of a mixed set of boarders whom Sylvia has had to take in to try to make ends meet. The 'very ordinary' takes a right-angle turn and thanks to one of the lodgers the girls end up as pupils of the formidable Madame Fidolia at the Children's Academy of Dancing and Stage Training.

Their progress there over the next six years owes much to Noel Streatfeild's own career, she having trained and worked as an actress for some twelve years before turning to writing. The disciplines, opportunities and disappointments of a theatrical education are laid out with a clear authority, but the book is saved from being an embryo 'career story' of later times by the verve with which characters, child and adult alike, are portrayed.

As it turns out, while the central plank of Madame Fidolia's curriculum is ballet and while Posy (she of the ballet shoes legacy from her mother) is destined for balletofame, there are fuller accounts of Pauline's rise to success in theatre. She progresses from a matineé of Maeterlinck's *Blue Bird* – where seven and a half pages are taken up with a direct quotation from the script – to increasingly professional engagements in *Alice in Wonderland* and *A Midsummer Night's Dream* (along with authoritative details about the crucial administrative requirements of child-licensing, and the equally crucial crises of getting or losing parts).

Petrova is to some extent the odd-girl out, being of a practical disposition and more enthusiastic about helping Mr Simpson, one of the lodgers, in his involvement with motor cars than performing with her sisters. When, on the last page, Gum eventually returns it is he who solves her career problem. While Pauline is off to Hollywood, and Posy to the Czechoslovakian ballet maître Manoff, he will take Petrova to live near an aerodrome where she can learn to fly. 'I wonder,' she remarks to Streatfeild's readers as much as to her sisters,' if other girls had to be one of us, which one they would choose to be'.

Commentary

Ballet Shoes, which was illustrated by Streatfeild's sister, Ruth Gervis, was her first book and was a runner-up for the Library Association's 1937 Carnegie Medal. It was followed by *Tennis Shoes* in 1937 and *The Circus is Coming* in 1939 which did win the Medal. The 'shoe' theme in the title was attractive to Streatfeild's American publishers who labelled the latter *Circus Shoes* and retitled several subsequent stories in similar fashion, thus, *Curtain Up!,* (1944), a partial sequel to *Ballet Shoes*, became *Theatre Shoes* in the United States.

-57-

THE HOBBIT: OR THERE AND BACK AGAIN
BY J. R. R. TOLKIEN (1937)

The general assumption that *The Hobbit* has never been out of print since its first publication is questionable. True it had a *succés*

'The Mountain-path'. 4-colour printing of a pen and water-colour drawing by the author, *The Hobbit* 2nd ed. (London: Allen & Unwin, 1937).

d'estime in September 1937 after heroic work on its production by Allen & Unwin's enthusiastic editors. (Encouraging the author to illustrate it, linked to their negotiations with Houghton Mifflin over an American edition involved much tortuous correspondence). But the coming of war, the destruction of stock, and the difficulties of reprinting almost certainly led to a hiatus in the production of reprints, added to which was its disappearance as any sort of critical landmark in children's literature.

That may seem strange from our present vantage-point, but *The Hobbit's* publication had occasioned doubts as well as praise. It had been passed over for the librarians' Carnegie Medal in favour of Eve Garnett's little stories of *The Children from One End Street* and was deemed by some critics both in Britain and America to be too frightening for the little ones. (Surprisingly, Richard Hughes had written to Stanley Unwin warning him that 'many parents ... may be afraid that parts of it are too terrifying for bedtime reading'.) Indeed, it is probably fair to say that up to 1953 *The Hobbit* was an unknown book.

Strictures on 'terrifying' would not do for Tolkien though. At the time of writing *The Hobbit* he was already working on *The Silmarillion*, the first part of which was to be *The Fellowship of the Ring* and his whole career since the end of the First World War had been a preparation for his imaginative endeavours. He had a mastery of both Anglo-Saxon and early English and the mythologies of those times (when he wrote *The Hobbit* he had been more than ten years the Rawlinson and Bosworth Professor of Anglo-Saxon at Oxford). As adjunct to his studies he had developed interests in the nature and naming of the creatures of Germanic mythology, in runes, and in primitive maps, so that the book had an authentic infrastructure of which 'terrifying' aspects were a necessary and component part.

'There and Back Again' is both the delight and the reason why bedtime parents might neglect Mr Hughes's 'snag' in the composition. (And large parts of the story were told to Tolkien's own children over the dozen years of its composition.) There is an assurance at the start that Mr Bilbo Baggins, elected much against his will by thirteen dwarves to burgle a dragon's lair, will come back safely and, in the conduct of his adventures, any terror present is mitigated by his never relinquishing his unheroic desire for a comfy night in his hobbit hole with eggs and bacon for breakfast in the morning. The great round-trip through the Wilderland to the Misty Mountain and back sees a panoply of traditionary creatures possessed of good and evil intents – dwarves, trolls, elves, goblins, and Smaug the dragon himself – as well as the invented Gollum, who appears to such ominous effect in *The Lord of the Rings*. (In fact the episode in which Bilbo meets Gollum in the underground caverns and they have their riddling competition had to be rewritten for later editions of the book to meet requirements reflecting back from the longer work.) Through it all too, though, the Professor-Storyteller maintains a reassuring conversation with his readers as to the events that they may be witnessing.

Commentary

Much can be learnt of the making of *The Hobbit* from the immensely detailed descriptive bibliography of Tolkien's works by Wayne Hammond (1993). He tells of the acceptance of the manuscript (following a positive report on it by the publisher's ten

year-old son, Rayner Unwin, who received a one shilling fee for
it) and follows the workings of the editorial process in fascinating
detail. And, to complementary discussions of the text, are those
on the treatment of the runes and the maps and especially of the
author's illustrations. These were planned as monochrome plates
with a coloured frontispiece, but the American publishers asked for
more colour which Tolkien duly supplied, the colour blocks then
also being used for the second English edition of the book. Those
early editions have a homely quality to them, fit for a hobbit's
bookshelves, but the fame of the *Silmarillion* project has been such
that various heavy and pompous editions have been marketed for
shelves from which the books may well never be taken.

-58-

THE ADVENTURES OF THE LITTLE
WOODEN HORSE
BY URSULA MORAY WILLIAMS (1938)

Bedtime stories recently got a government seal of approval. Our new
Enlightenment is in process of acclaiming and supplying consumer-
tested advice for what past generations regarded as a natural human
activity.

What to choose for them is also easy enough for anyone who
does not have a tin ear for language and can discriminate between
the genuine and the meretricious in today's vast output. But the
transitions are worth noting: from simple to more complex picture
books, from picture books to story collections and to those full-
length stories that split up naturally into bedtime-sized chunks.

The Little Wooden Horse and his adventures are an ideal example
of this last. The book has nineteen chapters, none of which is longer
than eleven pages of generously-spaced letterpress (in the first
edition anyway), and all of which are organised in classic storytelling
fashion – one crisis after another down to the happy resolution.

But there is more to it than that. The story begins by establishing the bond of affection between the little wooden horse and Uncle Peder, the toymaker who constructed him. The horse's efforts to help his master, who falls upon hard times, lead to a series of accidents which carry him further and further away from his home surroundings (perhaps with Carlo Collodi somewhere in the background, influencing the proceedings). Some of these accidents themselves result in the little horse incurring debts of gratitude which amount to stories within the story. Thus, he is diverted from taking a reward to the miner's son, who cleaned him up after a pit explosion, by having to run in a royal horse-race and then by getting a job as a tightrope walker (!) in a circus. Such divagations supply tensions of their own and help to give an organic unity to the whole narrative as the ravelled-up incidents are finally unravelled.

So who wrote it, and when? Ursula Moray Williams, who was born in 1911, was prominent among the writers for younger children from the thirties onward. Her first book, *Jean-Pierre*, (1931), verses illustrated with her own scissor-cuts, was a notable debut and was rapidly followed by a succession of stories and plays, including two collections for Brownies. More adventurous experiments, like *The Pettabomination* of 1933, were precursors for *Adventures of the Little Wooden Horse* which came out in 1938 with illustrations by Nina K. Brisley, sister to the author of *Milly-Molly-Mandy*. Later the little horse was to team up with another particularly engaging Moray Williams character, *Gobbolino the Witch's Cat*, who first arrived in 1942.

Having been told stories and lived with stories from childhood on, Ursula Moray Williams seems never to have needed to learn her craft, and the secret of the *Little Wooden Horse*'s success lies in its plain, undemonstrative telling. Nothing else would have done, for managing the suspension of our disbelief involved writerly feats rather like the wooden horse negotiating his tightrope on two wheels. Readers and listeners must be persuaded that her hero is not only a walking, talking, living wooden horse, but one who can pull barges, shift coal, and outrace stallions. And indeed, at the point when he has, literally, lost his head he more or less functions as a disembodied spirit. Only Ursula Moray Williams's self-assurance, 'quiet and strong' like the horse himself, and her unadorned language can do the persuading.

'Long out of fashion' says the shopkeeper to the gentleman who wants to buy the little horse to try to quell his unruly children, voracious for new toys. But, rough and rowdy though they be, they never want to give him up, and the incident is emblematic of the potential that extremely simple things may have for nurturing the child's imagination. This horse belongs with Edward Gordon Craig and *The Book of Penny Toys* (1899) and Lovat Fraser with the tumblers and whistling larks of his *Book of Simple Toys* (1917) – an assertion of creativity against the ersatz products of the plastic mills.

Commentary

Ursula Moray Williams's archive is at Seven Stories: the National Centre for Children's Books and it includes her long-hand manuscript and corrections for the *Little Wooden Horse*. A biography, *Through the Magic Door* by Colin Davison, with a listing of sixty-three of her principal published works was published in 2011.

–59–

THE SWORD IN THE STONE
BY T. H. WHITE (1938)

Let's begin: 'Then it was lesson time: Divinity, French, History, and Latin. Divinity was easy as it was about Noah's Ark …'

Oops! Sorry. Start again:'On Mondays,Wednesdays and Fridays it was Court Hand and Summulae Logicales while the rest of the week it was the Organon, Repetition and Astrology …'

That's better, but the muddle over curricula is forgivable. The misspeck to begin with was from the first page of John Masefield's *The Midnight Folk* (see above no.50) and its likeness to the first page of T. H. White's *The Sword in the Stone* is no accident. 'A *chef d'oeuvre* of the *imagination* ... a book which I love this side of idolatory' said White of *The Sword*'s predecessor, published some eleven years earlier, and the two books share a quality of free fantasy that sets them above most of the more leaden-footed explorers of spacetime.

The Wart (to rhyme with Art) as Arthur is known in the Castle of the Forest Sauvage has much in common with Kay Harker among the Midnight Folk. Both are being brought up under guardianships and are at once stoutly independent and immensely likeable characters. Each, in quest of what the Wart's Sir Ector calls 'eddication', ventures among animals, becoming privy to some of their ways, and each encounters, for good or ill, figures from local myth. And both have their stories told with a captivating brio.

The difference, though, lies in the management of the narrative. From the very start Kay's adventure is directed by a desire to find Grandpapa Harker's lost treasure, while the Wart is at the mercy of his creator's quicksilver imaginings. T. H. White certainly founded his story on the first book of the *Morte D'Arthur* by Sir Thomas Malory, to whom *The Sword* is dedicated and from whom some phrasings are taken direct, but a huge tissue of authorial invention is interposed between the child Arthur, being first brought to Sir Ector's castle, and his eventual drawing of the sword from the stone. (As in Malory, that famous dramatic moment arrives with only minimal preparation in the final few pages of the book.)

What precedes it is a romp. Eddication for the Wart and for Sir Ector's son (another Kay) requires a tutor and the magician Merlyn arranges for himself to be so appointed and then generates most of the events of the story. It's an episodic affair, conducted with occasional glimpses of Malory as a source, but mostly as a series of riffs by White on those elements in the myth that attracted his practical imagination. He was a man who needed to know how things worked, whether medieval tournaments, the hunting of boar or the inner nature of hawks or fish, and, with Merlyn as his surrogate, he opens up Arthur's understanding to the world and the people around him.

It's hardly a conventional schooling though. White has no truck with lecturing either his pupil or his readers. The formalities of chivalry are matter for Quixotic farce as King Pellinore and Sir Grummore Grummurson joust together; Art discerns the nature of fish by swimming in the castle moat as a perch and having an almost too daring interview with Mr M, the giant pike King of the Moat ('remorseless, disillusioned, logical, predatory, fierce, pitiless; but his great jewel of an eye was that of a stricken deer, large, fearful, sensitive, and full of grief'). Such prose, often deriving from a close knowledge of whatever subject comes to hand contrasts strangely with the book's hilarious use of anachronism ('"Couldn't send 'em to Eton, I suppose?"' inquires Sir Grummore during the eddication debate over a bottle of port) and this runs through both phrasings and events. Thus, Merlyn is living his life backwards so is found smoking a meerschaum pipe and owning 'a complete set of cigarette cards depicting wild fowl by Peter Scott', while one of the book's central adventures is a raid on Morgan le Fay's Siege [i.e. fortress] of Air and Darkness carried out in company with Robin Hood and Maid Marian. But far from alienating the reader these ploys serve to involve him within the fantasy, presenting, say, mewed hawks metaphorically as taking formal dinner in an officers' mess, or touching a high pitch of pathos with the death of the hound Beaumont at the boar hunt.

Commentary

The reader of *The Sword in the Stone* must beware though, for it is not a stable text. It achieved instant success both in Britain and the USA when it was published in 1938 and that led White not only to devise three sequels (seen more as continuations for an adult rather than a child readership, and gathered together in 1958 under the title *The Once and Future King*) but also to rework the original story. At least three versions of this can be found with chunks and lesser details deleted or added. Thus, Morgan's Siege is retitled the Castle Chariot; she herself may at one time be 'a very beautiful lady wearing beach pajamas and smoked glasses' or, at another, fat, dowdy and middle-aged 'with black hair and a slight moustache', or just not present at all, and the place may be guarded by a single griffin, or a troop of griffins and wyverns, or a

collection of Anthropophagi. You don't get much guidance in any
one edition as to how it relates to the others, but for me anyway
the first is pre-eminent for the joyous freshness of its wit and its
storytelling.

<h2 style="text-align:center">–60–</h2>

<h2 style="text-align:center">A TRAVELLER IN TIME
BY ALISON UTTLEY (1939)</h2>

More than one journey must be made by most readers who will
traverse the histories of this tale.

Foremost is that which falls to the storyteller, Penelope
Taberner Cameron, who goes from her home in Chelsea with
her brother and sister to stay at their aunt's farmhouse in the
Derbyshire uplands. Thackers is an ancient manor, not far from
the ruined mansion of Wingfield where, briefly, Mary Queen of
Scots was held under surveillance. It is also deemed to be the
one-time country seat of the Babingtons whose scion, Anthony,
was devoted to that Queen and whose endeavours on her behalf
would lead to his barbaric execution on a scaffold in Holborn.

Allowing that this confluence of past events can somehow
be sustained in the atmospherics of the present place, young
Penelope finds herself involuntarily drawn into the sixteenth
-century life of Thackers (whose housekeeper is an ancestor of
her own aunt). 'Sharing the ether with those unseen ones' carries
her intermittently from present to past in sojourns that take place
outside the clock-time of her own life.

Thus it is that she follows, with a grim foreknowledge of its
outcome, Anthony Babington's hopeless venture in tunneling
through from Thackers to Wingfield in order to rescue the Queen.
Thus it is that Alison Uttley is able to interlink the two centuries
with memories, tales and tokens that have survived through the
generations – ballads echoing on, a lost jewel that cannot be
carried back in time, a bobbin-boy made by a dumb child who

nonetheless seems to have a sense of Penelope's otherness. (It's worth speculating on whether a relationship exists between *A Traveller in Time* and Philippa Pearce's *Tom's Midnight Garden.*)

The second journey that today's reader must make is into Penelope's own time. For although few clues are given as to the dates of her visits to Thackers it is reasonable to set them in the years before the First World War when Alison herself was Penelope's age. For Thackers is, of course, the farm near Dethick in Derbyshire where she was brought up and her 1931 novel of reminiscence, *The Country Child,* contains passages directly equivalent to some in the later book. But those years are near enough a century away (and *A Traveller in Time*, published in 1939, is itself eighty years old) and the Chelsea children and Uncle Barnaby and Aunt Tissie and all the life of the farm may seem as far away to some readers as the Babingtons. (Think tractors.)

This double dislocation of time coupled with Uttley's absorption in her own version of pastorale may pose difficulties. For one thing, the twentieth-century story is hardly a story at all but rather a setting – a retreat – against which the historic drama may be played. And for another thing that drama defies expectations of what 'time-slip fantasies' ought to do. The irruption of Penelope in her modern garments and with her modern patterns of speech into the life of a sixteenth century manor house seems to be explained all too casually ('Oh, that's Mistress Taberner's niece just arrived from Chelsey'). Her rather flakey awareness of what happened in history – which could have got her burned as a witch – and her wholly irregular comings-and-goings, are passed over without recourse to any intricate – and surely unavailing – explanations.

To ask for such is to mistake the nature of the book, judging it according to over-conventional criteria. It is a 'slow' work. It does not set out to exploit startling juxtapositions. It is rather a 'dream-story' (something in which Uttley was very interested) where the sleeper experiences events with such clarity and emotions with such intensity that they override the need for a rational accounting. Uttley is offering us in Thackers's double manifestations a take-it-or-leave-it world where what matters is not so much events as the impact of a felt past. Her lyrical prose – rejoicing throughout the book in such things as 'white roses foaming over walls' or the sight of 'pigs' pettitoes soused and tansy puddings' – encompasses with scarcely suppressed nostalgia a now-vanished rural life and the inevitability of its vanishment.

Commentary

The first edition had dashing, but eccentric scraperboard headpieces by Phyllis Bray, little known as an illustrator, which were replaced in the Puffin edition of 1977 and subsequently. A handsome account of the wayward life of Mary Queen of Scots by Susan Doran was published by the British Library in 2007. Richly illustrated with contemporary portraits and manuscripts, its judicious text helps to bring home the fascination exerted by the Queen not just on Anthony Babington (or Penelope Taberner-Cameron-Uttley) but on almost every generation since her doleful execution.

–61–

THE LITTLE PRINCE
BY ANTOINE DE SAINT-EXUPÉRY (1943)

Born in Lyon on 29 June 1900, St-Ex as he was known, was a hulking six-foot tall aristocratic French *comte* from a traditionally reactionary Catholic background. He was also a pioneering aviator (he learnt to fly when he was twelve) and philanderer whose mistresses were resented by his Salvadorean wife Consuelo. Despite the couple's stormy relationship, St-Ex promised to return to her after the war, saying that if he was killed: 'I will have someone to wait for in eternity'.

St-Ex had joined the air force and had been decorated during the fall of France. He took refuge in the US but rejoined his squadron in 1942 although officially too old to fly Lightnings. He died on a reconnaissance mission flying over the littoral of southern France near his childhood chateau on 31st July 1944.

He carefully cleaned out his active volcanoes. Full page water-colour by the author, printed in four colours (275x185mm.). From page 61 of the augmented quarto Gift Edition (Heinemann, 1997)

The recent discovery of St-Ex's identity bracelet, 300ft below the surface of the Mediterranean, engraved with Consuelo's name and contact address in New York, implies that she was indeed still close to his heart, something that was refuted after his death by his family. They reviled Consuelo's memory, trying to exclude her from biographies and denying that *The Little Prince* was a metaphor for his relationship with her. One mistress, the aristocratic Hélène de Vogüé, even wrote a biography which reduced Consuelo to one paragraph. St-Ex's mythophile descendants are now opposing a seabed search for his wrecked aircraft.

The Little Prince was first published in New York by Reynal & Hitchcock in French, and almost simultaneously in an English translation by Katherine Woods. It was dedicated to Léon Werth, a Jewish Trotskyist art critic ('the best friend I have in the world'), but as the dedication statement continues it decides to address rather 'the child from whom this grown-up grew' and amends itself to: 'Léon Werth when he was a little boy'.

What's It About? (1) An airman is repairing his plane which has crashed in the desert. He is approached by 'un petit bonhomme' who requests that he draw him the picture of a sheep. This little fellow [Woods = 'little man'] is *le petit Prince*, sole inhabitant of Asteroid B-612, who has travelled to Earth (taking advantage perhaps 'of the migration of a flock of wild birds') via several other asteroids inhabited by eccentric personages: a lone king, a conceited man, a boozer, a business-man, a lamplighter, and a geographer. He is fleeing from his association with a flower on his own planet whose behaviour embarrasses him, but a meeting with a philosophical fox persuades him that he must follow the dictates of his heart and take responsibility for his flower. He helps the airman to find a well in the desert and then, after a pre-arranged and fatal meeting with a yellow snake, he vanishes – presumably returning (with the drawing of the sheep) to his own asteroid.

What's It About? (2) St-Ex meets his child self in a fable of innocence and experience. It is not hard to make a case for this eccentric story being rooted in his dismay over his difficult marriage, with the asteroidal, adenoidal rose, being the hypochondriac spendthrift Consuelo. Confused adult uncertainties bang against the ruthless assurances of childhood ('One runs the risk of weeping a little if one lets himself be tamed'). The metaphor becomes an excuse for ruminations on freedom and responsibility. Existential Angst enters children's literature and you must work out the interpretation for yourself.

The book belongs among those whose text can only at peril be divorced from, or rearranged round, its illustrations. Exupéry's watercolours and monochrome wash drawings (now, with his manuscript, in the Pierpont Morgan Library, New York) are closely integrated with the text, which often refers to them. Their naïveté ('I was discouraged [from painting] when I was six years old') chimes with, and hence lends conviction to, what has often been seen as an absurd, not to say perverse, piece of whimsy.

Is that so? The recent trawling up of the silver identity bracelet from the bottom of the Mediterranean has encouraged renewed discussion about the status of this 'children's book for adults'. It could be classed, amongst disparate examples from Rabelais and Swift to *Alice* and *The Water-Babies*, as what the critic Northrop

Frye calls 'a Mennipean satire' – which is to say a stylised dialogue playing with and making fun of human activities as distinct from life as she is actually lived. As with Kingsley, though, the satiric energy can be blunted by an intrusive sentimentality.

Commentary

As a writer, Exupéry was a master craftsman and his pellucid French mitigates the inherent soppiness of the child's transactions with his flower. That seems to suit the francophones, who have put the little chap on to pre-Euro bank-notes, and it may well suit foreign readers coming at the French text and rejoicing in its accessibility as well as its content (Heinemann used to publish it as a schoolbook). But who knows what the readers of the hundred or so translations make of it? Katherine Woods can be ungainly – and has been called 'ponderous' – but for English readers any successor to her *Little Prince* has been blocked by Europe. The recent decision to 'harmonise' our copyright limitations with those of Germany (i.e. extending them to seventy years after the author's death) prevented Pavilion Books from reprinting a new, and more satisfactory, translation by Alan Wakeman, with its highly discussable pastiche illustrations by Michael Foreman. One is moved to reflect that there should be an asteroid reserved somewhere for *les grandes personnes bruxelloises*.

-62-

AUTUMN TERM
BY ANTONIA FOREST (1948)

By the time lessons begin in the autumn term at Kingscote, the chief participants have already answered the register: Miss Keith, the headmistress who, surprisingly, has allowed her niece Thalia, or Tim for short, to be entered as a pupil in the Third Remove, Miss Cartwright, the form mistress, the six Marlow children and their potential antagonists Marie Dobson and the senior, Lois Sanger.

The fact that there are six Marlows at the school simultaneously (almost as many as the total population of Mrs Teachum's academy in *The Governess* [see no.5 above]) presupposes a remarkable income for their father, who is but a Naval commander.

The youngest of his daughters, the twins Nicola and Lawrie, are entering Kingscote for the first time this autumn term and the book is a serial account of the happenings that occur. The most

dramatic is probably right at the start when Nicola's treasured Swiss army knife gets dropped out of a train window and she pulls the communication cord and stops the train in order to recover it. But the central issue results in their being suspended from the school's Girl Guide Company in which they had only just been proudly enrolled. Too young to be cognisant of their responsibilities is, on the face of it, a sufficient reason, but, in a situation common to many a school story, they are paying a price for trying to be honest when those with more to

Jacket design by Margery Gill
(210x135mm.), London: Faber, 1948.

lose (la Dobson and la Sanger) are rearranging the evidence.

They are redeemed to some extent before everyone goes home for the Christmas holidays. Under Tim's direction the Third Remove put on an impressive production of a dramatisation of Twain's *The Prince and the Pauper*, which reveals Lawrie to be a born actor. At the same time, the wretched Marie finds herself giving away her compromised role in the Guide débâcle, a revelation which is met with contempt rather than condign publicity among her peers which would be the natural result in most fictional schools.

Speaking of which it must be noted that Kingscote as such has a strange, slow-motion history. Forest's depiction of school, staff, and pupils has a contemporary setting for 1948 but when we return there for a new school year two terms later no fewer than eleven real-time publishing years have passed. *End of Term* was published in 1959 and, with even more laggardliness, the closely-following *Cricket Term* and *Attic Term* did not come out until 1974 and 1976. Within the fictional time-frame however four other books about the Marlow family – out of school – develop further what is unique to Forest's children's books: parallel themes of religious argument involving both Catholic and Jewish orthodoxy.

Commentary

The devotion of adult readers to the genre (primarily) of the girls' school story led to a widespread movement, associated perhaps with the development of feminist theories. Books were published discussing particular authors or series such as Elsie Oxenham and the Abbey girls, or Elinor Brent-Dyer and the Chalet School books; publishing ventures were set up to reprint (often via print-on-demand services) swathes of favourite titles and from 1990 to 2013 the sixty numbers were published of the joyous magazine for aficionados *Folly* (i.e.,'Friends of Light Literature for Youth'!). Two of the prefects responsible for that jolly jape, Sue Sims and Hilary Clare, were also the editors of *The Encyclopaedia of Girls' School Stories* (Ashgate, 2000), just across the formroom from Robert Kirkpatrick among the boys.

–63–

THE LION, THE WITCH AND THE WARDROBE
BY C. S. LEWIS (1950)

Before Harry Potter or even his creator were born, and before anyone had met Frodo Baggins, the founding of Narnia, which was to have a like celebrity, had occurred. Furthermore, if you look at the first couple of chapters of this foundation document, the roots of its phenomenal popularity may be observed.

Lucy Pevensie, youngest of the four Pevensie children, finds her way through the back of an ancient wardrobe into the land of

Narnia where she meets and has tea with Mr. Tumnus, a faun. For the reader she is at once, and will remain, a figure as appealing as she was to the author (the book is dedicated to Lewis's god-daughter, Lucy Barfield). The wardrobe as a gateway to fantasy is a nicely everyday object (we will find Lyra hiding in one when we get to Sir Philip Pullman's *Northern Lights*), and Mr Tumnus bears witness to Lewis's gift for taking over and naming intelligent creatures from myth and fable (cf. such later heroes as Reepicheep the mouse and Bree the talking horse).

To those first readers the book as a whole must have seemed a new exploration of what was to become, under its influence and that of the hobbits, the theme of war between the powers of darkness, where 'it is always winter and never Christmas' and those of peace and joy. The four children – Sons of Adam and Daughters of Eve as they are referred to by Narnians – enter the kingdom where it has been foretold that such beings will inherit the rulership of the land. Such an event would end the power of the White Witch who has usurped it from the lion Aslan and, through the treachery of one of the children, Edmund, she bids fair to have her way.

It is this treachery which is the fulcrum of the story for, by the Law of Narnian Deep Magic, the Witch has the right to take Edmund's life, but Aslan, on his behalf, bargains that she may take his own life instead. In consequence he is slaughtered on the ancient Stone Table of sacrifice but is able to draw upon the 'deeper magic from the dawn of time' which is unknown to the White Witch, and gain resurrection. There is a battle at which the forces of evil are defeated and the children are crowned rulers, 'as foretold', in the castle of Cair Paravel. As such they grow in honour and power over many years until, adventuring together in chase of a white stag they find themselves on the threshold of that old facilitator, the wardrobe, and, plunging through it, return to discover that no time has elapsed while they have been away.

The baldness of that plot summary may seem hardly to justify the critical esteem in which the book has been held and its world-wide popularity among children. There has certainly been a querulous reaction as to how far it draws upon the story of Christ's sacrifice and resurrection and how far young readers either notice or care about such a reference. Lewis and his advocates are perhaps more culpable for not glossing the work's technical defects as a piece of storytelling. Narnia as a country is given no physical or social presence, the only representatives of its population being Mr Tumnus, a couple of beavers, and an undifferentiated mass of flailing bodies in the final battle. The introduction of Father Christmas as precursor of Aslan and bearer of some essential magical gifts, is forced, and the galloping conclusion summarising the children's long reign is embarrassed by a descent into sham olde Englysshe: ' "I know not how it is, but this lamp on a post worketh upon me strangely" '.

Above all, the author is guilty of juggling the plot to suit himself rather than its genuine needs. The sins of Edmund, the traitor (for the sake of a sinful craving for Turkish Delight) hardly have the weight demanded of them, while Aslan's application to the magic from the dawn of time for his return to life is special pleading. No white witch, however spirited, can stand up to an author who is able so to stack the cards against her.

Commentary

Unlike the saga of the *Silmarillion* by his friend Professor Tolkien, the seven books of Lewis's 'Narnia' series were written to no initial plan and may be seen as merely episodes in an undefined project, although one unifying factor has been the vital presence throughout the series of its illustrator, Pauline Baynes. In a similar way the sequence of publishing was split between the first five stories which were issued by Lewis's friend and main publisher, Geoffrey Bles, and The Bodley Head who published the last two books (Collins having taken on the Bles list after his retirement in 1954). This double fragmentation, together with the fact that only the last, and weakest, volume, *The Last Battle* (1956) was awarded the Carnegie Medal (a sort of consolation prize?) while only one other volume had the status of a 'runner up' adds to evidence that the series was very slow to take on the immense popularity that it later enjoyed. (My own feeling is that that movement started when Kaye Webb produced a united boxed set of the series as

Puffin Story Books, and promoted it with her customary panache through the Puffin Club.) From the 1970s the series was well away as a family of books within which child readers liked to move, and with HarperCollins acquiring the serial rights in 1994 the set was ripe for large scale commercial exploitation. The question of a reading sequence for the books: whether to read them chronologically by date of publication or by date of historical events in Narnia itself (jumpy though they be) has been answered, amid objections, in favour of the latter by the publishers who have used it in their numbered sets of the volumes and in their hefty compendium with the complete stories in one volume.

-64-

FINN FAMILY MOOMINTROLL
BY TOVE JANSSON (1950)

The saga of the Moomins has no beginning and no end. Like remnants of some skaldic history, bits of the story jut up out of the silent tundra to be gathered and chronicled by their discoverer.

Tove Jansson was well qualified for the task. She was born in Finland in 1914, the gifted daughter of a sculptor and a variously-talented mother (who seems, uncannily, to resemble Moominmamma, the pivotal figure in the saga). The family's first language was Swedish and the conjunction of the two Norden cultures, along with a passion for the sea and for life on remote islands, was to be fundamental to Tove's work.

Art too was significant. She studied painting in Stockholm and in mainland Europe, and as well as fine art she found great satisfaction in writing and illustration and indeed, while still at school, she had produced an illustrated story of her own, *Sara och Pelle*, which was published in 1933. Her technical command of drawing in both pen and ink and watercolour was complete, as was her interpretative vision (she did some remarkable illustrative suites for Swedish editions of *Alice*, of *The Hunting of the Snark* – almost a Moomin story itself – and of *The Hobbit*) and any assessment of her texts must stress the perfection of their graphic accompaniment. It unites and gives coherence to what sometimes seems a fragmentary masterpiece.

Moominpappa and the wet Muskrat. Scraper-board drawing by the author (88mm.square) on p.28 of *Comet in Moominland* (London: Ernest Benn, 1951).

Finn Family Moomintroll gave English readers their first sight of the saga in 1950, although it had been preceded in Sweden by a long-running cartoon strip in the paper *Ny Tid* which would gain world circulation in 1954 when strips in English began to be published and syndicated by the *Evening News*[22]. An earlier story, *The Moomins and the Great Flood*, had appeared in Swedish in 1945 but was not translated till 2005 and its successor, *Comet in Moominland*, came out in English a year after *Finn Family Moomintroll*. Together, these establish the character of the Moomin family: Pappa, Mamma and Moomintroll, and begin the introduction of the many eccentric creatures who pop in and out of these bits of the saga that Tove has preserved for us. Near-permanent figures are Snufkin, the wandering harmonicist, and the Hemulen, philatelist and failed natural philosopher, and they

22   Five hardback volumes of 'Tove Jansson Comic Strips' have been published in Britain by Drawn & Quarterly. They are seriously deficient in bibliographical information.

are joined by Moomintroll's chum, Sniff, and by the Muskrat, who, later on in the saga, drop out of sight. A prodigality of walk-on characters materialise all through, and in later books Mymble and her sister, the tough Little My, come to prominence with the boy Toft and the hysteric Fillyjonk. Strangely ominous, at the edge of events, are the tribe of Hattifatteners who can neither hear nor speak 'with no object in life but the distant goal of their journey's end', and the lowering Groke, beneath whose feet the ground itself will freeze.

And the arbitrary is in charge. Such a register of characters may give a hint of the saga's independence from all literary ancestors (unless, like the Moomins' Ancestor they have been immolated in the stove). Any attempt to sum up the point of it all is defeated however by the arbitrary and sometimes barely connected succession of narrative events. ("'Does anything matter anywhere?'" asks Little My at one point. "'No,'" her sister replied happily. "'Don't ask such silly questions.'") What may be helpful though is to note that the weight of the saga is present in the eight books that run from *The Great Flood* to *Moominvalley in November* (1971), while some incidental goings-on are recorded in three picture books with texts in verse. A kind of coda, *The Dangerous Journey*, came out in England in 1978; this was preceded by the ballad, *Who Will Comfort Toffle?* (1960) and an early novelty-book, featuring pages with holes in them, *Moomin, Mymble and Little My* (1952) which is written out in a playful script.

So does anything matter? Yes, Mymble's sister, happily it does. Do not be put off by the unusual narrative structure of the seven books of the canon. Ignore the *reductios* of the Blytonians that page-turning is the highest good. Tove Jansson's rags, tags, and bobtails march to a different drum, wakening minds and imaginations like no other. These exhumations from Moominland are best read successively and complete, from *Comet* onwards, because – for all their inconsequence – they take the reader into an exploration of the wellsprings of personality. Their persuasiveness does not lie in cranking up factitious conflicts. Instead we get an existentialist comedy (whose genius storytelling is remarkably well translated by, in sum, three different translators) with the participants wobbling across the paths of their fellows in quest of what may prove only a precarious self-fulfilment.

You keep reading because these oddballs turn into friends. You want to glimpse how they might be faring. And in the great culminating episodes of *Moominpappa at Sea* and *Moominvalley in November* you realise that they may be living your dilemmas too and that a consolation is not impossible – even for Fillyjonks.

Commentary

While, thanks to the Moomins, Jansson became a writer and illustrator of world renown, she was also a gifted painter and cartoonist. (It was just as well that Sweden was not invaded by Germany during the war or became a Soviet satellite after, for she produced ferocious cartoons of Hitler and Stalin alike,) A large touring exhibition of her paintings and graphic work, with a catalogue, light on information but heavy on pictures, was set up several years ago and arrived for a spell at the Dulwich Gallery in 2017.

-65-

THE THIRTEEN CLOCKS
AND THE WONDERFUL O
BY JAMES THURBER (1950 AND 1957)

Observe always the two sides of the coin of the singer of tales. On the obverse, with varying degrees of glitter, are the chills, the thrills and the giggles of his fanciful sport, but turn it over and there lurk its more shadowy implications.

The combinations vary. I think you'd be taking things a bit far to read nuclear pessimism into 'Tittymouse and Tattymouse' in Joseph Jacobs's *English Fairy Tales*, but what of the chthonic reverberations of 'Yallery Brown' or 'The Rose Tree'? It is part of the magic possessed by the singer of tales that his simplicities may hide such depths.

And where better to see it than in these two new-invented variants: double fancies by a single storyteller, urgently demanding

to be read aloud, but composed for print and visually united by
the perfect collaboration of his illustrator? *The Thirteen Clocks*,
published in 1950, came first but was, in fact, the fourth children's
book by Thurber, the great *New Yorker* cartoonist and satirist.
(His first, *Many Moons,* had won the 1944 Caldecott Medal for
its illustrator, Louis Slobodkin, and its two successors, *The Great
Quillow* and *The White Deer,* are as worthy of reissue as the present
books.)

As is proper, *The Thirteen Clocks* follows the formal pattern of those

'He tampered with the clocks to see
if they would go', by Marc Simont
(80x100mm.) reproduced by colour
lithography from a paperback edition
of *The Thirteen Clocks* (nd).

tales that feature the wooing of a
princess immured in a tower – on this
occasion by a villainous and false
uncle ('a cold Duke, afraid of Now'
whose thirteen clocks have long been
frozen at ten-to-five in the afternoon).
The hero prince must fulfil an
impossible task to rescue her (the
garnering of a thousand jewels in
nine-and-ninety hours, so timed that
on his return the clocks of the castle
shall all be striking five). And there is,
of course, a helper, the irrepressible
Golux: 'a little man … in an
indescribable hat [whose] eyes were
wide and astonished as if everything
was happening for the first time'.

Needless to say, the task is fulfilled,
for the devising and solving of fairytale problems is one of Thurber's
gifts. (In *Many Moons* a way is found to satisfy a young princess's
desire to be given the moon.) But while a traditional structure is
the foundation for the story's authenticity it gains a wholly 'modern'
character from the manner of its telling – 'modern' here intended to
point up its place within an ageless tradition where now even the
rawest of folktales come to their audience through print and pictures
rather than through direct telling.

Within that dispensation, Thurber is superb. For sure, there are
some elaborate literary turns ('It was cold on Hagga's hill and fresh

with furrows where the dragging points of stars had plowed the fields') and these are conjoined with frequent and entirely successful shifts towards verse within prose sentences ('You'll never live to wed his niece. You'll only die to feed his geese. Good bye, goodnight and sorry.') But Thurber's lightness of touch and continuing comic presence enhance the joyousness of the whole narrative enterprise. Laughter, not fear, lies behind all the dark doings.

The Wonderful O, however, which was published seven years after *The Thirteen Clocks*, is the different side to the coin: the tale as fable, where the storyteller casts aside 'happily ever after' and is liable to offer a Moral Application instead. Marc Simont, the accompanying illuminator, who had concluded *The Thirteen Clocks* with his only picture coloured in vernal greens and blues, is now driven back upon muted blues and greys as Thurber takes us into a startling and problematic narrative.

'Somewhere', the tale o-fully begins, 'a ponderous tower clock slowly dropped a dozen strokes into the gloom'. And the ominous toll of that sentence contrasts with the o-less advent of Littlejack, 'a man with a map' and his alliance with Black 'a man with a ship' in a buccaneering quest for treasure. They sail in the *Aieu* (all the vowels but 'o' and 'sounding a little like a night-bird screaming') for Black has a fixated hatred of the letter 'o', and hence of their destination which is the island of Ooroo ('like the eyes of ghosts leaning against an R'). Their invasion of the place, ostensibly for treasure, turns into a crazed rampage against o-ness. An edict forbids the use of the letter (so that a bootmaker becomes a btmaker and '*Love's Labour's Lost* and *Mother Goose* flattened out like a pricked balloon') but the ban is spread from denominator to denominated and, category by category, those things and creatures possessed of o-ness are driven out or destroyed.

This assault on o and its innocent adherents gives Thurber the opportunity for a virtuoso raid on the thesaurus: oboes, pianos, bassoons giving way to fifes, drums and cymbals, dominoes and ping-pong to tiddleywinks and mumblety-peg. There are jokes over o-less spellings (look at the name by the doorbell of poor Miss phelia liver), and a continuing flow of his trademark rhythmic, rhyming sentences. Triumph comes with a kind of celestial dance of o-full

literary heroes:'Donalbane of Birnam Wood, Robinson Crusoe and
Robin Hood, the moody Doones of *Lorna Doone*, Davy Crockett
and Daniel Boone, out of near and ancient tomes, Banquo's ghost
and Sherlock Holmes …' Such lightnesses mitigate the Orwellian
undertow to the fable and also, in the fairytale ending, a rather
clunking Moral Application.

Commentary

Despite the difference in publication dates the two books have a
unity of purpose which was reflected in their reissue as a matching
pair by the publishing arm of the *New York Review of Books*.

–66–

THE BORROWERS
BY MARY NORTON (1952)

One of the most ruthless takes on bedtime stories is 'Paul's
Tale' which Mary Norton wrote for James Reeves's wonderful
anthology (perhaps the best ever) *A Golden Land* (1958). Paul's
godmother, Aunt Isobel, has started to read him a Blytonesque
fairytale but he interrupts to say that he prefers told stories to read
ones: '… real ones … so you know it must have happened …'
Pressed further he asks for a tale about a little man 'as high as that
candlestick on the mantle shelf' and as the poor godmother tries to
meet his wishes he gradually takes over the story himself. He does
so to such effect that he persuades her that he has actually met and
tamed the little man and keeps him in a cake-tin in the bedroom
cupboard. Distressed about such behaviour the godmother finds
the tin, which accords to Paul's description, intending to free
the little man. She drops it and, of course there is nothing there.
"That's what I mean", says Paul, "About stories. Being real …"

There is a like ruthlessness behind Norton's telling of the story
about the little people, *The Borrowers* (no Aunt Isobel she). It is
necessarily given a rather complex wrapping to enhance the

possibility of its reality, it being told to a young girl, Kate, by Mrs May, an elderly relative who lives in the same house. But it is not Mrs May's tale, rather one which she was told by her younger brother who (like Paul?) was a bit of a tease and much given to making up strange stories. So it is inevitable that Mrs May must tell Kate of her brother's encounter with Pod, Homily and Arrietty, the borrowers, many many decades before.

At this point the narrative voice shifts from Mrs May to, in effect, Mary Norton and we are taken under the kitchen floor of 'the old house' out Leighton Buzzard way to which Mrs May's brother had been sent as a boy to recover from rheumatic fever. (Mary Norton, incidentally, had been born in Leighton Buzzard.) The scene is set as we meet the tiny family who have made a home for themselves in this hidden place, the ways and property

'She thinks my father comes out of the decanter'.
Full-page pen drawing by Beth and Joe Krush
(160x110 mm.) for the American edition.

of the 'human beans' who dwell there being adapted to the needs of the little folk. There is much ingenuity in describing how they convert common objects to their miniature existence: an upturned drawing-pin for a candle-holder, match-boxes for drawers, puncturing a water-pipe with a pin and then stoppering it so that they can turn the supply on or off as required.

Drama arrives when Pod, Arriety's father, is seen by 'the boy' while he is borrowing a cup from a dolls' house tea-set. Big though the house is, it is usually occupied only by the bed-ridden Aunt Sophy, Mrs Driver her cook and housekeeper and, intermittently, by Crampfurl, the gardener, and Pod is not expecting anyone to be present up in the nursery where the old dolls' house is. The boy then becomes complicit in the activities of the family, scared like them of their discovery by unsympathetic characters like Mrs Driver, and the story builds to a climax as – in a great fright and beyond her believing – she does discover them and devises means for their destruction. Mr Rich Williams, local rat catcher and pig-killer, will be the man for the job.

It is left to Mrs May to tell Kate what she knows of the outcome for that must depend upon her brother's testimony as both witness of, and agent in, the last-minute escape of the Borrowers from the house. It occurs, though, almost at the moment when a taxi arrives to carry him away to join his parents in India so that he never knew whether they *did* escape or what became of them. But Mrs May did know since, as a girl, she came to visit the house before it was sold and her speculations were confirmed by what she found – evidence that cried out for a sequel …

The Borrowers met with great acclaim when it was published, winning the Carnegie Medal for 1953. It was distinguished too in physical terms, its perfect illustrations by Diana Stanley being printed in sepia with its endpapers, bearing a stunning double-spread image of 'the boy' looking at the Borrowers through the floorboards, which was never reproduced in the book's text. For some inexplicable reason, the American edition, which also achieved wide praise, was illustrated with monochrome line drawings by Beth and Joe Krush.

Commentary

The expected sequel, *The Borrowers Afield*, was published in 1955 and the family are found *Afloat* in 1959 and *Aloft* in 1961, each with Mrs May or Kate in a confirming role. In 1966 Norton contributed a side-story, 'Poor Stainless', to an anthology: *The Eleanor Farjeon Book,* and, surprisingly, she rounded off the series in 1982 with *The Borrowers Avenged*, illustrated by Pauline Baynes.

-67-

CHARLOTTE'S WEB
BY E. B. WHITE (1952)

'A little girl is one thing' said Farmer Arable 'a runty pig is another'. But the little girl, Fern, his eight year-old daughter, was making the point that it was a matter of justice that neither should be chopped up with an axe at birth. As a result her Pop gave her the pig to look after. She called it Wilbur, 'the most beautiful name she could think of'.

For five weeks Fern and Wilbur get along well together but then Mr Arable makes the practical point that the pig must be sold (he had already sold the rest of the litter) and Fern sells him to her uncle, Mr Homer L. Zuckerman, who farms down the road where she can visit Wilbur in the barn.

Up to this point the affair has been conducted in a naturalistic manner. In chapter three however, where Wilbur is standing around in the yard waiting for Fern to turn up, he is recorded as complaining that 'there is never anything to do round here'. In this he is at once contradicted by the farm goose who shows him a loose board in the yard fence and encourages him to get out and enjoy himself:' "Go down through the garden, dig up the radishes! (the goose is a fast-talker) Root up everything! Eat grass! Look for corn! Look for oats! Run all over! Skip and dance, jump and dance! ..." '

Needless to say, the escape is spotted, but Wilbur is glad to be brought back – he's too fond of regular meal-times for freedom – but the story has now opened up to become a beast fable. The barn becomes a site for casual conversational interchanges with the geese, or the sheep, or even with Templeton, a crafty rat, who lives under Wilbur's trough. More intimately though are those with Charlotte A. Cavatica, a grey spider who has set up a web over the barn door and sets out to foster a friendship with the pig.

'At last Wilbur saw the creature...' line block in text (105x90mm.) by Garth Williams on p.36 of *Charlotte's Web* (New York: Harper & Brothers, 1952).

Here lies the central drama. An old sheep, who knows the way of the family warns Wilbur that, as a spring piglet, he is now being fattened up to provide the Zuckermans with smoked bacon and ham at Christmas. She's seen it all before. This creates consternation out of which Charlotte devises a rescue strategy by weaving into her web the message SOME PIG, later to be succeeded by TERRIFIC and HUMBLE. The astonishment they cause amongst the local farming populace is sufficient to bring Wilbur a medal at the county fair and a fame which it is confidently assumed by Charlotte will save him from being turned into a Christmas joint.

Although Fern was Wilbur's initial saviour she drifts to the edge of the action as the animal participants take over. From her visits to the Zuckerman barn as the plot is developing she is a spectator, apparently understanding the animal conversations and reporting them, to her mother's concern, back at the farm. (Mom consults the family doctor who takes a very civilised view of both Charlotte's messages and Fern's reports: 'It's quite possible that an animal has spoken civilly to me and that I didn't catch the remark because I wasn't paying attention. Children pay better attention than grown-ups'). Nevertheless, it seems a bit precipitate that, by the time of the County Fair, Fern is more interested in riding the ferris wheel with Henry Fussy.

Those concluding chapters return us to the life of the barn dwellers as Charlotte's natural life comes to a close but with Templeton bribed by Wilbur to rescue the sac that contains the five hundred and fourteen eggs of her offspring. This Wilbur guards in a hidden corner through the long months of winter and then, as Charlotte had foreseen in her valediction:

> The song sparrow will return and sing, the frogs will awake, the warm wind will blow again. All these sights and sounds and smells will be yours to enjoy, Wilbur – this lovely world, these golden days…

Wilbur is there to greet the first grey spider as it crawls from the sac and after Charlotte's multitudinous family has taken off for

who knows where three daughters remain, building their webs in
the top corners of Wilbur's barn door.

Commentary

Charlotte's Web was one of five Honor Books in 1953 when
Ann Nolan Clark's *Secret of the Andes* won the American Library
Association's Newbery Medal. All, including the medal winner
are now forgotten books whereas *Charlotte's Web* has become one
of the most-loved classics of the post-war period. It was published
by Hamish Hamilton in London in the same year, a firm that
had also instantly accepted White's earlier children's book, *Stuart
Little* (1945). The ALA had been leary about that work and
especially its hero who was a mouse born as the second son of
Mrs Frederick C. Little and it got no honours although it is now
almost as celebrated as its successor. As noted above [no.55] White
had suggested Garth Williams as its illustrator (it was to be his first
commission) and he went on to illustrate *Charlotte* too.

–68–

HOBBERDY DICK
by KATHARINE BRIGGS (1955)

Philip Pullman and Richard Adams are not the only storytellers in
our roster to give the chapters in their fictions apposite epigraphs
from literary works. Pretentious, say some ('Look! I've read *Paradise
Lost … Jerusalem … The Faerie Queene …*') but such introductions
can lend a kind of authentication to the text, placing a new story
in an old tradition.

That is certainly true of the epigraphs which Katharine Briggs
chose for the twenty-five chapters of *Hobberdy Dick*, and these also
bear witness to her pre-eminence as a folklorist. Nursery rhymes,
border ballads, snatches of folktale, seventeenth-century poetry are
all aptly laid under contribution in order to root her historical
romance in the ambience of its times.

The romance, set in Nollie Cromwell's time, is conventional

enough: a puritan Cheapside merchant has ambitions for the squirearchy and moves his family to Widford in Oxfordshire. His son by his first wife, now dead, has a taking for country life, and also – in the teeth of parental opposition – for his stepmother's waiting-gentlewoman, last survivor of the old family that owned Widford Manor. Straight-dealing – and the discovery of some handy buried treasure – ensure that:

'The little red hen is different from the rest' Pen and wash drawing by Jane Kingshill.

> Jack shall have Jill,
> Naught shall go ill;
> The man shall have his mare again,
> And all shall go well.
> (Epigraph to Chapter 24.)

The story that is layered in with these events is what turns the book from the conventional to the classic. For there, on the fringe of things, subsisting in parallel with human activity, are the chthonic powers: the ghosts, bogles, lucifugi and such, whose time is not our time and whose irregular interventions in our affairs may have unpredictable consequences.

Hobberdy Dick is the house-spirit of Widford since 'time out of mind' – a shadowy, raggety, unkempt apparition, occasionally caught in the corner of someone's eye, and with a deep-rooted concern for the right management of house and land. It is his benign working in favour of the lovers (and, somewhat melodramatically, in preventing the abduction of a daughter of the house by witches) that swings the plot towards its happy conclusion; but it is his character as ancient guardian that holds the reader. For the true conclusion is that sanctioned by fairy lore: the offer of mortal cloth for Dick to wear which will bring him eternal release from servitude.

The intertwining of the strands in this tale is carried out with practised ease. Katharine Briggs loved writing and was devoted to the study of folk customs from childhood on (her D.Phil at Oxford, much curtailed, was on 'Some aspects of folklore in early seventeenth-century literature') and, by choosing the period of the puritan regime after the Great Rebellion, she supplied her story with that dramatic tension between old belief and new enlightenment which is of permanent concern. (Have not present generations abolished Whitsuntide, advanced tinned goods as proper fare for a Harvest Festival, and determined to cut Easter loose from the phases of the moon?) Katharine Briggs's absorption in 'the personnel of fairyland' gave a naturalness to the supernatural goings-on in her story, while the precise attention she gave to its setting reinforced this. Much of her youth had been spent in Scotland but in 1939 she had bought a house in Burford and her love of the Cotswolds, with their green roads, their barrows, and their standing stones brought accuracy to her portrayal of both landscape and local dialect.

Commentary

Hobberdy Dick was first published unillustrated and later came out in an edition from Puffin Books in 1972 with illustrations by Scoular Anderson. In between those however was an edition which, at the time of writing, is not to be found in either the British Library or the Bodleian. Published in 1969 by the Alden Press at Oxford it was furnished with strange wash drawings by Jane Kingshill, who was Dr Briggs's god-daughter and is presumed to be a short-run private edition, not subject to the demands of legal deposit.

Briggs's later book for children: *Kate Crackernuts* (1963), which draws upon her profound attachment to Scotland, is a novelised reconstruction of the folktale with the same title. It is a powerful story which could be seen as something of a forerunner to Janni Howker's incomparable *Martin Farrell* [no.96 below].

-69-

A SWARM IN MAY
BY WILLIAM MAYNE (1955)

Praise him with the sound of the trumpet. 'A superb, unconventional writer … rare and intense quality … a complete original, a damn-your-eyes individualist …'

Aw! You can not be serious. 'A writer whom children will not read … sound narrative technique, misdirected psychologizing … he remains obstinately unread by children …' (To which, in the present example, can now be added assaults on current sensibilities, seen here as elitism – all that Latin and posh music – and exclusiveness – not a female in sight, apart from a queen-bee and, possibly, a resident cat.)

Such strictures were not heard in 1955 when *A Swarm in May* first appeared and other dispensations prevailed. It was Mayne's third book and was greeted with universal praise, although both it and Philippa Pearce's *Minnow on the Say* were passed over for the Carnegie Medal in favour of a selection of Eleanor Farjeon's previously published stories reprinted in *The Little Bookroom*.

Ostensibly the book was 'a school story'. After all, most of the action occurs among schoolboy-boarders with a line in genuine argot: 'Potty Fido … chiz … well done ye …' but none of Mayne's work is made for predetermined categories. The school is a choir-school and the narrative is focused upon the duties of John Owen as youngest Singing Boy present for the summer term. To him has fallen the lot of performing in the four-hundred-year-old ceremony of presenting a candle to the Bishop in the service following Ascension Day. It's not something he cares to do though and he resists in a manner disparaged by all.

His conversion to the path of duty occurs through his own remarkable discovery within the cathedral's wall of the ancient beehive (a tiny room hidden in a tower) whence came the medieval candle-wax and the concomitant ceremony of blessing. By shifts and stratagems he and the head chorister rescue enough ancient wax to make a candle, while his further discovery of a globe, formed of a strange substance attractive to bees, enables him to bring a tethered swarm before the Bishop's throne: 'They hung in an egg-shaped brown lump, with a faint buzz coming from them; but they were perfectly docile.'

John Owen's conquest of his aversions and his role in reviving the old custom may seem the point of the story, but in truth they are an excuse for a more telling inquiry. This choir-school is at Canterbury, where Mayne himself was a scholar (the book's dedication reads 'for my fellow choristers') and what is really being celebrated beyond the discrete story is the working-life of a *societas* – cathedral as hive. The relationship (wonderfully conveyed) between teachers and taught is essentially collaborative rather than conventionally oppositional. As the headmaster, Mr Ardent (drawn after an actual teacher) says in a successor story: 'We are only here to do one thing: sing the Cathedral services.'

That one thing cannot help but implicate both building and music in the events of the story. It is no accident that we first meet John Owen as he returns to the Cathedral precincts at the start of a new term. For as he makes his way through the dark grounds the building looms as a presence that dominates the lives of its servants and their toils. Nor is it an accident that the book concludes with a poetic evocation of the Cathedral's music as the organist, Dr Sunderland (a mighty character) sweeps the reader along towards a final diminuendo.

What Mayne achieves here is a *tour de force* of the writer's craft, having the capacity permanently to shift the reader's sensibility. Workaday authors given this story would plonkingly explain settings, routines, activities – what a buttress is, or how bees swarm. With Mayne, however, our apprehension of these things is almost assumed so that his story gains an extraordinary density through the trust placed in the reader's own imagination. Less demonstrably means more.

Nor is this an isolated magic instance. Homely examples occur in the three successor stories (they are hardly sequels[23]) – but later in his career William Mayne presents us with a host of startlingly dramatic, wondrously varied examples of the storyteller's craft, a succession of imaginative explorations of unparalleled richness. *A Swarm in May* has no primacy among them. There are a dozen at least that equal or exceed its classic status – but, as is the way of things, they are all out of print.

Commentary

'The way of things' was lamentably exacerbated in 2004 when Mayne was sent to prison for two-and-a-half years for having abused small girls some thirty years previously. His in-print books were all withdrawn and no one was willing to continue publishing him. He was, though, a born writer – it was his life as well as his profession – and he set up his own print-on-demand imprint, The Starrabeck Press, whose first product was the short novel *Every Dog*. Soon after it appeared, however, Mayne died, leaving a quantity of never-published novels and short stories in manuscript among which was a fifth 'Choir School' book featuring the son of the original John Owen. There are plans to publish this and several novels, two of which are among the finest things he has written.

23   These were *Choristers' Cake* (1956) and *Cathedral Wednesday* (1960), both published by OUP and illustrated by Walter Hodges but the third one, *Words and Music* (1963) from Hamish Hamilton had some disconcertingly different drawings, especially the portraits of characters, by Lynton Lamb.

-70-

THE HUNDRED AND ONE DALMATIANS
BY DODIE SMITH (1956)

You would have thought that Mrs Dearly would have done her best to avoid Cruella de Vil when she found they were near neighbours in the houses on the Outer Circle round Regent's Park. They may have been at school together but Cruella had been expelled for drinking ink and does not seem a very comradely person. But ' "Do come in and meet my husband," she said' and insisted that the dogs come too:' "They are so beautiful I want my husband to see them too." '

Well the dogs are Dalmatians, Pongo and Missis (who is about to have puppies), and Mr de Vil is a furrier. Cruella is struck with an idea:' "Wouldn't they make enchanting fur coats? ... For spring wear, over a black suit. We've never thought of making coats out of dogs' skins." ' Ominous words and clearly remembered by Pongo, who is a markedly intelligent dog, after the appalling kidnapping of Missis's fifteen puppies once they have been weaned.

Mr and Mrs Dearly and Nanny Cook, who is their cook, and Nanny Butler, who is their butler – in striped trousers and a fetching frilly apron – are devastated. Expensive adverts are taken in all the papers, but the dogs know a better strategy than that. Encouraging their owners, whom they take to be their pets, to take an evening walk on Primrose Hill they engage in the Twilight Barking. This doggy custom, not familiar to their human pets, is an example of a primitive social medium by which messages may be barked across country in a chain of vocal communications.

Although drawing a blank for two evenings Pongo and Missis are successful on the third when a Hampstead Great Dane is the recipient of news that has travelled sixty miles through no fewer than four hundred and eighty collaborating wuffers. The puppies have been sighted incarcerated in the grounds of a lonely mansion in Suffolk where they are being tended by the Baddum brothers, servants of Cruella who owns the place along with a seething mass of what are found to amount to eighty-two more of the same breed. The address is known and an itinerary can be arranged if Pongo and Missis can find a way to make the journey.

It takes five chapters for the anxious couple to get to Dympling in Suffolk where they are greeted by a Sheepdog, known as the Colonel for his military pretensions, and a plan is drawn up for a large-scale rescue operation. The logistics for canine travel both there and back – food, water, shelter – are fixed by the Twilight Barking; the Colonel instils some discipline into his young troopers, but the scheme is almost wrecked when Cruella turns up, frightened by all the publicity, demanding the immediate destruction of all the animals. Pongo and the Colonel are flexible tacticians though and after another five chapters of hair-breadth escapes the whole party turn up back at the Outer Circle in a furniture van on Christmas Eve.

There is much to admire in Dodie Smith's presentation of her inventive plot. Her experience as a playwright gives assurance to her portrayal of the dog-owners and Madame de Vil and the walk-on parts of the Splendid Veterinary Surgeon, the aged Sir Charles who believes Pongo and Missis are the Dalmatians of his youth (bearing the same names) and even the removal men who come in at the end. The Starlight Barking (of whose spread we are given a pictorial map) is an ingenious idea, decidedly more polite than the system now run by the dogs' pets. In 1967 it was used as the title and theme of an unsatisfactory sequel.

Commentary

Both the book and its sequel were illustrated by Janet and Anne Grahame-Johnstone, and in 1969 the book was turned into a very successful animated film from the Disney studio. In turn, that engendered a variant movie in 1996.

-71-

RANSOM FOR A KNIGHT
BY BARBARA LEONIE PICARD (1956)

It is 1315, a year after Bannockburn where ten year-old Alys de Rennville's father and her brother Robin, his squire, have been killed. Now under the guardianship of Baron Walter, her father's overlord and Lady Ermengarde, his cousin, she is the juvenile mistress of the manor of Little Merdon in Sussex. Her sole companion, of sorts, is the pig-boy, Hugh, who was foster-brother to Robin and brought up with him, hoping one day to serve him as his squire. Now though he must needs return to serfdom on the estate.

One day, Alys observes a strange and sorely injured knight making towards the manor and, on meeting him and bringing him in to be tended, she learns that he had been with the army in Scotland and that her father and Robin were not killed but are being held for ransom by a Scottish lord in a castle beyond Perth. Unfortunately though, having delivered a message that her father and brother may be ransomed for a hundred marks, the knight becomes delirious and loses all memory of his commission.

The ransom arrives. Sole full-page pencil drawing by Walter Hodges (220x145mm.) for *Ransom for a Knight* (London: Oxford University Press, 1956).

Since only Alys has faith in his message (she is thought to be convinced of it merely from wishful thinking) no move is made to discover its truth and it's left to her, summoning help from Hugh, to devise a scheme for secreting jewels and gold to carry to Scotland to deliver the ransom. Getting away is a wild plan but successfully carried out except that Alys has mistakenly carried off a bag of silver coins rather than gold, as they set off at midnight on the mare, Blanche.

As might be expected, this turns out to be no easy journey for a small girl, however determined, and a fourteen year-old pig-boy, however loyal. Almost at the start, when they take respite in a nunnery in Surrey, they find that the abbess intends to return them to Merdon, and must make a precipitate escape, and from then on they undergo a long succession of near-disasters as the journey extends through a long winter of hardship. The money runs out (and Alys will not touch the ransom resources, which almost get stolen at one point); injury and illness occur; the gallant mare, Blanche, is found to be in foal and during a terrible lodgement at a farm near Alnwick (where Alys almost dies of a fever) gives birth to a handsome colt.

There are always countervailing circumstances though (otherwise no story!). Even when barefoot, Alys retains her family pride – and her ability to speak French, which allows for a brief moment of comedy when they stay at the house of a *nouveau riche* merchant in Nottingham. Most surprising for the two of them, though, was an event following their arrival in Scotland where they believe that only English-hating barbarians live (!). In trying to steal a hen from a farmer somewhere beyond Edinburgh, they are caught, but instead of receiving condign punishment, are kindly treated and brought safely to their journey's end. The heart-stopping moment when the ragged little girl hands over the ransom jewels to her father's captor in the great hall of his castle is one of the great climaxes of children's literature.

Commentary

Barbara Leonie Picard was one of the foremost talents in the great assemblage of new authors that John Bell garnered for Oxford University Press in the years after the Second World War. She had little formal education after leaving school but became a gifted folklorist and historian and, as the Historical Note at the end of *Ransom for a Knight* suggests, her often densely descriptive travelogue of fourteenth-century Britain is based upon close research. The pen-drawn headpieces for the book's twenty-four chapters are by Walter Hodges, pre-eminent among the period's illustrators, and it is of interest to note that the denouement in the Scottish castle is furnished with the book's only full-page drawing.

Picard, who was confessedly of an anti-social disposition, became increasingly reclusive (one thinks bizarrely of the Northumbrian witch in *Ransom*) and she died in 2012 at the age of ninety-four.

-72-

THE SILVER SWORD
BY IAN SERRAILLIER (1956)

There were three children in the Balicki family in Poland in 1940: Ruth who was twelve, Edek eleven, and little fair-haired Bronia, only three. Their father, Joseph, was headmaster of a local school but his wife was Swiss which was to be of consequence when the Nazis invaded. They hauled the father off to a prison camp in the mountains of Southern Poland, but she was deported to Germany to work. With some forethought, however, they had earlier determined that if calamity befell them they would try to get to Switzerland where her parents still lived.

At the time of her arrest the children were left in the house, but Edek, who had a rifle, foolishly fired on the van in which his mother was being carried off, hitting a soldier in the arm. There was no immediate response as the van drove off but Edek knew they would be back and managed a hasty and perilous escape for the three of them across the winter rooftops. That was just as well since, when the soldiers returned, they blew up the house, leaving it a mass of rubble with the children presumably dead.

From this point on the tale tells of the travails of this divided family in their quest for safety which is achieved in part through the agency of the silver sword – a decorated paper-knife that survived the destruction of the house. It is found by Joseph after he has escaped from the prison-camp and returned home, only to discover the loss of his children. He passes it to Jan, a street-waif and most accomplished thief, instructing him that if he should find the children in the chaos of Warsaw he must tell them to make for Switzerland where he too will attempt to travel.

Only at the war's end do the children discover the sword with Jan (who has forgotten the message anyway), but, amid much confusion, and with the streetwise talents of Jan, the journey is thrillingly concluded. And the family are brought together again (we hear next to nothing of the travails of Father and Mother) and in a coda the post-war futures of the children are summarised almost as a genuine report on their progress after helping to found and run the first international children's village.

In 2011 the Folio Society brought out their own edition of *The Silver Sword* with an Introduction by the children's novelist, Anne Fine, and an Afterword by Ian Serraillier's daughter, Jane. Here she enters into the details of how her father, a Quaker, came to conceive of and write the book, drawing upon much contemporary evidence, with the child characters loosely based on records from the International Tracing Service that had been set up to try to solve the many refugee problems following the end of the war. The paper-knife actually exists, having been sent (from Toledo) by Serraillier's brother and arriving in the post on the breakfast table at a time when, fortuitously, it proved a turning-point in the fashioning of the story.

Commentary

Ian Seraillier was a teacher and editor by profession and began publishing poetry and stories for children immediately after the end of the war. In 1950 Jonathan Cape published his *There's No Escape,* a tale of derring-do in a fictional war between Yugo-Latia and Silvania. Conventional in its plotting, it nonetheless showed a care for detail in its treatment of both landscape and character and can be seen as writerly preparation for *The Silver Sword,* work on which, though it was a much shorter book, took five demanding years.

Both *There's no Escape* and *The Silver Sword* were illustrated with line-drawings by Walter Hodges, but the Folio edition had seven atmospheric two-colour plates by Raul Allen.

-73-

THE EAGLE OF THE NINTH
BY ROSEMARY SUTCLIFF (1957)

'That's not a sandcastle,' said the busy child on the beach, ' I'm building a temple to Mithras'. So reported Rosemary Sutcliff, giving evidence to a bevy of librarians, of one child's reception of *The Eagle of the Ninth* not long after it was published in 1957. In all probability the temple-builder's enthusiasm for the work came from hearing its famed serialisation on 'Children's Hour' but (perhaps unlike television serials) the wireless version sent listeners straight back to the book to get the author's full-dress narrative to go with the spoken one.

They were keen readers, those librarians – our first critics, long before the academic brigades were mustered – and for them, at that time, the landing of *The Eagle of the Ninth* had something of the force of a revelation. True, it did not come from an entirely unknown author. Miss Sutcliff could be seen as one of the new post-war talents in the writing of children's books (several, like her – as noted elsewhere here – being fostered by John Bell and his editorial colleagues at the Oxford University Press) but of the five books with her name on them at that time only the most recent, *Simon* of 1953, suggested a voice suited to something beyond what she herself later referred to as her 'books for little girls … too cosy … too sweet …'

The Eagle of the Ninth revealed how quickly that voice had matured and now, in retrospect, we can see that its development is closely related to her imaginative apprehension of a subject that was lying in wait for her: the matter of Roman Britain. Her five earlier historical stories had not come near that period, being set mostly in post-medieval times, but Rome had been implanted in her mind well before then. There had been what sounds like a rather frenzied youthful attempt at a novel: *Wild Sunrise*, a 'very bad ... saga of the Roman invasion, as Victorian-English as anything out of Whyte-Melville's *The Gladiators*' and that, in turn, had been influenced by her mother's early reading to her of Kipling, 'especially the three magnificent Roman stories in *Puck of Pook's Hill*' [our no.40].

Those were not separate tales, but rather three episodes in the career of a British-born legionary who is sent from Sussex to help defend the Wall. It is no longer Rome's hey-day in England, but the time when the Empire is crumbling at the edges – the 'decline' adumbrated in the first two volumes of Gibbon – and what Sutcliff found there was a complex of subjects of great dramatic potential: civilising discipline set against tribal barbarities, the servants of Empire with an allegiance also to a homeland within its borders, the selfless devotion, on either side of the equation, to causes and to overarching human relationships (and even those between man and beast).

It looks as though the realisation of this potential almost forced Sutcliff to find a match for it through her storytelling. For the tremendous adventure of *The Eagle of the Ninth*, which sees Marcus, a lamed hero, and his companion, the freed slave Esca, journey from Sussex to the Pictish lands beyond the Wall, has an emotional density that cannot be denied. The wide-ranging geography of the book, the diverse characters who people it, are delineated with an unhurried confidence which gives substance to its episodic plotting (and even – a Sutcliffian hallmark – its happy coincidences), all building towards its Romantic denouement. Even now, I find it a 'gulp book' for its admittances of untainted chivalry – the manumission of Esca, say – and its resolution of taut moments of crisis – the return of Cub, the wolf-dog and the ensuing discomfiture of the Tribune Placidus.

Decline and fall was too resonant a subject to be encompassed by a single story and *The Eagle of the Ninth* was the begetter of a chronological sequence that would carry the reader through centuries of warfare in disintegrating Roman Britain towards a kind of resolution four books later in *Dawn Wind*. (One of those four is the substantial novel for adults that seeks to establish an historic Arthur: *Sword at Sunset*). The sequence is given continuity through the presence throughout of descendants of the *Eagle's* Marcus and the flawed emerald ring that he inherits from his father, and it confirms that Sutcliff's narrative technique deployed in the first book proved more than dependable in the making of its successors. Dramatic construction, the significance of landscape, a workable solution to the patterning of ancient speech, and, above all, an unflinching recognition of the disasters of war sustain the credibility of the saga. (John Terraine, the eminent military historian, claimed that Sutcliff – crippled from childhood by Still's Disease – had a more refined concept of what it was to be a fighting soldier than most of the specialists in the field.)

Commentary

Her insight into the violence of the times about which she wrote is certainly surprising, given her largely wheelbound life, but her illness also presented no bar to the making of her prodigious output. (Her spirited, and sometimes amused, courage shines through her brief autobiography, *Blue Remembered Hills; A Recollection* of 1983.) Although the Roman stories are perhaps central (she received the 1959 Carnegie Medal for *The Lantern Bearers*) she treated of many historical and mythical subjects in fiction and non-fiction and in picture books and short stories as well as novels. She was always well-served by her illustrators and, while contemporaries were puzzled by the substitution of Charles Keeping for Walter Hodges for the Roman books after *Eagle of the Ninth*, his fierce response to her texts made him a perfect choice

Rosemary Sutcliff was appointed OBE in 1975 and promoted CBE in 1992.

-74-

THE WARDEN'S NIECE
BY GILLIAN AVERY (1957)

It was Germany that brought about Maria's despair. In the interests of improving her command of geography she had had to make a map of the place and enter in its chief towns and industries and the like. But she couldn't draw and the spelling was tricky and she had to keep rubbing things out so that there was a hole in the middle of Saxony. It must all be done again by six o'clock and if it was not neat, clean, and correct she would be made to wear a label saying 'Slut' for a whole week.

In the cloakroom at lunchtime, brooding on her woes and on the six years that lay before her at this terrible new school, she found herself almost involuntarily buttoning on her walking shoes and putting on her coat and hat. There was clearly nothing for it but to run away and, creeping out by the garden door, she made her way to the town station, intending to catch a train back to Bath and the house of her elderly aunt Lucia.

The date is 1875 and we may fear that we are in for a tale of irresponsibility and redemption. It is certainly comforting that the ticket-man and the porter at the station are more interested in discussing homing pigeons than accusing a little girl of being a runaway and sending her back to school. She's missed the train for Bath though and can only get as far as Oxford that day, so she gets on that. Her great-uncle is warden of Canterbury College in that city and she fancies that he may help her. Semphill House Ladies' Academy fades from the scene.

To Maria's surprise, after she arrives, rain-soaked, at the Warden's Lodging, she finds that her Bath aunt has just died and that Uncle Hadden, who is thus her guardian, seems happy to adopt her. So begins a new life under the care of the housekeeper, Mrs Clomper, who had not bargained for such an additional duty, and her sharing a tutor with three boys next door, the lively sons of the Wykeham Professor of Ancient History. Even more liveliness comes on stage with the arrival of the said tutor, the Reverend

Francis Copplestone, 'the tallest and thinnest man in Oxford', who proves to be possibly the most eccentric as well – and that takes some doing.

The substance of the story lies in Maria's interest in a print in her uncle's study of Jerusalem House, just up the river from the city. As an historic building it may be visited and one afternoon the children and their tutor row up to join a party getting a guided tour. Through a conjunction of circumstances, which lead to hilarious set-pieces in the Bodleian Library and back at Jerusalem House, Maria is able to garner information about the death of a young boy at the time of the Civil War. It is honest-to-goodness 'research' which she hopes will please her uncle and which leads to him suggesting she present it at a meeting of the Kentish Historical Association: 'They would rather hear a child-prodigy than an elderly man … and if you feel the paper is rather short, you can tell your audience what it feels like to crawl out of the Bodleian Library, past the Librarian, on your hands and knees'.

Commentary

The Warden's Niece, illustrated by Dick Hart, was the first of some fifteen novels and shorter fictions for children by Gillian Avery, several of which include related characters. Most were set in Victorian times and she was also an authority on the children's literature and the education (especially of girls) of the period. Her study *Nineteenth Century Children: Heroes and Heroines in English Children's Stories 1780-1900* (1965) broke new ground in examining a complex period extremely difficult to survey. In 1994 she published a history of 'American children and their books', *Behold the Child*, which, thanks to her work on English sources, gave a stronger view of the subject than most studies from native scholars.

-75-

GUMBLE'S YARD
BY JOHN ROWE TOWNSEND (1961)

Round about 1960, as editor of the *Manchester Guardian Weekly*, John Rowe Townsend was working on an article on the National Society for the Prevention of Cruelty to Children. Living in Knutsford and travelling daily into Manchester by train he noticed, while crossing a bridge over a canal, a canal-side warehouse on the edge of a working-class estate. It coincided in his thoughts with the subject of his piece and triggered the idea of a story to be told.

The result, published in 1961, was *Gumble's Yard* which was the tale of two orphaned children, Kevin and Sandra, who are living with their uncle Walter and his two younger children, Harold and Jean, and is shacked up with the unlikeable, 'cross and shrill' Doris. There is also a friend, Dick, and they all live in The Jungle, so called because the streets are all named after tropical flowers. It's hardly a garden village though: 'it's a dirty old place and one of these days the Corporation are going to pull it all down – if it doesn't fall down of its own accord first'. And down at the edge is the warehouse complex, all empty and partially vandalised, of Gumble's Yard.

It is Kevin who tells us what happened there, beginning when his uncle and Doris – feckless both of them – clear out and leave the children on their own. He knows well enough that if they go to 'the police or the Cruelty' there would be a strong likelihood of the family being split up which they didn't want at all and thanks to friend Dick, who's a knowledgable fellow, they end up fleeing to the warehouse down by the canal. Working out how they can gain access to an upper storey there, which had obviously been used as someone's quarters at some time or other, persuading the younger children how they can scramble up to it, and then moving vital goods, including a bed, down to the Yard, makes for exciting reading and turns the book briefly into a kind of Robinsonade.

Clearly it can't last, for Townsend is no Romantic, but the arrangements are a temporary success. Twelve year-old Sandra is a shrewd manager, Dick and Kevin devise ways of earning money – a paper-round, selling firewood – but it's not long before adults (helpful and understanding adults, a curate and a teacher) intervene. They accept the need for the family to stay together and – after the conclusion of a sub-plot in which Uncle Walter is marginally involved in some smuggling – a solution is arrived at. But when, at the end, wise Sandra says: 'What else can we do? We'll be all right'. You can almost hear doubt as well as hope.

Gumble's Yard, with gritty illustrations by Dick Hart, has a notable place among post-war children's books as being among the first to try to treat the lives of working-class children and their environment in a realistic, and for the most part, uncompromising and non-didactic manner. (Townsend was aware of pitfalls, having described a 1937 predecessor by Eve Garnett, *The Family from One-End Street,* as 'condescending'.) By using a very literate Kevin as his mouthpiece and setting the tale in a believable environment he was a precursor of the 'city-street' novels of later decades which often bore a family resemblance to the concerns of the evangelical writers of the later nineteenth century who had been led by Hesba Stretton (no.19 above).

Commentary

Irene Slade, working as a young editor of children's books, had been impressed with *Gumble's Yard* when it came out and had travelled to hear a lecture by Townsend on his interest in children's literature. This led to her commissioning his entertaining *Written for Children* (1965), a select history of the subject written with more panache than its more scholarly predecessors. (Later expanded and revised editions sacrificed some of the fun for a more comprehensive status.) Joined by a survey of some contemporary authors, *A Sense of Story* (1971) and coupled with his work as Children's Books Editor of the *Guardian* (founding the *Guardian* Prize, awarded annually for a new children's book) he figured as a leading authority on the subject. Furthermore, *Gumble's Yard* led to a continuing activity as a writer of children's novels with a tally of over thirty titles for both younger and 'young adult' readers, ranging from contemporary realism to time-slip and dystopian fantasies. There were not only sequels to *Gumble's Yard* but it appeared as a site in other novels too, including what many regard as his masterpiece, *The Intruder* (1969).

–76–

THE WOLVES OF WILLOUGHBY CHASE
BY JOAN AIKEN (1962)

Willoughby Chase? Up north? How did the wolves get there? Ah, we are in Aikenland. Although the date is some time round 1835, good King James III of the House of Stuart is on the throne and a Channel tunnel has just been completed between Calais and Dover. Thence come the wolves, fleeing the severe weather in Europe and Russia.

Wolves prove not to be the only danger for Bonnie Green, daughter of the jovial Sir Willoughby of the Chase. For he is having to take his ailing wife on a sea trip and has engaged Miss Slighcarp, a tutoress and fourth cousin, once removed, to look after Bonnie and the house while they are away. Bonnie is joined by Sylvia, a first cousin of her own from London, and once Papa and Mamma have departed the two girls and the house itself are subject to villainy unconfined.

Joined by an accomplice, a skilled forger, Miss Slighcarp implements a predetermined scheme to gain not only ownership of the Chase but Sir Willoughby's fortune too (he and his wife were cunningly booked on to a sailing vessel that was barely seaworthy and was expected to sink). The house staff are all laid off, except for a footman, while Bonnie's maid secretes herself in an attic in order to minister to the girls on the sly. They also have a semi-feral friend, the goose-herd Simon, who lives in the woods, and is wise to what is going on.

At the nadir of their fortunes, the girls are dispatched to a prison-like orphanage in the local town of Blastburn from which Simon is able to effect their escape and the three of them make

a slow journey to London (with the geese) where they are able
to unravel Miss Slighcarp's dark designs. Bow Street constables
and the family lawyer travel back to Willoughby Chase which
the governess has converted into a Seminary for the Daughters
of Gentlemen and the Nobility (it bears a resemblance to Miss
Minchin's establishment in *A Little Princess* [no.39 above] and
in a triumphant conclusion, not only is a rightful order restored
but Mamma and Papa return having survived their shipwreck. It
seems that that misfortune had a pronounced curative influence
on Mamma's depressed state.

The larkiness implicit in the story from the start assures readers
that they are in for burlesque rather than a crushing drama and
one can imagine Aiken smiling over her characters and their
activities as they took shape on the page rather as she imagined
Dickens smiling over his. Although the book had been preceded
by two volumes of short stories and a short novel, its arrival in
1962 came as the revelation of a new talent and its faux-historical
setting clearly asked for more attention. *Black Hearts in Battersea*
appeared a year later, bringing Simon back to London and
although Bonnie and Sylvia remained in the comfort of the north
(apart from the wolves) they were succeeded by the irrepressible
cockney Dido Twite who was to survive and blossom over many
sequels. They possessed too, almost to the end, the indispensable
accompaniment of drawings by Pat Marriott, too fine-drawn to
survive their ghastly reprinting in paperback editions.

Commentary

If a Gold Cup were to be awarded to our most neglected
children's writer then Joan Aiken should be the winner. Around
the armature of the dozen or so 'Dido Twite' novels (some titles of
which at least achieved the non-status of 'runners-up' for awards)
there is an array of short story collections of unconfined originality,
mostly accompanied by leading illustrators. Any putative volume
of *'The 100 Best Short Stories for Children'* should surely be headed
by *The Winter Sleepwalker* with its fine illustrations by Quentin
Blake (Jonathan Cape, 1994

-77-

CHARLIE AND THE CHOCOLATE FACTORY
BY ROALD DAHL (1964)

It must be admitted that *Charlie,* while probably Dahl's most famous, rather than his best, children's book, exhibits what has often been regarded as one of his least endearing characteristics. Charlie, his parents and his four grandparents are living in extreme poverty when he wins one of the five Golden Tickets which will allow their winners into a tour of Wonka's secret chocolate factory. The other four children, though necessarily winners at random, are portrayed as a repulsive lot: Augustus Gloop, a fat, greedy boy, Veruca Salt, spoilt daughter of a peanut millionaire, Violet Beauregarde, who chews gum from morning till night and Mike Teavee, a besotted television addict. And what is not random about these choices is that the winners all represent traits to which their author has great objection and they will hence be in for an unhappy factory tour.

Creating such fall guys was to be a regular feature of Dahl's

storytelling and could already be found in Aunt Sponge and Aunt Spiker, the 'horrible people' who get squashed flat in Dahl's earlier children's novel, *James and the Giant Peach* (1961) and are much in evidence in such works as *The Twits* and *George's Marvellous Medicine.* As leading early characters, both James and Charlie first found a home for themselves under the imprint of the New York publisher Alfred Knopf and it seems as though the sorority of British children's book editors were too tender of their readers (and too unaware of what profits the future held) readily to bring out editions in London and it was not until 1967 that the two books

Pencil drawn vignette of Willie Wonka by Joseph Schindelman (120x100mm.) page 162 (New York: Alfred A.Knopf, 1964)

were belatedly shepherded into print by Rayner Unwin of Allen & Unwin.

In planning the English editions of these, Unwin not only anglicised Americanisms (elevator>lift, etc.) but, to save expense, re-illustrated them: *James* with drawings by Michel Simeon from the French edition which had already been published and *Charlie* with drawings commissioned locally from Faith Jaques. These replaced the American illustrations by Joseph Schindelman which are arguably the finest among all the subsequent visualisations. Here again, though, Dahl's cavalier progress received a setback for, by circa 1970, sensibilities over the nature of the Oompa-Loompas, the three thousand workers 'imported direct from Africa' who are Mr Wonka's workforce, demanded a change. He had to re-write their presence, now as dwarfish hippies, and Schindelman had to revise his earlier illustrations. A revised English edition had to wait till the Puffin reprint of 1973.

The squeamishness that undoubtedly delayed *Charlie's* publication in England probably relates to the drastic come-uppances received by the luckless children who, through their arrogance, disobey Mr Wonka's orders and become victims of their own greed. This occurs in a manic text with much screaming, shouting and jumping about, the fate of each child then being the subject of Bellocian chants on the part of the Oompa-Loompas. In a cataclysmic ending they leave the factory, sadder and perhaps wiser, while Charlie and his Grandpa Joe, who has accompanied him through the factory tour, hurtle around in the boss's magical flying elevator, the whole family having won the golden prize as inheritors of the factory itself.

Commentary

Flight Lieutenant Roald Dahl published his first book, *The Gremlins*, in New York in 1943 as a base for a Disney production about the interfering creatures in RAF folklore responsible for many a mysterious technical malfunction. It already shows his liking for extremes of fantastic narrative that were to be staple to his children's books, achieving a less raw and frenetic treatment in such later stories as *The BFG* (1982) and *Matilda* (1988). These appeared within the period of his very fruitful collaboration with the illustrator Quentin Blake which had begun in 1978 when Cape's editor, Tom Maschler, teamed the two of them for Dahl's *The Enormous Crocodile*. An essay on their work together within the whole context of Dahl illustration was undertaken by myself for an exhibition at Seven Stories in 2007.

An absurd sequel, *Charlie and the Great Glass Elevator,* was published with Schindelman's illustrations in New York in 1972. English editions illustrated first by Faith Jaques and then by Michael Foreman came out in 1973 and 1986, with Blake's edition coming in 1995.

-78-

ELIDOR
BY ALAN GARNER (1965)

A pivotal book in two respects. Published in 1965 it marks the summation of a period far more thrilling than the present, when intelligent experiment in books for children (rather than for teenagers) was rife, encouraged by creative editors who were not ham-strung by normative edicts or the demands of conglomerate tradesmen. And pivotal too in its author's career, a high Romantic tale, separating those two beginner fantasies that Alan Garner once more or less disowned – *The Weirdstone of Brisingamen* (1960) and *The Moon of Gomrath* (1963) – from the contorted narratives of *The Owl Service* (1967) and *Red Shift* (1973).

High Romantic? Not 'alf. Admittedly four children, marked down to save a Tolkienian secondary world from desolation, may seem a corny plot. They are messing about on the way home from school when they are drawn into their role as ordained by an ancient Elidorian manuscript (although how this is recognised in twentieth-century Manchester is never adequately vouchsafed). They enter its parallel kingdom through the agency of a damaged lord, a fisher-king, or Titurel, figure. There they gain four treasures:

sword, spear, cauldron and stone, which they must take back to their world and guard against the time when the four regions of Elidor may be freed.

The fantasy is underpinned by the verities of myth and folktale: Childe Roland and Elidurus who both broke through to 'fairyland', the heroic fairies of Ireland and their Treasures and Findhorn, the unicorn – emotional centre of the book – dying in the lap of the 'mayde that is makeles'. The mystery gains potency through contrast with the everyday environs of the children's suburban life ('even the toadstools are made of concrete'), the Blytonesque caricature of parents and neighbours, and, above all, by Garner's ingenious recognition that the power of the treasures, which have been converted into every day objects – a railing, a toy sword, a tea-cup and a coping stone – has a disruptive force on the electric power around their location.

And also 'Classic'? What gives the fantasy its classic status (enhanced by Charles Keeping's tremendous pen drawings) is the manner of its crafting. Garner's quick prose attunes itself to both of the worlds that you encounter: Elidor, with its 'air as thick as water', and Dad's back garden, where a startled bird 'braked in the air, shot sideways and flew back to the chimney'. Undemonstrative quotes perhaps, but declaring a command of diction which convinces right through to the moments of tense drama, above all to the concluding death-song of the unicorn on Helen's lap in a building site in Manchester.

Strange to say, the book was only 'commended' in the Carnegie Stakes for 1965 (and who now remembers the winner: Philip Turner's *The Grange at High Force*?) but the fashioning of its story and the energy of its writing stand in happy contrast to the laborious, self-reflexive plod of some of the medallists *de nos jours*.

Commentary:

Elidor, set primarily in Manchester, and its successor *The Owl Service,* set in Wales, are the two children's books where Garner moved away from his home site of East Cheshire, an area whose topography, customs and dialect are deeply implanted in his being. His recent modest account of his childhood, *Where Shall We*

Run To? is specific on many details but the four short fictions of 'The Stone Book Quartet' (1976-8) dig deep into a legacy from craftsman ancestors and the interplay of local attachments. It is also worth noting that Garner's antipathy to his first two books, despite their devotion to their Alderley locale, seems now resolved by *Boneland,* which brings the boy Colin to adulthood and the author's storying to a decidedly more recondite pitch. Perhaps too, for the present volume, one should record another authorial reject, the nativity play *Holly from the Bongs* for which the musical accompaniments were written by William Mayne.

-79-

THE MOUSE AND HIS CHILD
BY RUSSELL HOBAN (1967)

At Bowness on Windermere is to be found a well-appointed 'visitor attraction' called The World of Beatrix Potter. The name is apt since what you find there is a co-mingling of both characters and scenes from all Potter's little stories, not in discrete groups according to their texts but scattered promiscuously through what is indeed their own 'world'. The visitors are mere intruders in what is essentially a people-free zone and who can tell what may go on – what wanderings, strife and cosy tea-parties – when the doors are closed in the evening upon the departed guests.

So too in *The Mouse and His Child.* For sure, the book is not a set of tangentially-related tales, but rather a single history of several strange surprising events taking place in an anonymous countryside, but, as with the Bowness crowd, these events are of concern only to their protagonists – toys and animals living their secret lives in a people-free zone. There's a toyshop prelude (that surely owes much to Hans Christian Andersen) when we are introduced to the eponymous heroes whose adventures lie all before them: clockwork tin toys with the mouse father swinging the child up and down in directionless circles. They stand on a counter in front of a handsome dolls' house and alongside two associated wind-ups: a snooty elephant and a performing seal, and in his innocent liking for this company the mouse-child conceives a longing for permanence – for a home, with a family and a Mama.

Such dreams can hardly be the province of shop toys however. The goods are dispersed to their various purchasers, where the fate of all children's playthings awaits them. For the mouse and his child it comes fortuitously – they are crushed by a falling vase and end up in the dustbin – but they are rescued from its depths by the single human agent in the story, a wandering tramp seeking leftovers, and he repairs them to the extent that they are now able to move in a straight line rather than round and round. 'Be tramps', he says as he sets them down on the high road, and from that time forth they must make what way they can in a phantasmagoric world.

Manny Rat is their nemesis. It is he who finds them when the tramp has gone – Manny, the Godfather of the town dump with its rat-run bars, its greasy-bacon-rind stalls and its orange-box music-hall (no Ginger and Pickles village shops in those parts). He press-gangs the mice into his team of foraging wind-ups, but despite their degradation he is unable to subdue the mouse-child's rooted faith that a Home Territory awaits him out there somewhere or other and, against the fatalism of his pragmatic father, he nurtures the dream.

In the manner of a picaresque romance and against all the odds, this is finally fulfilled. The wind-ups are unavoidably inhibited by the impossibility of taking much in the way of independent action – someone must always be present to turn their the key or, for good or ill, carry them aloft through the air and that is what engenders the story's episodic progress. Their escape from Manny Rat (thanks to a beneficent frog) takes them to the Caws of Art Experimental Theatre where a couple of crows are rehearsing *The Last Visible Dog*, a Beckettian drama not too distant from *Endgame*. 'The meadow isn't ready for this yet', says a local field-mouse critic to his wife – a judgment soon ratified when mayhem is set up by the weasels in the audience, the wind-ups escaping, courtesy of the house parrot, to the den of an algebraist muskrat.

Promised a theorem by this logical gentleman which will solve their pressing need to find a method of self-winding independence, they first allow themselves to be harnessed to a wildly ingenious tree-felling project ('$XT = Tf$' is the formula: 'X times Tree equals Treefall' with X turning out to be the mice harnessed to an axe). A catastrophe not calculated for at the start however, plunges the put-upon pair into a broken beaver-dam and a subaqueous encounter with C. Serpentina, turtle-thinker, scholar and eminent author of *The Last Visible Dog* who treats them to a dose of linguistic philosophy. (With some justice, critics have complained that the satire in these central episodes makes few concessions to readerly inexperience, but that is to neglect its farcical character and the continuing energy with which it is bound in with the fate of the wind-ups.)

Contrivance follows contrivance, bearing witness to Hoban's delight in designing ingenious mechanisms of rescue. Manny Rat however, obsessed by a desire for revenge on his escaped wind-ups, is never far away and in an extended denouement he becomes the unwitting agent of the drama's catharsis and eventually a reformed character – *Uncle Manny* indeed. Bashed around by bitter experiences, the characters first gathered on the toyshop counter come together again, piece by fortuitous piece, and their secret history (imagined with consummate skill through the line-drawings of Lillian Hoban) comes to a climax with a grand Christmas party.

It is said that Hoban was not entirely content with such a lenitive ending. The villain who had softened into a domesticated Uncle Manny had already overcome one reversion to type when he had tried to blow up the dolls house, and could well revert again in the pages of some Manny Redux sequel. But Hoban recognised, I think, that there was a uniqueness about *The Mouse and His Child* and that no later ending could supersede its present one. For the hobo who set the story going to begin with returns while the party is in full swing and, peering through the dolls' house window, utters two further, all-conclusive words of human speech: 'Be happy'.

Commentary

American author Hoban and his first wife Lilian, an illustrator, published a series of seven much-loved picture books about a girl-badger, Frances, from 1960 and *The Mouse and His Child* proved a radical departure from those slender conversational texts. First published in New York, the book met with a decidedly more enthusiastic reception when, a year later, it was published in London by Faber. Hoban and his family came on an extended visit and although the family returned he remained and the rest of his life, including a new marriage and family, was spent in London. It was here that he was inspired to write an extensive oeuvre of imaginative works for both adults and children. Among the latter his two hilarious books about Captain Najork forged a close working relationship with their illustrator, Sir Quentin Blake, to make classics of the picture book genre.

–80–

FLAMBARDS
BY K. M. PEYTON (1967)

It is 1908 and Christina Parsons, orphaned, age twelve, is leaving the care of her Aunt Grace to go to live at Flambards Hall, forty miles out of London, where for five years she has been genteelly brought up among ladies of limited means. The change could not be more dramatic. As the pony-trap carries her from the station to the Hall she moves into a world of men, boys and horses, dominated by her crippled Uncle Russell who rules all with a single-minded violence.

Smashed up, when a horse fell on him some years previously, he remains obsessed by the hunting field, its customs, and the intercourse with his like-minded neighbours. The farm and the house itself count for nothing beside the winter meets and, during the summer, the plans for the next season. Money is clearly running out thanks to the extravagance of his passions and Christina, who is wise for her years, is already aware that the hospitality extended by Uncle Russell (which is non-existent) has been devised to effect some future marriage with his eldest son, Mark. For, when she is twenty-one, Christina will inherit a fortune.

Adaptable as well as wise, Christina wins a place for herself in the scheme of things, discovering a surely inherited pleasure in riding, which she is taught be a stable-hand, Dick, and which wins a modicum of praise from Uncle Russell. She also develops a powerful sympathy for Mark's younger brother William who earns nothing but bitter scorn and ferocious beatings from his father, for he is antipathetic to, and incompetent at, riding, being himself obsessed by the new science of aeronautics. Not only is he a skilled modeller of early aeroplanes but has formed a secret friendship with a wealthy neighbour who is an authority on the science of flight. They are trying to build a plane.

As the story develops over five years there is much scope for interlocking emotional tensions to generate a succession of dramatic stand-offs. Dick departs from the story, being sacked for helping Christina save her horse from the knacker's yard and then, later, thrashing Mark for impregnating his sister, a servant girl at Flambards. Mr Dermot, the scientist, supplies a contrasting stability of behaviour and good humour as he and William work on their flying-machine and, in the final climax, it is he who assists in Christina's return to Battersea and Aunt Grace, the dressmaker. There has been a growing rivalry between Mark and William over a possible marriage to her and the book ends in a final flourish as William drives her away from Flambards to Battersea in Mr Dermot's Rolls Royce.

Commentary

Peyton published her first book, *Sabre, the Horse from the Sea*, illustrated by herself, in 1949 under her birth-name, Kathleen Herald, for she was only nineteen. By that time she had already written several long stories, and before she married Mike Peyton she had already published two further stories as Herald. By the time *Flambards* arrived she was well on her way to creating an oeuvre

of over fifty highly regarded books for children and teenagers.
Flambards itself was followed by three sequels, the second of which,
The Edge of the Cloud (1969) won the Carnegie Medal. All three
were illustrated with line drawings by Victor G. Ambrus.

Peyton was awarded an MBE in 2014 for 'services to children's
literature'.

–81–

THE CHILDREN OF THE HOUSE
by Brian Fairfax-Lucy
ed. by Philippa Pearce (1968)

One day the editor Grace Hogarth was given a confused bundle
of paper which were the rambling memoirs of the horseman
and author Brian Fairfax-Lucy of the family that for centuries
had owned the mansion of Charlcote House in Warwickshire.
(Shakespeare is said to have gone poaching in its grounds).
On examination the papers, under a general title of 'The Back
Stairs', did not recommend themselves as a biography but Grace
perceived within them the substance of what might be a book for
children and, with the author's blessing, they were turned into just
that. Charlcote became Stanford Hall, whose Stanford family had
now become Hattons, following the marriage of its last, indigent
member to a Yorkshire industrialist in hopes of saving the estate.

In a prefatory note, Fairfax-Lucy concedes its fictional nature
but remarks that it was 'written from the memory of a way of
life now vanished' and it proves to be a threnody on that theme.
The children are four: Tom, who at the start is about to return from
boarding school for the summer holidays, Laura next, then Hugh,
who will also be off to school shortly, and then little Margaret, less
boisterous than the others and said by the servants to be only nine
pennorth to the shilling.

It is the servants, who may be in the wings but are the dominant
forces in the events of the story. Certainly Papa, Sir Robert Hatton,

is dominant in that he is a martinet who holds his children in fear. Boisterousness is not to his taste and their inventive plans must be executed beyond any chance of his discovery. He is obsessed by the financial demands of the House and its upkeep and his children are kept on the shortest of commons as to food and raiment and have few connections beyond the great park with its encircling fence three miles long. In consequence it is to the servants that the children turn for relief and even sustenance if that can be cunningly managed and the servants supply a devotion and sympathy upon which they can depend. (But beware of Lady Hatton's French maid, Hortense, who is a *spy*.)

Perhaps because of its manuscript origins the events of the story are episodic. The first half is confined to the children's activities during the summer vacation that began it because that emerges as a turning-point after which disturbing changes will set in. An early morning raid on the fruit garden, the lucky finding of a half-crown with which presents can be bought for the servants, Hugh's sketchily-noted night adventures with Victor, son of the radical village schoolmaster, fill out tellingly the constraints of their frustrated existence. But then the clock moves faster, first with an explosive rebellion when they confront Lady Hatton with the poverty of their lives and their more than physical hunger and then with the movement towards war. Tom is for Sandhurst and Hugh for the navy.

There is great emotional power running through even the simplest of scenes: playing cricket with Walter Mark the butler while the parents are in Yorkshire, secretly eating cakes purloined by a housemaid who reckons that 'we are better off in the servant's hall than you are here'. With the coming of war, the history moves to a sad diminuendo with only an echo of vanished children's voices.

Commentary
Readers may find this entry a rather specious attempt to smuggle in a second book by Philippa Pearce. I am unabashed. Brian Fairfax-Lucy is the first, if not the onlie begetter and what seeker after the best children's books would wish to exclude this beautiful and touching example?

In 1969 a new edition of the book was published as the first in a soon aborted series of 'Acorn Children's Classics' which Gollancz projected with the National Trust (who now own the house). The title was changed to *The Children of Charlecote*, a pen-drawn frontispiece and chapter-heads replaced the earlier illustrations by John Sergeant (the new artist was barely acknowledged) and Brian Fairfax-Lucy's widow, Alice, a novelist herself and a daughter of John Buchan, extended his original brief Note into an informative Foreword.

-82-

BLACK JACK
BY LEON GARFIELD (1968)

Take a little minced Fielding, add some spiced Dickens and you should be well on the way for a ragout Leon Garfield.

His arrival on the scene was with a maritime novel submitted to Messrs Constable. They could not see a book for adults in it but (as also occurred with *The Children of the House* [no.81 above]) they passed the manuscript to their children's books editor, Grace Hogarth, who worked with Garfield to turn it into *Jack Holborn*, which was at once acclaimed as giving a new flavour to the post-war festal-board of English children's fiction.

The eighteenth-century background and the orotundities of Garfield's prose were to figure through much of his writing life but are especially marked in his early novels which achieved an added uniformity through the accompaniment of the masterly pen drawings of Antony Maitland. *Black Jack* was the fourth of these (and was dedicated to Grace) and marks as well as anything Garfield's serpentine plotting and the prodigality of his characterisations.

Black Jack himself, 'a vast ruffian, seven foot high', is first met with on his way to Tyburn to be hung for his crimes of murder and mayhem. He survives the drop because, unbeknownst, he has furnished his gullet with a steel tube which defeats Jack Ketch's noose. Its success is not known either by Mrs Gorgandy, who with the help of a young draper's apprentice, Bartholomew Dorking, has brought him back to her house, pretending to be his 'mint-new widder'. In fact she is nothing of the sort but plans to sell his corpse to the surgeons.

Batholomew, to his dismay, is left with the coffin as she goes about her dealings and thus is not only present when Jack comes back to life but is hauled off by him to act as an unwilling companion in his escape. They first visit an apothecary for something to soothe Jack's painful throat and a description of the 'varnished room' of the shop gives some idea of the Garfield manner:

'It seemed to be built out of varnished cupboards, varnished drawers with china handles, and varnished shelves on which were crowded – in supernatural numbers – pots, bottles, jars, beakers and flasks all reflecting the apothecary's candle with an air of obedient but nervous gloom'.

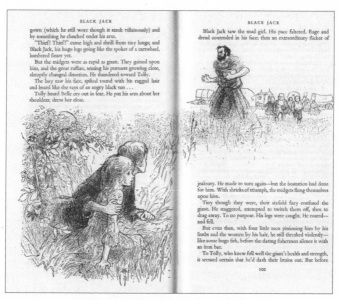

Black Jack lumbered faster yet. Pen drawing diagonally across
the page-opening by Antony Maitland (220x160 mm.)

From here on the two are conjoined, to Bartholomew's terror, in journeying southward in the course of which Jack devises a means for upsetting a coach so that his help in its re-establishment will result in due reward. In the course of the action however a young girl, Belle, assumed to be congenitally mad, escapes from her guardians who were carrying her to the Islington Bedlam-house. From here on the frame of the novel widens to admit not just the parson and doctor who run that profitable care home but the members of a decrepit travelling fair, including Dr and Mrs Carmody, specialising in selling bottles of a quack medicine, and other assorted hucksters including Hatch, their young apprentice in this trade, who is to be responsible for subsequent knavery and murder.

What is at the centre of the tale is the candid innocence of Bartholomew and Belle in the midst of a society riven by cupidity and trickery. Belle, who regains her sanity, falls in love with the boy who first rescued her but then, to his despair, fearing her disease truly to be hereditary, she gives herself up to the Bedlamites. Black Jack, whose initial scorn for Bartholomew (' "It aint every hanged criminal what can travel with a whey-faced weasel of a saint" ') gradually eases to tolerance and then admiration. At the climax, in a London that has been seized by a wild fear of a coming Judgement Day, his energetic power and violence serve to snatch Belle from the madhouse, follow a clue to discover that her illness was not congenital at all, and bring the couple safe together. Thanks to Garfield (and Black Jack) we have been given one of the few love-stories at the 1960s feast.

Commentary

Most of Garfield's stories are contained within 'his' imagined eighteenth century, always with touches of humour shared with their reader. (*The Strange Affair of Adelaide Harris* (1971) edges into farce with delightful drawings by Fritz Wegner.) Of particular interest are the twelve short books spinning yarns about the experiences of apprentices to various trades but more interested in the story potential than any educational purpose. In 1970 he and Edward Blishen, as joint authors, won the Carnegie Medal for their telling of a train of Greek myths, *The God Beneath the Sea*. It was not something for which his elaborate style was fitting, the necessary ferocity of the myth-maker being better reflected in powerful images by the illustrator, Charles Keeping. (These were not to the taste of the book's American editors who replaced them with slimy, sometimes near-pornographic, pencil-drawn images by Zevi Blum, although – unintentionally? – retaining the third part of the book's dedication to Keeping's wife.)

-83-

THE IRON MAN
BY TED HUGHES (1968)

Poetic licence is required (and Hughes was, of course, a poet). When the Iron Man tumbles over the cliff-edge – CRRRAAAASSSSSSH – he breaks up into his constituent pieces on the shoreline. Then he begins to be reconstituted by a couple of seagulls. But we are told that this huge creature has a head 'shaped like a dustbin but as big as a bedroom', so how the dickens can a seagull pick up an eye, 'like a headlamp' and probably at least as big and heavy as a medicine-ball? Not even an ostrich could do it.

But folktale licence is in force – after all, Jack managed to get the giant's harp down the beanstalk – and *The Iron Man* is nothing short of a modern folktale with the *de rigueur* moral. Once the seagulls have also found the Iron Man's hand – 'like a strange crab', but it must have been gigantic – the body-parts start to re-assemble themselves and this visitor from who-knows-where is ready to get on with the story.

At first he causes mayhem, eating up the local farmers' tractors, earth-diggers, ploughs, with a salad of barbed-wire to finish off. The boy Hogarth though, who first saw the creature and doesn't like the idea of blowing him to bits, suggests a means of trapping him – the traditional covered-pit trick, like the Trap that Pooh and

Piglet dig to catch a Heffalump.

The scheme works and the farmers are able to bury the Iron Man under a great hill of earth which becomes a notable picnic spot until the Iron Man eventually breaks out of it, severely incommoding a family about to have lunch.

'A giant hand reached down...' after a wood engraving by Andrew Davidson (vignetted 105x75mm.) from a paperback edition of *The Iron Man* (London: Faber, 1989).

A solution is eventually found by installing the fellow in a scrap-yard where there is a regular supply of succulent gas ovens and the like, and it is from there that he is summoned to save the world from a terrible space-bat-angel-dragon that has arrived from outer space and is currently resting across most of Australia. A great contest is held, trial by fire, through which the Iron Man triumphs and the cowed dragon is sent to live on the moon whence every night he swims through the ether singing the music of the spheres. Bliss descends to earth and 'all people wanted to do was to have peace to enjoy this strange, wild, blissful music from the giant singer in space'.

As the book concludes we may see that some illustrator's licence is also required. When the Iron Man reconstituted himself on the sea shore he couldn't find his right ear, although when he returns to land he seems to have found it. Not so. It was lodged in the seagulls' nesting ledge and, for all we know, it's still there.

Commentary

Ted Hughes's high status as a writer for children has tended to be obscured by his fame as a poet and the notoriety of his marriage to Sylvia Plath. His first children's book, the nonsense poems of *Meet My Folks* appeared in 1961 and was followed by other collections intended for young readers, including *Poetry in the Making*, based upon some BBC Schools broadcasts in 1967. *The Iron Man* was preceded by the 'origin fantasies' of *How the Whale Became and Other Stories* (1963) and followed by *Tales of the Early World* (1988). A sequel, *The Iron Woman,* of 1993 was a disappointment, perhaps occasioned by the growing fashion for 'social balance' in cultural affairs.

-84-

A WIZARD OF EARTHSEA
by Ursula Le Guin (1968)

The archipelago will not show up on any atlas nor be reached by
any transport starting from Platform 9¾ on Kings Cross Station.
Its 30,000 square miles of water and islands are bounded by oceans
at the four points of the compass from which no adventurer has
arrived and from whose crossing none has returned.

For the islanders at the centre of the archipelago (there are
dragons and hostile raiders at its outer edges) a wizard is a welcome
figure, for this is a region impregnated by magic. Humble witches
or conjurors, possessed perhaps by small communities, are lowest
in the hierarchy while above them are the sorcerers and wizards,
whose master-craft may be taught by the mages whose college
dominates the island of Roke.

And it is to Roke that the boy goatherd, Sparrowhawk, is sent
when he is discovered to have preternatural powers in the exercise
of magic. He is well enough aware of this himself when, under
first tutelage from the wizard on his home island of Gont, he
experiments with a spell to summon the spirits of the dead. He is
saved from incipient calamity of that deed by his master, but, when
sent to Roke, he forgets the lesson. Arrogant in his awareness of
his growing powers and jeered at by a rival apprentice he again
performs the spell of summoning and releases into the world a black
shadow of evil.

Now, as the mages know – as does their historian, Ursula Le
Guin – there is an economics of magic. Whatever your powers, you
do not get something for nothing and if you transgress the system
the system will demand payment. Sparrowhawk is saved from
obliteration by Roke's archmage who forfeits his life in the act, but
the living Sparrowhawk has disturbed the balance between real and
enchanted phenomena and the ancestral pattern within which high
magic may only answer only real need. From now on he is to be the
prey of the spirit that he has unleashed.

Also at work is the power of names. In Earthsea all creatures have their secret names behind those of common use, keys to their very essence which will give power to any who may know them[24]. Sparrowhawk was named Ged by the wizard who first tutored him and part of his defence against the shadow that hunts him is to discover its name. (In one subsidiary episode, he is able to elicit a binding promise from the Dragon of Pendor, of 'an older race than man' through knowing the Dragon's secret name.)

Ged's search for redemption carries him through much of *Earthsea*, with other subsidiary adventures: temptation to gain universal power from the evil stone of the Terrenon, compassion for two aged castaways marooned on an unnamed island (from the woman he receives – rather as the hobbit does in his adventure – a broken ring which will be a lead into *A Wizard of Earthsea's* successor story). Eventually he discovers in a revelation that the hunt must be reversed and that it is he who must seek out the Shadow and challenge him in a trial. A final confrontation where 'man and shadow meet face to face' takes place in the far waters of the East Reach: 'Aloud and clearly, breaking that old silence, Ged spoke the shadow's name and in the same moment the shadow spoke without lips or tongue, saying the same word, 'Ged'. And the two voices were one voice.' The quest has ended.

It does not do to attempt a callow explanation of what Le Guin is up to in Earthsea. She has herself said that she discovered the archipelago as an explorer rather than invented it as an engineer, and much must be taken on trust. The society and its implied ancient history are a given for the sake of the story, and the mixed magics are present as much as anything for the dramatisation of Ged's journey. We never know how he came to name his adversary and it is probably best to admire his triumph as an act of Eddic heroism rather than a laborious quest to mend a split personality.

---

24   So too, it seems, of cats for Old Possum writes of their 'ineffable, effable, effanineffable, deep and inscrutable, singular Names'.

Commentary

Earthsea was first published in the United States and took three years to find an English edition when Kaye Webb chose it for Puffin Books, happily retaining its maps and the beautiful, quasi woodcut decorative chapter headpieces by Ruth Robbins. It later gained its original American hardback form and was followed thus by the sequels *The Tombs of Atuan* (1971) and *The Farthest Shore* (1972).

Eighteen years later in *Tehanu*, the author published a revisionary volume, governed less by the demands of the fiction than by a 'wrestle with the angels of the feminist consciousness'. Earthsea however would not let her go, and she undertook research 'in the Archives of the Archipelago' which brought forth five *Tales from Earthsea* (2001) which explored and extended certain aspects of the saga and preceded a final novel *The Other Wind* (also 2001).

-85-

CHARLOTTE SOMETIMES
BY PENELOPE FARMER (1969)

Sometimes, every other day, she would be Clare. It all depended on the tricksy bed with little wheels …

Apparently, it wasn't conventional but when Charlotte Makepeace arrived for the first time at her new school she was haled from the bus by an older pupil, Sarah, and taken straight to 'Cedar', her bedroom for the term, even though it was the custom for new girls to report to the staffroom first. Roommates were offended by her jumping the gun but adjudged it 'snooty Sarah's' doing.

'She thinks she's queen of the school, that's all, just because her sisters were here, and her mother, donkey's years ago.'

When Charlotte woke up in the night, though, she saw outside a cedar tree which she had not thought present when she arrived and in the morning not only was it still there but the whole little dormitory had changed. There were only four other iron bedsteads instead of five and when the little girl next to her wakes up she proves to be one Emily, who clearly thinks that Charlotte is Clare and her own sister.

Charlotte's confusion as a new girl in one school finding herself now to be the new girl in another, with a sister as well, inhibits an immediate demand for explanation. She is treated so naturally that she doesn't see how she can explain the situation and what with bells going, the others waking up, and severe Nurse Gregory coming in and treating her as Emily's older sister, she rides with the scene. After all, as a new girl, she is not expected to know the routines as yet. In any case it must be just a long and complicated dream.

So it seems when she wakes up next day and finds herself where she ought to be – no cedar tree, planes taking off from a nearby airport, and the dormitory companions that she had met earlier. But within a minute of her waking she discovers that she had missed a day – it is now Monday and not Sunday and the dream visit to the church with Emily and her 'other' classmates was a reality. Moreover, it is clear that she has not been missed but that her place must have been taken by the true Clare. This is confirmed by Clare herself who had the bright idea of using a school notebook, labelling it the private diary of Charlotte Makepeace and then using it to communicate a message to Charlotte by the simple process of leaving it on their bedside table.

Nothing further seems possible as the girls go on living their alternate daily lives, with Charlotte discovering that she and Emily are present in the closing months of the 1918 war. A solution looks in sight when a decision is made for Clare and Emily to leave the school dormitory in order to go into the town as lodgers, day-girls, because they are occupying beds in the school sick-room. They realise that the bed has dictated the changes and work it out that if Clare is resident in it on the day of the move her removal will break the spell.

Ah 'the best of plans …'. When the time comes there is a hold-up with the result that it is Charlotte who moves with Emily to the lodgings (under the charge of the unsavoury Mr and Mrs Chisel Brown) and now has to spend every day among the events of 1918. As it turns out though, rampagious local celebrations as the war ends bring the girls back into the school as boarders and before the end of this extraordinary term the final change is effected.

It would be a spoiler to enter into the final revelations except to say that the bed never explains itself and we know not if it was ever an agent in other transactions. We must imagine how on earth Clare coped with the post-Second World War society in which she found herself for she was seemingly quite a strait-laced, almost Victorian child, but Penelope Farmer's subtle handling of all the impossibilities of her plot is itself a powerful spur to its acceptance. And her portrayals of Charlotte and Emily, and indeed, the absent Clare make for a moving conclusion.

Commentary

Time-slip fantasies have a long history from the folkloric traveller entering a faery mound for a brief time while years pass outside (cf. *Rip Van Winkle*). They also may entertain by allowing visits to the past, as in Nesbit's *Five Children and It* and its successors, or they may become metaphors of psychological disturbance as in the complex *Red Shift* by Alan Garner. *Charlotte Sometimes* is an unusual variant in that the time gap between the events experienced by the two 'travellers' is small enough for each to find the alternative time within their intellectual compass. There is a slightly similar connection in Philippa Pearce's *Tom's Midnight Garden* with its touching conclusion where the two participants finally meet in 'real time'. In *Over the Hills and Far Away*, William Mayne engages with a crossover between a woman from Roman times and contemporary children, who thus find themselves in a land 'before the map knew about it'. As with *Charlotte,* the reader longs to know, but can only speculate on, what the visitant from the past made of her spell in a changed world.

-86-

WHEN HITLER STOLE PINK RABBIT
BY JUDITH KERR (1971)

Anna's Papa was a celebrated journalist and theatre critic during the first three decades of the twentieth century. He was also a socialist and a Jew which were not good things to be in Berlin in 1933. One night just before the general election that brought Hitler to power he got a phone call from a well-wisher advising him that, if the Nazis won, his passport would be impounded, so when Anna woke next morning he had vanished. He had gone to Prague.

That was the start of the serial journeyings that seven year-old Anna, her older brother Max, and her parents had to undertake over the next three years. First, and most terrifyingly, the family had to get out of Germany as fast as possible – by train over the Swiss border to Zürich. There Papa tried to re-establish himself as a writer, although Swiss editors were cagey about running pieces by emigré Germans. France seemed to have more to offer, since other emigrés were publishing a German-language journal which would be pleased to have Papa among its contributors, so they moved to Paris. It was, though, the time of the Depression and the going got tough and it was only through the acceptance by an English agent of a film script that Papa had written that brought them across the Channel to London.

Through all this Anna and her brother live a life of resilient acceptance. They seem to accommodate themselves to the loss of their comfortable past life in the spirit of experiencing new encounters. There are foreign children (although at the Swiss hotel where they lodge they have a bad moment when it is visited by a Nazi family *en vacance*). There are foreign schools and teachers and, when they get to France, the confrontation with a foreign language. Papa may be fluent for he had had a French governess in his youth but for the others it is a sudden immersion in an unknown sea.

Nor is that all. For they are also now living in an apartment of their own and Mama, formerly accustomed to all-round household help, must learn the domestic arts. (Papa is hopeless and there is a hilarious scene where he proudly brings home an ancient and entirely defective sewing-machine by way of a helpful contribution.) These Parisian trials make up the core of the story as a demonstration of challenge and response. Mama masters the art of low-budget cooking, Max, hitherto a reluctant scholar, blossoms in his *lycée,* and Anna, after determined but seemingly frustrated, efforts, discovers what has been often found, that quite suddenly, overnight, she begins to think in French and hence to speak it quite naturally.

When they get to London though it will be all to do again ...

Commentary

Happily not so fraught with crises as the journeyings of the children in *The Silver Sword* [no.72 above] Anna's story is also closely based on what had occurred to the Kerr family when, just in time, they got out of Germany. The English sequel, *The Other Way Round* (1973), dealt primarily with their life in London during the Blitz and what followed and told how the growing children proved more adaptable to the new place and the new language than did their parents. Anna, who went on to art school was, of course, Judith Kerr herself, the much-loved creator of *The Tiger who Came to Tea* (1968) and, from 1970, the picture book series about Mog the Forgetful Cat, and it is she who draws the chapter headpieces for the present book.

Kerr was the subject of a major exhibition at Seven Stories in 2012. Her archive was placed there on long-term loan and, following her death in May 2019, is now in the Centre's ownership.

-87-

WATERSHIP DOWN
BY RICHARD ADAMS (1972)

In case you didn't know, this is a more or less five hundred-page story about rabbits. We are first brought to see the creatures in a warren by Sandleford Down in Berkshire where we are given a view of their life and social hierarchies: a Chief Rabbit, his lieutenants, and a miscellaneous population of rabbits and does. In this case however there is a small rabbit, Fiver, who is something of a seer and he persuades a comrade, Hazel, that danger is abroad and the warren must be abandoned. Much derided, since his fears lack any evidential foundation, he and Hazel and one of the warren lieutenants, Bigwig, nevertheless determine upon flight, but they know not wither.

Much of the central part of the book is taken up with their adventurous trek to Watership Down in Hampshire which, as Fiver foresees, possesses ideal circumstances for the setting up of a new warren and, as this is accomplished, they realise the need for does that its population and future may be sustained. This engenders the final adventures of the warreners in attracting female companions for the rabbit population, which makes for a complex and dangerous mission ('twas ever thus).

Obtaining a couple of home-bred does from a farm where they live safely in hutches is but prelude to abortive negotiations with the large, neighbouring warren of Efrafa, ruled like a fascist state by General Woundwort. Despite a cunningly devised plan by Hazel, executed with great courage by Bigwig with the aid of a black-headed gull, Kehaar, the arrival of the does at the Down is fearfully jeopardised through a revenge attack on the warren by the General and his cohorts. A not-wholly-well-managed interplay of scenes between the battle and a mission by Hazel to engage as ally an unsuspecting dog eventually brings victory and a lasting peace descends upon the warring warrens. The General disappears, becoming a mythical figure, like old Boney, for rabbit mothers to frighten their kittens with at bed-time.

This whole adventure story in which people and other animals, apart from the wonderfully portrayed Kehaar, hardly ever appear, is chronicled with great authority by its historian. Adams admits to gaining rich insight into the 'working life' of rabbits from the authority on the subject, R. M. Lockley and, powered by the potential of the theme, he developed it (rather as we shall see Peter Dickinson doing with *Tulku*) while driving his children through the very sites of the action. A map in the first edition of the book, replicated and improved upon in the large edition illustrated by John Lawrence, gives evidence of 'the real place' that Adams owns to using for his imaginings of rabbit life. He likes to see parallels in the social organisations of people and rabbits and the immense success of his picaresque fable owes everything to his persuasive characterisation of sensitive Fiver, of the sometimes self-doubting thinker, Hazel, of the gung-ho Bigwig, and, above all, of Kehaar – an alien presence, with but a small command of Lapine ('I 'elp you 'ow you like. Den when you getting mudders I leave you dere …) but rendering heroic thanks for a kindness extended to him by these strange creatures who do not know how to fly.

Commentary

The book was first published by a small, under-capitalised publisher, Rex Collings, after it had been rejected by the big names of the trade. Its instant success both with an adult and a juvenile audience (it was awarded the Carnegie Medal in 1974) and also in the United States led to its transfer to a publisher, Penguin Books, who had previously rejected it. That gave Adams, a former civil servant, the confidence to engage in further novel writing and the creation of two picture books in verse: *The Tyger Voyage* (1976), illustrated by Nicola Bayley and *The Ship's Cat*, (1976) by Alan Aldridge.

One of the features of the epic was the inclusion of several tales, common to the rabbit community, which punctuated the journeys of the travelling group. These later inspired an entirely separate publication: *Tales of Watership Down* (1996). There are nineteen of them, many 'traditional' rabbit tales of El-ahrairah, and stories told after the peace with the Efrafians. After a television production of the story in 1999 there was a predictable debasement of Adams's work (which presumably he permitted) involving oversimplified re-tellings, a dozen pages each with unmentionable colour illustrations and also board books of the 'concept' genre: *Count with Fiver* (1 to 10), *Pipkin's Rainbow* (different colours) etc.

Adams retired to the Isle of Man where he developed his great book collection, the subject of a posthumous sale at Dominic Winter in 2017. Its catalogue gives evidence, if such were needed, of his love of the printed word. Among fine editions of some of the children's book that feature in this 100 may be noted: *The Wind in the Willows, Winnie the Pooh,* and *The Three Mulla-Mulgars,* noting his remark that it was a 'milestone of importance' and one of the most important influences on his whole life.

-88-

THE DANCING BEAR
BY PETER DICKINSON (1972)

Tulku, published in 1979, was the first of Dickinson's two books to win the Carnegie Medal, and was set, for the most part, in Western China and Tibet. In an interview with an American admirer he was asked how much time he had spent in those far off places researching his copy. 'Well,' he said, 'most of the work was done behind my steering wheel, driving the children to school'.

That too may have been the research site for the Dacian adventure of *The Dancing Bear,* for Dickinson had an intellectual curiosity and a power of invention almost sufficient unto itself. His story here begins with Silvester, an intelligent slave, bear-keeper and student of medicine who is owned by Lord Celsus, the Count of the Outhouses in sixth-century Byzantium. He is also a kind of foster brother to the Count's daughter, Ariadne, whose betrothal day feast is about to take place. Unfortunately, through the machinations of a scheming Greek, an army of marauding

Huns is let loose in the city with much slaughter and the carrying off into servitude of the Lady Ariadne.

Silvester and his bear, Bubba, manage to escape the mayhem and they set off to try to trace and ransom the Lady Ariadne, accompanied by the stylite Holy John who comes down from the pillar on which he dwells enthused with a mission to find the Huns' encampment and convert them to Christianity. The journey would be tough enough for three such assorted travellers, but becomes the more dangerous when Silvester discovers that, because of his escape, he has been put on The Lists, the register of wanted men whose capture will end only in torture and death.

The success of their journey and the finding of Ariadne in the Hun camp – an immense trek of about a thousand miles, out of Byzantine territory and into the lands across the Danube – is facilitated after they have saved a Hun warrior, badly wounded during the attack on the city. Silvester's medical knowledge is sufficient to treat him (although he can no longer walk) and since he proves to be cousin to the Great Khan himself their reception is more welcoming than might be expected. In the end Silvester, whose name will never be erased from The Lists, and Ariadne, who has no desire to return to an unwanted betrothal, escape from the camp and find a home for themselves and Bubba in a Dacian village, where they marry and become honoured members of the community. The Holy John remains among the Hun, confident in his capacity to bring them to the True Faith.

Throughout this enthralling travelogue the reader is absorbed by Dickinson's imagined realm, although he does claim that 'the main history is as true as I can make it'. The excitement is enhanced by his marvellous portrayals of the travellers (especially Bubba), and of key figures on the journey – Urrguk, the wounded Hun, the Khan Zabergan, and Antoninus, a devotee of the virtues of Republican Rome, in whose Dacian house their journey ends. Even the many walk-on parts: a shepherd, a barge-conductor, the Emperor's eunuch despatched to capture Silvester, the Khan's blind Greek counsellor, have a wholly three-dimensional character.

Commentary

The Dancing Bear, which is illustrated by David Smee with rectangular 'icons' set into the text at the start of each chapter, was the fifth children's book by Dickinson and demonstrates as well as anything his outstanding versatility. The first three had been in his dystopian 'Changes' series, each one a sequel to the one following it: *The Weathermonger* (1968), *Heartsease* (1969) and *The Devil's Children* (1970) – a later single-volume reprint reversed them into a correct chronological sequence. They were followed by a tricksy contemporary story on the theme of the Loch Ness Monster, *Emma Tupper's Diary* (1971), and then this journey to Byzantium. From here on, all his twenty and more children's books (and, until 1999 they were matched by novels for adults) show a writer playing with ideas that demand varying treatments of time, place, subject and narrative schema. Thus, unlike the novel *Tulku*, his second medal-winning book, which came only a year later, was the first, *City of Gold*, a re-fashioning of individual stories from the Old Testament, while *The Blue Hawk*, which won the *Guardian* Prize, is a fantasy set in a wholly indeterminate landscape and time. The only author of the post-war period to equal him in diversity and depth of response to his themes is William Mayne.

-89-

CARRIE'S WAR
BY NINA BAWDEN (1973)

'Auntie Lou' had a fluey cold so twelve year old Carrie and her ten year old brother Nick had to go and collect the Christmas goose from the farm at old Mrs Gotobed's. They'd not been there before – up out of the village, along the railway line, and down into the valley through a grove of yew trees. Nick was frightened in the late December gloom especially as a gobbling monster seemed to be following them down to the house and they tore through the nearest door they could see and into a warm and comforting kitchen. Hepzibah, Mrs Gotobed's carer, had been making mince pies, and there was Albert, a school friend that Carrie hadn't seen for ages, and in came the author of the gobbling noises, Mr Johnny, a brain-damaged man, nursed by Hepzibah since childhood. Before the goose was packed up and ready to go there was a celebratory feast of mince pies and ham and goloptious farm butter.

Such things were marvellous at the time, especially to Nick, a renowned feaster, for he and Carrie, had been evacuated from their London home to escape German bombs and had been billeted in a Welsh mining village with Councillor Evans, grocer, 'a good man', as 'Auntie Lou', his put-upon sister said: 'but strict ... and very strong Chapel'. He is also the disaffected brother of the goose-supplying Mrs Gotobed, with whom he had broken off relations when she had married the local pit-owner and gone up in the social scale. Temperamental in his behaviour towards the children (Carrie has moments of sympathy towards him while Nick owns at times to hating him) it is the defection of his older sister, now drifting towards death, and his bitterness towards kindly Hepzibah, whom he sees as a usurper, that has eaten into his soul. Carrie's war is not a matter of drums and trumpets but one where she is observer of and to some extent participant in a family feud.

But it doesn't last long. The children have been in the village for less than a year before their mother writes to say that she has removed to Glasgow to a place where they can resume a family life. As they prepare for departure however, a triple drama erupts. First, Mrs Gotobed dies intestate, leaving Hepzibah and Mr Johnnie to face eviction at the Councillor's hands, while Albert (who has evinced a quiet passion for Carrie) must go and lodge with the local Minister. Then 'Auntie Lou' who has been a meek and kindly buffer between the children and her brother suddenly reveals an unexpected steel to her character and elopes with an American soldier (a Major no less) from the Base down the valley. It is left to a chastened Mr Evans to see the children on to their train and, as it departs and they look their last on the yew tree grove they see that the farmstead below is engulfed in flames.

Long, long after this traumatic episode in her life and but a month or two after the sudden death of her husband, Carrie makes an unpremeditated return to the village as she drives her own children into Wales. It is a drear place, with the pit closed and the railway Beechingified, and she must needs explain to her young why on earth she has brought them to spend a night in so unprepossessing a spot. Before they depart in the morning though the children's exploration of the destroyed farm below the grove brings a moving revelation of what the future had held for Auntie Lou and Mr Johnnie, and Hepizibah – and Albert.

Commentary

The massive internal immigration programme of the 1939 evacuations may have been occasioned by the outbreak of war but its impact on children's literature had little to do with military hostilities. Thousands of children would find themselves uprooted from a familiar to a strange environment (neither being necessarily as comfortable or as uncomfortable as the other) in a kind of involuntary holiday adventure. As with *Carrie's War*, the narratives tended to present essentially domestic dramas, initially recorded in fictions at the time of the evacuations themselves (Kitty Barne's *Visitors from London*, for instance, which won the 1941 Carnegie Medal, or several comic takes in the contemporary 'William Books', he never being allowed anywhere near a Medal). Many more are written in historical terms, although Nina Bawden, in an Afterword to the second edition of her book in 1995, recalls the – for her – exciting time of her own evacuation. By contrast, other authors, such as Michelle Magorian had not even been born at the time of the events recorded in her famous *Goodnight, Mister Tom* (1981).

The first edition of *Carrie's War* had been illustrated with chapter headpieces by Faith Jaques. Their replacement by equivalent stippled drawings by Mark Edwards makes for a demanding exercise in comparative visualisation and graphic technique.

Many references to evacuation stories can be found among the 372 titles of the descriptive bibliography of World War II children's literature by Farnell Parsons, *Prelude, Conflict and Aftermath* (St Louis, Missouri, 1999).

-90-

THE SLAVE DANCER
BY PAULA FOX (1973)

Man's inhumanity to man is on display before the ship has even put out for Africa. Thirteen year-old Jessie Bollier is kidnapped on his way home to the single room in New Orleans that he shares with his widowed mother and sister. Wrapped in a sack he is carried out of the town and brought to the clipper *The Moonlight*, setting off on a slaving trip to Whydah in the Bight of Benin. Interviewed by the Captain (who 'likes to eat well and likes to beat men') he is found to answer too sharply and has his ear bitten into till it bleeds.

Jessie has been pressed for one reason only. One of the sailors had heard him playing his fife for money at the New Orleans market and has kidnapped him to replace a boy who had run away and who was to play for the slaves when they are carried across the Atlantic for America. Bought from the barracoon at $10 a head they will only bring profit if they arrive back in good physical condition so they will be daily brought up from their ghastly entombment below decks in order to dance to Jessie's fife.

Paula Fox spares nothing in her descriptions of the rigours of both the voyage out and the return. She gives the telling to Jessie himself as eye-witness of his own fate and this has the effect of building a close-viewed portrait of the ragbag mariners who are on the voyage solely for the end rewards and also a direct report of the horrors which confront him as an unwilling participant in the venture.

The sea, though, brings an unlooked-for ending. When the Spanish slave-master joins the ship at Cuba to examine his merchandise two things happen. First, Jessie plays for a final dance which is interrupted when they find an American patrol ship bearing down upon them, necessitating their throwing the slaves into the sea. Then that is interrupted by the arrival of a ferocious storm which drives the ship out of control across the water. Jessie who has rescued a native African boy from the confusion on deck hides the two of them in the hold whence they manage to get into the sea, clutching a spar as *The Moonlight* goes down with all hands.

The storm it seems has driven the boat to the Mississippi coast of America, where the two boys make landfall on a beach backed by what looks to be a deserted forest. In fact it is the hideaway of a black man, himself an escaped slave, who 'had founded this place of liberty for himself in the forest'. He looks after Jessie and the boy, Ras, until he is able to implement a plan to get the boy on a journey north and he directs Jessie on a route to New Orleans. The quiet ending is fitting, as Jessie, eventually an apothecary, looks back from his northern home on Rhode Island, with some part of his memory 'always looking for Ras'. Impossible to find him, of course, and his life goes on 'much like my neighbours' except that he can no longer bear to listen to music.

Commentary

Paula Fox wrote twenty books for children, most notably: *How Many Miles to Babylon* (1967) and *Blowfish Live in the Sea* (1970), probing the lives of city teenagers. The delightful *A Likely Place*, about a young boy's encounter with an elderly gent in Central Park is for younger readers and was illustrated by Edward Ardizzone. *The Slave Dancer*, illustrated by Chris Mowlan, caused a critical stir when it was first published (an early offender against 'cultural appropriation') but was nonetheless awarded the American Library Association's Newbery Medal. The distinction of the whole of her work up to 1978 resulted in her gaining the major international award of the Hans Christian Andersen Medal.

– 91 –

THUNDER AND LIGHTNINGS
BY JAN MARK (1976)

Nothing really happens. The book doesn't seem to be much more than simply a vignette of a twelve year-old boy and his obsession with aircraft.

The Mitchell family have just moved up to a cottage in Norfolk, Dad having got a new job in Norwich. Mum, who used to be a librarian, is looking after the new baby and Andrew is to start a new school. On his first day, his class teacher Miss Beale suggests that he might make a start on a General Studies project – yes, motor racing or guinea pigs would do:' "Perhaps Victor would show you round so that you can see how the others set about it." '

Victor seems an odd choice. He is doing fish:' "I do fish every time. They're easy. They're all the same shape" '. And when Andrew looks at some of Victor's examples he finds 'Braem. Tensh. Carp …' accompanied by pictures that were indeed the same shape ('as slugs') except for the shark 'which had a row of teeth like tank traps'. He clearly takes a relaxed view of the educational process, but turns out to live just down the lane, 'the loke', from Andrew and the two commence a local friendship. It is Victor who has the aircraft obsession, and especially on the Lightnings: Rolls Royce Avon-powered turbojets, which fly from Coltishall military base, just a modest bike ride from the village.

The simplicity of the vignette here takes on a vital depth as the contrast between the friends and their upbringing is revealed. Andrew, bright, but unsure of himself, is the child of easygoing, amused and amusing parents, comfortable in a chosen lifestyle; Victor is the victim of an inbred village family, narrow and unencouraging. When, astonished at the clutter of the Mitchell menage with the messy baby, the guinea-pigs, the books all over the place, he remarks that 'our house is too clean', he summarises the restricting priorities of his circumstances.

An unobtrusive observer, Jan Mark contrives in incident after incident to bring out a native wisdom and humanity in Victor which has been given no chance of expression before the arrival of the Mitchells. He becomes instantly devoted to Edward, the baby, whom he dandles and perambulates around in a way that Andrew would have found profoundly embarrassing. He engages in blunt satire of teachers and a local librarian who seem not to understand the limitations of their trained approach to knowledge. He would never attempt a project on aircraft for them: 'If I started doing that for school, I wouldn't be interested in them any more. I don't care about fish, so I don't mind doing them … I don't want to learn things, I just want to find out'. The depth of that genuine passion animates not only the plane-spotting adventures in the book but also its emotional heart when Victor – hearing of the likely withdrawal of Lightnings in favour of the newer Jaguars brings what may be a last sight of them to a close: ' "Everything go. Everything go that you like best. That never come back" '.

Commentary:

This, Jan Mark's first book, came to publication through a competition in 1975 run by the *Guardian* and the publisher Kestrel Books to find 'the most outstanding first novel by a new writer for children'. So perceptive was the judges' choice that the book went on to win the 1977 Carnegie Medal. Mark would later win a second medal with *Handles* in 1983, another take on the foibles of contemporary youth. As such it belongs to the core of a body of equally diverting long stories, around which are ranged collections of short stories for older and younger readers, stories that play high jinks with their plotting, and demanding futuristic novels. The consistency and readability of her whole oeuvre makes the choice of a single example invidious and *Thunder and Lightnings* allows us to see the start of a distinguished career, which included the regular running of writers' workshops.

– 92 –

THE BATTLE OF BUBBLE AND SQUEAK
PHILIPPA PEARCE (1978)

Funny things, book-awards and suspect from end to end. Time was when there were only two or three of them for children's books but now they are like sands upon the Dead Sea shore and a fat tome like Ruth Allen's *Winning Books* (Pied Piper 2005) will give you summary listings of the most notable. But thick though the information may come we are rarely told, from occasion to occasion, who the people are who were responsible for picking the winners. What matters surely is not the gongs, the statuettes and the red, red roses but one's respect for the judges and the diligence with which they can be shown to have pursued their task.

I dare anyone to claim that *The Battle of Bubble and Squeak* did not deserve the accolade accorded to it when it gained the Whitbread Prize for a children's book in 1979 – I was there on that heartwarming occasion. But I was somewhat taken aback when the judge assigned to deliver the encomium (Beryl Bainbridge) referred throughout to the author's delightful handling of the *guinea-pigs* who were the subject of her story. I was bothered to know whether this was a mental aberration brought on by the lavishness of Messrs Whitbread's luncheon or a judging procedure that was all-too casual (after all, the thing was only a book for children).

And a like sloppiness pervades summary descriptions too, as in the description of the story that is found in the recent four-volume Oxford *Encyclopedia.* The author of the article is Maria Nikolajeva, an eminent Cambridge academic. She is seven years out in her dating of the book's first publication, she mentions neither the illustrator nor the award of the Whitbread Prize, and her summary of the work is simply that it is 'a nice domestic story involving two pets and the children's struggle to keep them'. (Well, at least that's a mention. She doesn't find in her article on Philippa Pearce any room at all for the masterly re-working of Brian Fairfax-Lucy's *The Children of the House* [no.81 above].)

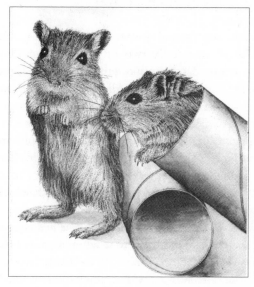

Line and wash drawing (125x115mm.) by Alan Baker, in text on p.23 of *The Battle of Bubble and Squeak* (London: André Deutsch,1978).

If that lukewarm judgment were its due then *The Battle of Bubble and Squeak* could hardly qualify for a place in any list of classic children's books. Perhaps the book's brevity provoked Mme Nikolajeva's rather dismissive attitude, for the story occupies only some two-thirds of its generously-printed eighty-eight pages. But brevity does not preclude intensity – and indeed may foster it – and it is the powerful emotional currents that lie below the surface of the tale that turn it from 'a nice domestic story' to a small-scale, but intense, human drama.

Miss Bainbridge's guinea-pigs are, of course, gerbils and are indeed at the centre of the narrative, but it is necessary to stress that they are not 'pets' but animals who are given a character wholly independent of the humans amongst whom they find themselves. We are told that they are modelled on a pair of gerbils owned by Philippa Pearce's daughter (and actually called Bubble and Squeak) and the author's close observation of their antics provides one of the joyous ingredients of the book. Whether they are gnawing the best curtains, or scurrying around inside the boy Sid's clothes ('pop-eyed gerbil faces popped out of trouser-ends'), or are merely present with their household clutter on the table (one of them 'sat up on its hind-legs behind [a] tube, on which it rested one front paw, as if to begin public speaking') they persuade the reader to join Sid and his two sisters in caring about their fate.

And that fate is a more complex business than is implied by Nikolajeva's 'struggle'. Certainly, gerbils and children alike are up against the implacable force of Mum, 'an expert at preventing mess'. She is appalled when the creatures are found, secreted overnight in her pantry, and half the book concerns her efforts to get rid of them. But the tension thus generated is emblematic of strains within the family itself. For the children's birth-father is dead and their forceful mother is married again to a kindly and accommodating man. But she seems assailed by what? – regret? jealousy? uncertainty? – over her place within the family circle. Those question marks are necessary because Philippa Pearce is not one for plonking psychological explanations or for the stereotyped portrayal of family rows. You must make what you will of the hints and suggestions that are touched into the text, but as the story approaches its climax with Bubble, 'the quiet one', having been set upon by a cat, it is Mum who heart-stoppingly resolves the drama in which she has been the central non-gerbil participant.

Commentary

Philippa Pearce's first book, *Minnow on the Say,* was commended for the 1955 Carnegie Medal which she won for her second, *Tom's Midnight Garden*, in 1958. This was hailed by John Rowe Townsend in 1974 as the 'single masterpiece of English children's literature' to be published since the war – a judgment which has been frequently echoed since. It must therefore seem perverse to have included here what may be seen as a lesser and slighter book but, as noted, one that succeeds in the more demanding task of creating a moving story in the world of an ordinary contemporary family. The book was a most satisfying production with a jacket and illustrations by Alan Baker that were like beautifully composed stipple-engravings (a pity though that he deprived Jimmy Dean's cousin of his anorak in the final denouement). It was dedicated 'To Pam [Royds]' whose mentor Philippa had been when she succeeded her as editor at André Deutsch: 'Not a gift but a tribute'.

-93-

TRUCKERS
BY TERRY PRATCHETT (1989)

Arnold Bros. (est.1905) is to close down. As a general store ('All Things under one Roof') it has had its day and is to be replaced by an Arnold Bros. Leisure Centre.

Unknown to the Management however the Roof covers the dwelling place of the nomes, tiny people, four inches high, who have established a comprehensive way of life under the floorboards. Subsistence is easy for does not the Store hold everything that can be turned to good use and the nome population has divide itself into tribes related to whatever department under which they are living: the Ironmongerie, the Corsetrie and so on with the Stationerie as leaders, for they deal in books and some of them have learnt to read.

These good folk, sceptical that any world exists Outside, are also ignorant of the destruction that is soon to fall upon the store and are only alerted to it when strange nomes, who claim to live Outside are visited upon them – new people who are seeking a better place to live than the rough circumstances of a roadside cafe. They bring with them too what is known as The Thing, a black box, an heirloom of the tribe, which, once influenced with the electricity that flows through the Store, comes to life as a speaking computer. It is The Thing that warns them of the imminent demolition of their home.

It falls to Maskin, a reluctant spokesman for the tribe, first to establish their authenticity as nomes who *know* that there is an Outside and then to plan with some bright lads among the Store nomes a means by which the whole of the underfloor population might escape. They plan to hijack a lorry.

The daring of this undertaking is only surpassed by Terry Pratchett's *chutzpah* in thinking that he can convince his readership that the whole social set-up of nomedom is a credible Other World and then that a group of four-inch people can contrive an engineering feat, using mostly bits of wood and string, to take an x-ton lorry out of the town of Grimethorpe and into the saving countryside. Of course he can do it (by the time *Truckers* was published he had already charmed the world with the first half-dozen volumes of the '*Discworld*' saga.) His discrimination between the incoming Outsiders and the establishment figures of the Store nomes suggests a personal observation of their ways. The Store and its notices: Christmas Fayre, January Sales, Prices Slashed, etc. are shown to be interpreted by the Store dwellers as signs of the seasons or human personalities (the latter is a dangerous individual who lives in the basement) and there are many witty – and apposite – parallels drawn in the satirical view which the nomes take of the Store's staff and customers alike.

Pratchett has claimed that he is not over-fond of the Borrowers and their adventures, but it is impossible to escape a comparison and contrast between these little folk, 'strangers and afraid, in a world they never made'. Both are dependent on their skills at adapting materials to their needs, even though the technology at Grimetown is far more sophisticated than is possible in the countryside around. In both cases too, the little people are under constant threat from assault by other fauna or discovery by 'human beans'. The difference lies in Mary Norton's tender care for the lives of Pod, Homily and Arrietty and the exhilarating comedy as the truckers make their escape.

Put it down to their sheltered innocence that they do not realise that 'Road Works Ahead' means that it doesn't work, or that a roundabout does not have golden horses running round it.

Commentary

Truckers was preceded by Pratchett's children's book, *The Carpet People* (1984), his first ever published novel and although it too is about tiny people, here populating the pile of a carpet, they bear no relation to nomes. *Truckers* itself is the first of a trilogy, being followed by *Diggers* and *Wings* (both 1990 and both covering the same time period immediately following that of the first book, but from different points of view). These explain and complete the history of the nomes who, many generations before, had ended up on earth from a defective space-ship and now – ingenious as they are – find a way to return to their own planet.

-94-

THE KINGDOM BY THE SEA
BY ROBERT WESTALL (1990)

Harry's mam, dad and sister Dulcie are killed in an air-raid on North Shields up by Tynemouth. He'd been quick enough to get to the shelter but they had been delayed and the house suffered a direct hit.

After that, there seemed nothing for it but to go to his Cousin Elsie, which is what the authorities would recommend, but that held no appeal whatsoever. He'd rather die than go to Cousin Elsie's and he determined to tough it out on his own and see what happened. He found some temporary accommodation under an old, upturned boat on the seashore where he was joined by a young Alsatian dog who he guesses from the address on its collar had also been bombed out – a posh street that had been demolished by a stick of explosives.

War or no war the summer holidays were on and Harry and the dog, Don, begin a journey up the coast towards Lindisfarne through a parade of incidents that display the vagaries of human kindness, brutality and eccentricity. The dog saves him from being robbed by drunks; he saves the dog from being shot by a farmer. The two of them find lodging and work with a solitary beachcomber who lives in a shed under some cliffs but then, fearful of a visit from the police, they must leave, finding shelter for themselves in a Home Guard pillbox that was convertible to a snug hideaway. Lindisfarne, when he gets there after serving as an errand boy at a soldier's camp, proves a rather unholy, unwelcoming island and in escaping from it across the causeway he and Don are caught by the sea and just manage to gain safety in one of the refuge-towers erected for that purpose.

That would seem to be the nadir of their adventures. What money they had has been converted to a sodden mess by the sea from which he is brought down by a helpful man crossing the causeway, Don has a seriously injured paw through his being manhandled up the refuge-tower, and when they get to the coast road further journeying is impossible. However a passing motorist, struck by their plight, comes to their aid. Takes the dog to a local vet and carries Harry home with him to offer rest and sustenance.

It proves to be a final irony that their rescuer is a widower whose son, a young midshipman, had died when the *Repulse* went down. He is a master at the Duke's School at Alnwick – one of those perfect teachers who can inspire pupils with a desire to learn – and he can apply to adopt Harry. Of necessity though, and although Harry never wants to see North Shields again, they must return there to clear up the official details of Harry's orphandom. It is a crushing visit. They discover that Mam, Dad and Dulcie were not killed at all but blown into a neighbour's garden by the force of the explosion.

They are then re-housed – no one knows what's happened to Harry – in dingy quarters and not so much pleased to see him when he returns as to blame him for his disappearance and all ready to have Don put down. (" 'Fancy picking up a great hungry animal like that. Have you got no sense?" '). After his heroic journey through 'the kingdom by the sea' he must return to quotidian experiences which he has outgrown and to a family which, however loved, he perceives as holding no future for him. We are left with only a slender hope that it will be otherwise.

Commentary

Westall was born in North Shields and spent his years in the north-east until he graduated from the School of Art at King's College, Newcastle, then part of Durham University. He took first class Honours, majoring in sculpture, and went on to the Slade in London after his years in National Service in the army. He had worked at writing intermittently during this time but only after taking up a job as a teacher, moving eventually to Cheshire, did he cut his teeth as a part-time journalist and composed his story *The Machine-Gunners* for his son Christopher. Its publication in 1975, when it won the Carnegie Medal, unleashed a dormant talent which resulted in the publication of forty-eight children's books before his sudden death eighteen years later in 1993.

Although he did not write a formal autobiography, sundry essays (from which most of the above synopsis is taken) were gathered by his partner, Lindy McKinnell, and published as *The Making of Me* (2006). She there records, as his executrix, her decision to set up the Robert Westall Charitable Trust, making a grant of £100,000 which was vitally important in setting up the Newcastle foundation of Seven Stories, the National Centre for Children's Books.

-95-

THE STORY OF TRACY BEAKER
BY JACQUELINE WILSON (1991)

Aged ten years and two months Tracy Beaker takes the understandable view that her life 'hasn't been very special so far'. Her father is unknown and her mother 'keeps moving about' and may well be a luscious actress in Hollywood as much as anything else. Tracy had had to leave her after she took up with a Monster Gorilla Boyfriend who beat her up and the girl was thus taken into care.

Care is problematic too. There were a couple of abortive attempts to place her with foster parents which ended in anger and despair ('I've done a bit of stamping and shouting in my time'). Now she is in a children's home, looked after with other youthful residents on the fostering list by housemother Jenny, with a companionate social worker: 'My social worker is called Elaine and sometimes she's a right pain. Ha, ha'.

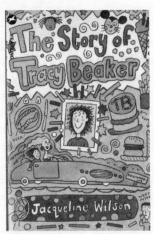

Full colour paperback wrapper by Nick Sharratt (195x130mm.) London: Yearling Books, 1992).

These insights are relayed to us direct from Tracy's own disenchanted account of her ten years and two months of being alive. The ordeals from the time of the Monster Gorilla onwards have given her a shrewd perception of the duplicities, well-meaning or otherwise, of the adult world, and the onset of stampings, shoutings and derisive engagements with her fellow inmates stem from a frustrated sense that the system does not allow for the eccentricities of non-conformity.

As a distorted version of a boarding-school story (she has read her Enid Blyton), Tracy's ruminations and antagonisms are flavoured by the circumstances of the Home. There is a thread of narrative that sees her despising 'dopey Peter Ingham', but mothering him in her worldly-wise way only to lose him as he is accepted for fostering. And this is paralleled by her jealous hatred of Justine Littlemore, whose nose she spectacularly punches at one point, but with whom there is a tentative reconciliation on the last page.

That is brought about by the central episode in which a local writer, Camilla Lawson, visits the Home, having been commissioned to submit a feature on it for the local paper. Tracy is fazed by Camilla – deploring her preferred shortening of the name to Cam – who does not ask 'endless stupid questions' or put on the pose that 'nothing-you-can-say-will-shock-me-sweetie'. Instead, she seems nervous and 'I was amazed to see that she bites her finger-nails'. Like many another practitioner, she confesses to a hatred for writing, summoning up the horrors of the waiting keyboard and the blank sheet of paper. Such a thing astonishes Tracy, the uninhibited autobiographer, who exudes confidence and before long letters are exchanged (we are shown facsimiles) and a feast is had at McDonalds. Seizing the moment, Tracy promotes a case for Cam to foster her and although long schooled in disappointments, she ends her story in bright hope.

Jacqueline Wilson, to whom the replication of Tracy Beaker's hopes and follies has been entrusted, does not buck the issues. She knows that when Tracy's eyes water it may not be down to hay fever or that the long-awaited visit from Mum may never occur, for she has a profound understanding of the stratagems by which this small castaway survives. And in this she is supported by Nick Sharratt's visualisations of what might be Tracy's own illustrations through which *The Story* becomes one of those texts whose physical essence lies in the conjunction of word and picture.

Commentary

Although she wrote stories from childhood on, it was *Tracy Beaker* that proved a break-through book for Jaqueline Wilson, being followed in the last twenty-five years or so by a hundred or so successors, most illustrated by Nick Sharratt. The mixture of compassion for the plight of children exposed to situations they are hardly fitted to endure coupled with an often hilarious demotic has made the partnership an immense success (especially, one suspects, among girl readers). With *The Lottie Project* in 1997, Wilson ventured a sideways engagement with her own interest in Victorian life and its presence in children's books and this was filled out with the first of three stories about the cast-off Victorian girl, Hetty Feather (2008) and also by a resurrection into modern times of E. Nesbit's Psammead in *Four Children and It* (2012).

Wilson has received many local and national awards and was chosen as Children's Laureate from 2005 to 2007. In 2002 she was appointed an OBE and raised to DBE in 2008. In 2017 she received the Special Award at the BAFTA Children's Awards.

-96-

MARTIN FARRELL
BY JANNI HOWKER (1994)

Martin Farrell, the fourth book by Janni Howker, was published by Julia MacRae Books in 1994. Fourth, but seemingly least remarked, its predecessors, the short stories of *Badger on the Barge,* and the gritty Lancastrian tales of *The Nature of the Beast* and *Isaac Campion* all found themselves be-wreathed in prizes or gaining lesser acclaim as runners-up for prizes. But *Martin Farrell,* eight years in the making, was *sui generis,* an experience foreign to awards committees, vagrant in a critical climate that was less attuned to its uncompromising accents.

For the book shifts from the vernacular of Bill Coward and Isaac Campion, those Lancastrian boys from mill-town and horse-breeder's farmstead. Instead, the voice comes from the more distant shores of the ancient singer of tales. 'This man,' he begins, 'he had no sort of name to waste breath on. He filled his mouth with drink. A swig and a slug before he had come through the door and like a horse at a trough at the wedding feast.' As in the sung ballads you are not vouchsafed the information you have been taught to expect. 'Nails o'God' we next hear the wedding-feaster fatally say of the bride, 'You dun mean to say he's thinking he's the first wi' her!' and so you must piece together, incident by incident, a double, triple, quadruple bloody drama.

Those words were spoken by Martin Farrell's foster-father, a slovenly peat-cutter, and not long after he ends up tongueless and meat in the black boar's sty. It is to be the first move in the end-game of the feud between the Solway Border clans of the Armstrongs and the Grahames and is a model for the ruthless, but essentially pointless, gang warfare that is not unknown to later generations. Here though it is intermingled with a primitive magic of summoned memory and dark foretelling, with the Galloway fiddler (who also meets a bloody end) shepherding Martin Farrell towards a lenitive ending as he discovers his inheritance and brings about the ending of the feud.

Attentiveness is what matters, as the tale is cast in the accents of the singer of tales. He questions his audience ('Are you roused? Are you listening?'); he interjects ('Ach, ye must wait. My bladder is full. Open the door, let me into the yard') and these serve not as distractions but as augmentations of what seems like a direct experience. Janni Howker has said that she was not herself writing the book, but (as Stravinsky said of *The Rite*) was the vessel through whom the story spoke. A unique achievement.

Commentary

But is *Martin Farrell* for children? Well, I would say 'yes' in so far as they too would have been in such a story's audience in the peat-hags among the high hills of the Border country and I would not deprive them of hearing such a masterpiece. Their ears are open to an imaginative, if not a literal, understanding of what is afoot and unlike the listeners of earlier times, they have the good fortune to be able to plumb the depths of the printed narrative. The storyteller stays with them on the page and richer meanings are yielded up by repeated readings.

-97-

CLOWN
BY QUENTIN BLAKE (1995)

How many chapters in this epic? Just one? Or perhaps eighty-two? Here's a possible enumeration:

I: Clown with a clutch of comrades – a startled teddy-bear, an upset parrot, a small elephant – is dumped in a dust-bin;

II: overhanging its edge, he manages to tumble out;

III: he is pleased to find, in another bin, a pair of shoes that fit;

IV: he runs off along the street in his new shoes and meets a little girl and her gossiping mum;

V: she is snatched away from him but he is picked up and entered for a children's fancy-dress photo-shoot;

VI: worried about the friends he has left behind, he tries to explain matters to a little participant dressed as a fairy and she carries him off to a very smart lady who hurls him out of a window;

VII: landing on the pavement, still worrying about his comrades, he is chased by a ferocious dog. He puts on a clowning act to distract the animal, whose muscle-bound owner arrives and once again hurls him sky-high;

VIII: he flies through an apartment window and lands at the feet of a girl who is trying to pacify her baby sister while mum is at work. His arrival distracts the baby and, although he explains about his absent friends, he helps to clean up the apartment so that they can venture out – baby in pram – on a mission to collect his old toy-friends;

IX: racing down the stairs – bumpetty, bumpetty, bump goes the pram – and along the streets, they find the forlorn castaways and pile them into the pram;

X: they then dash – bumpitty, bumpitty bump – back again just before mum gets back from work and there, in the tidied-up apartment, everyone celebrates the joyful conclusion.

There are, of course, gestures but no words in this exhilarating story. 'Readers' may (as here) undertake their own interpretations from the content of Blake's more-or-less eighty-two drawings which vary in size from the page of six drawings where Clown finds and puts on his shoes to the full-page scene of Clown and the girl racing home with the pram after their triumphant rescue of the toys. The whole sequence belies what may look at first sight like a casual display of sketches through Blake's capacity in almost the whole of his work to imbue the characters who inhabit his stories with a consistent and joyous life.

Commentary

Clown dates back to a form of narrative that can be found in some medieval illuminated manuscripts where a text may carry a matching sequences of pictures. Later, in prints for children, examples may be found in English, French, and German picture-sheets which, along with modern comic strips, *bandes-dessinées* and manga may tell novel-length stories with very few captions or (as here) with no words at all. Quentin Blake is an ideal artist to create such things for his swift delineations carry the story forward almost like a movie while the expressiveness of his subjects, picture upon picture – especially the gestures and look of his characters – need no words to convey the comedy and drama of the narrative.

-98-

HIS DARK MATERIALS: NORTHERN LIGHTS
By Philip Pullman (1995)

The Retiring Room at Jordan College, Oxford was sacred ground open only to Scholars and their guests, not at all to women, and not at all at all to eleven year-old girls. It is there though that we are presented with the first of Lyra Belacqua's daredevil escapades when she and her daemon, Pantalaimon, hide in a wardrobe and an adventure starts that is to continue over three large volumes.

Daemons are to be a matter of central importance in the world of this volume, which has many features of perhaps the 1930s but will be found to have many extraordinary differences. All children are born with them but only in adulthood will daemons settle in one animal form, a surrogate of the character of its possessor. (In the second volume where Lyra meets a boy from the world of contemporary Britain she seeks to explain his absent daemon as somehow internalised: 'It's inside you … You wouldn't be human else … Even if you don't know, you've got a daemon you have …').

From her eavesdropping in the wardrobe, Lyra becomes privy to a report to the Jordan Scholars given in a lantern lecture by a certain Lord Asriel. He is said to be her uncle and was responsible for her being housed at the College as an orphan but he is often absent, being a scientist and explorer, particularly concerned with studies in the Arctic regions from which he has just returned. Revelations in his lecture cause some consternation among the Fellows, not least about the presence of a mysterious phenomenon known as Dust.

The nature of Dust is not easily explained – a life force, pouring from the heavens, whose function is provocative of a profound controversy. It would seem to rouse particularly the antagonism of the Magisterium, the Church of the land, which exercises a near totalitarian power outside the quotidian political administration, and the preservation of Dust is to be one of the central themes of the trilogy.

Not long after her adventure in the Retiring Room, Lyra must needs take the first step in her journey beyond Jordan. Her ragamuffin dress and demeanour straightened out as best may be, she is bidden to a private dinner in the Master's Lodging where she meets and is enthralled by a Mrs Coulter, 'a kind of explorer' with an interest of her own in Arctic matters, and it is she who has come to collect Lyra from the guardianship of the College and launch her upon the adventure of the story.

Through four hundred pages her hoydenish experiences among the children of Oxford and her native wit carry her in the book's final pages to a strange meeting with Lord Asriel and Mrs Coulter under the radiance of the Northern Lights of the Aurora. Her hunt for a particular friend, Roger, a kitchen boy at Jordan, who has disappeared with a number of other children, takes her first through English waterways in the boats of a party of 'gyptians' and then on to very strange goings-on in Arctic islands and the company, among others, of witches and ... *panserbjørn* – military bears. She is much aided too by possession of a device presented to her in strict secrecy by the Master of Jordan, an alethiometer, a forecaster which she teaches herself to operate, which reveals the truth of given situations. One of only perhaps six examples it too will play an important part in events and it gives its name as 'the Golden Compass' to the American edition of *Northern Lights*.

The concatenation of plottings to be survived and the long and difficult journeys to be made gives the book the character of an enthralling and highly original fantasy adventure. But the ever-present machinations of the Magisterium supply a more oblique subtext. As a site of lifeless rationalism it is modelled by the author within a larger philosophical drama – his twentieth century

Republic – where a totalitian threat is mounted against Dust-given independence of thought and imagination. That is more baggage than a children's book is normally expected to carry and it is no surprise that the appeal of the subtext to adult metaphysicians has become as tasty as fighting is to *panserbjørn*.

Commentary

Northern Lights has a uniformity of place in the world of the Magisterium. In the two sequels, *The Subtle Knife* and *The Amber Spyglass,* the 'Barnard-Stokes' theory of the existence of parallel worlds is endorsed and one is transported from an 'actual' twentieth century Oxford to yet further realms. At the same time the Magisterium's power over Philip Pullman is such that the vision that makes *Northern Lights* such a powerful story is fractured into an authorial determination to drive the organisation and its Consistorial Court and its Oblation Board into oblivion (an exercise similar to but more extravagant than C. S. Lewis's demolition of the White Witch in Narnia). Too diverse a fantasy with too many new-minted characters distorts the storytelling.

Pullman's exploration of the idea of Dust is now set to generate a further trilogy as *The Book of Dust.* The first volume, *La Belle Sauvage,* which is a prequel to *Northern Lights,* sees Lyra as a baby arriving at Jordan College, appeared in 2017.

-99-

FIRE BED AND BONE
BY HENRIETTA BRANFORD (1997)

Times were very hard in the early years of the reign of Young King Richard the Second. The Black Plague had not long before hacked down the population and the potential for wealth for society as a whole. There were resultant poll taxes, even on poor folk. There was oppression from overlords, and down in Kent the labourers were drawn to hear seditious talk from itinerant preachers filled with the doctrines of John Ball:

> Whan Adam dalf, and Eve span
> Wo was thanne a gentilman

But there were spies about and lickspittle tenants and the cottagers, Rufus and Comfort, who were sympathetic to such radical ideas, found themselves arrested and shackled in a stable at the lord's Great House awaiting their being marched to Maidstone to meet rough justice.

We know of this, and especially the horror of their incarceration, through the telling of their fine and faithful hunting-dog. She – for she is in truth a hunting-bitch – is the reporter on events throughout their tale so that we not only hear of the fate of Comfort and Rufus (who will eventually be hung in Maidstone marketplace) but the intertwined story of the animal herself – who never gives her name – her puppy, Fleabane, and their dealings with the other animals in their doggie lives.

It is a brilliant device, for, as a dog born to work with a man: ('I am not, nor ever will be, truly wild … I have known fire, bed and bone'), her instincts and intelligence allow her to interpret the human and feral situations in which she finds herself. She gives heart to her people, at first by making a move that sees their children will be cared for while they are imprisoned, and then by staying faithful through later traumas. At the same time, through such events as the rescue of Fleabane from the hold of the cruel local miller, the main villain of the story, and the companionate hunting in the forests with wild dogs, she engages a double sympathy in her readers.

Henrietta Branford's storytelling also encompasses a double skill. The bitch's direct account of the events of her own life has a convincing immediacy. Hear her as the story opens with her giving birth to three puppies in the farm byre:

' "Oof!" she says as Fleabane arrives, "Welcome. Are you the last and latest, small new, smudged smidgen of a puppy? I think so. Yes, just three" '.

And then by what might be called 'sleight of voice' Branford preserves our conviction that the dog is able to give us necessary circumstantial detail as she recounts conversations or sets the scene for the dogs' own parts in the plot. A grim history is told and the measured final resolution is the more believable.

Commentary

Henrietta Branford came late to writing and left too early, a victim of breast cancer. In ten years she published more than a dozen books for children of varying lengths and subjects and *Fire, Bed and Bone* was one of five created in the last two years of her life. (An immediate successor was *White Wolf* which shares the characteristic of being told by its animal protagonist.) From the start however she showed a marvellous gift for storytelling with her often stark or near tragic plots tempered by her sense of humour and her graphic and poetic language.

Her death in 1999 coincided with that of her editor, Wendy Boase, also from cancer, and their names are linked in a Branford Boase Award at Walker Books, celebrating creative collaborations between children's book authors and their editors. The *Guardian*, whose annual award had been given to *Fire, Bed and Bone*, also established a Henrietta Branford prize for young writers and its annual announcement is shared conjointly with that of the Branford Boase.

–100–

HARRY POTTER AND THE PHILOSOPHER'S STONE
BY J. K. ROWLING (1997)

It would be a matter of more than passing interest to know who were the reported twelve publishers who returned Rowling's manuscript to her agent, thus depriving themselves of the biggest killing in book trade history. Even more interesting would be knowledge of the substance of their reasons for rejecting it, whether 'off-the-cuff' judgments as to its saleability or more closely argued readers' reports.

Lèse-majesté though it may sound, their unfavourable opinions are in many ways understandable because the book has many weaknesses which would be very apparent as coming from an author with no track record. Those opening chapters, for instance, have a Blytonesque animus against Harry's hapless guardians. The introduction of Hogwarts, for all its magical tincture, may be thought to rely on the tropes of the historic boarding-school story with its staff portraits and pupil rivalries (one wonders if Rowling knew of Ged's trouble with Jasper in *The Wizard of Earthsea* [no.85 above]). And the final chapters are a terrible pickle. How could Harry forget his Invisibility Cloak at the top of that tower? How was Ron's dragon bite repaired? And one must assume that the descent to gather the Philosopher's Stone is described with a speed designed to distract the reader from its several incredibilities. A very amateurish job for $100,000.

Bloomsbury's jacket for the children's edition, illustrated by Thomas Taylor.

Bloomsbury's readers, however, were astute enough to perceive that there were a lot of ideas thrashing about in this callow text that may have a more than casual entertainment value. A writer who could persuade you that it was possible to walk (unnoticed?) through a wall to do your shopping or similarly disappear onto Platform 9¾ at Kings Cross Station was not deficient in originality. The devising of a curriculum for Hogwarts with its classes in Potions and Defence Against the Dark Arts, and Transfiguration and the rest comes from an intelligence much at home with the occult as will also become very apparent with myth and the motifs of folktale. Above all, there is the driving force of the Miltonic impulse found in so much children's literature since the Second World War: innocence against corruption, good against evil, Harry against You-Know-Who.

This battle is touched on in varying ways from the beginning but it is only in the final quarter that it emerges as a dominating theme. The death of the unicorn in the Forbidden Forest (discovered during an implausible detention at eleven o'clock at night), the entry to the dungeons where the Stone is to be found and Harry's confrontation with the spirit of Voldemort display its potential. J. K. Rowling, who had for years harboured an awareness of this potential and the direction which its exploration might take, left dangling her hooks to the reader's curiosity to know more and We-Know-Now with what growing assurance she mastered the bright Art of her story-making.

Commentary

It will be equally interesting in the coming years to discover for how long a child readership will continue to devour the 3407 pages that constitute Harry Potter's schooldays. How much more easily they may be consumed from a seat in movieland? And will the same incentive be present to move from, say, the 636 pages of *The Goblet of Fire* to the 766 of *The Order of the Phoenix* without the initial stimulus of pre-publication hype? And will it finally be worth it? There are many occasions when young Harry might be done for but his creator (as we have seen happening in many a good-versus-evil contest) always manages to let him win the Snitch in the end and that holds good through the tangled logic, the hyper-magic, and all the screeching and shrieking of the last chapters (but one) of *The Deathly Hallows*. Lewis got the job done quicker with the White Witch and not so much argy bargy with death-defying wands.

RESERVES

Suggesting as we did in the introduction, that our one hundred might have been confined to players whose work had arrived *only* in the twentieth century, we find waiting in the pavilion the following players who did not make it to the first team. The list is a strong one and many spectators may regret that some of them were not initially selected.

1902 P.G.Wodehouse *The Pothunters.* A.& C. Black
1903 Jack London *The Call of the Wild.* New York, Macmillan
1917 Dorothy Canfield *Understood Betsy.* New York, Holt
1920 Hugh Lofting *The Story of Dr Dolittle.* il. author. New York, Stokes
1921 Mary Tourtel *The Adventures of Rupert the Little Lost Bear.* il.author. Nelson
1925 S.G.Hulme Beaman *The Road to Toytown.* il. author. Oxford University Press
1933 Norman Hunter *The Incredible Adventures of Professor Branestawm.* il W.Heath Robinson. John Lane
1934 Patricia Lynch *The Turf-Cutter's Donkey* il. Jack B.Yeats. Dent
1934 Pamela Travers *Mary Poppins.* il. Mary Shepard. Collins / New York: Reynal
1936 M.E.Atkinson *August Adventure.* il. Harold Jones. Jonathan Cape
1936 Barbara Euphan Todd *Worzel Gummidge.* Burns Oates
1937 Eve Garnett *The Family from One End Street.* il. author. Muller
1937 J.B.S.Haldane *My Friend Mr Leakey.* il.Leonard Rosoman. Cresset Press
1937 Katharine Hull & Pamela Whitlock *The Far-Distant Oxus.* il. P.W. Jonathan Cape
1938 Enid Blyton *The Secret Island.* Oxford, Basil Blackwell
1939 C.Walter Hodges *Columbus Sails.* il. author. George Bell
1939 Hilda Lewis *The Ship that Flew.* il. Nora Lavrin. Oxford University Press
1939 Violet Needham *The Black Riders.* il.Anne Bullen. Collins
1940 Eric Knight *Lassie Come-Home.* il. Marguerite Kirmse.

Philadelphia: Winston

1940 Geoffrey Trease. *Cue for Treason*. Oxford: Basil Blackwell

1943 Esther Forbes *Johnnie Tremain*. Boston: Houghton Mifflin

1943 Malcolm Saville *Mystery at Witchend*. Newnes

1944 Eric Linklater *The Wind on the Moon*. il. Nicolas Bentley. Macmillan

1947 Monica Edwards *Wish for a Pony*. il. Anne Bullen. Collins

1948 C. Day Lewis *The Otterbury Incident*. il. Edward Ardizzone. Putnam

1950 Anthony Buckeridge *Jennings Goes to School*. Il. S. van Abbé. Collins

1958 Michael Bond *A Bear Called Paddington*. il. Peggy Fortnum. Collins

Further Reading

Compared to the thousands of books on imaginative literature for adult readers, those about children's books and their illustration are few in number often unreliable, and, at present, mostly out of print although possibly accessible through electronic sources. (Currently the subject figures mostly in essays found mostly in various 'companion' compendia, noted below, or in volumes on discrete subjects generated by students contributing to 'research excellence' activities.) The major history, which has been labelled unsurpassable, is that by F. J. Harvey Darton *Children's Books in England; five centuries of social life* which was first published in 1932 and was edited for a new edition in 1999 by the present writer (British Library). Two more summary but very approachable accounts from more recent times are *The Natural History of Make-Believe* by John Goldthwaite (OUP, 1996) and *Written for Children* by John Rowe Townsend, first published in 1965, but much augmented up to its latest edition of 1995 (Bodley Head).

'Companions' in the form of alphabetical reference books, while breaking up historical or critical discussions into small gobbets, may nonetheless offer cross-referenced trails through the subject which can make for entertaining exploration. The leading example was the *Oxford Companion to Children's Literature* edited by Humphrey Carpenter and his wife Mari Prichard (OUP, 1984). It was modelled on its famous predecessor, Harvey's *Companion to English Literature,* by being entirely composed by its editors. That gave it the quality of having a single 'voice' even though the complexity of its contents and the poor state of children's book bibliography burdened it with many errors. (The Carpenter character was much weakened in a new edition published in 2016 and the errors continued.) Other alphabetic companions have also been published, but edited by scholars who have difficulty in obtaining consistency in the bibliographical and critical penchants of their many contributors. Much more common now are volumes of essays which label themselves as 'companions' and may include a variable coverage of writing for children.

From the days of Charlotte Yonge, advisors of one sort or another have published what amount to expanded book-lists recommending books for the children of their own generation.

Outstanding among these was *Intent Upon Reading* by Margery Fisher (rev. 1964, Brockhampton Press) whose division of her subject by categories and whose perceptive critical eye makes it still a work of larger address than that for an audience of the 1960s. It has had no equivalent successors. Mrs Fisher's energy took her also to adjunct works, such as *Who's Who in Children's Literature; a treasury of the familiar characters of childhood* (Weidenfeld & Nicolson, 1975), to editing reviews of children's books for the *Sunday Times* and, more systematically, for *Growing Point*, the journal which she wrote and published herself for thirty years from 1962 to 1992.

So far as children's book illustration is concerned, there is very little for the general reader that measures up to the demands of its technical and aesthetic history and its graphic function. Only the now somewhat dated *History of Children's Book Illustration* (John Murray, 1988) by Irene Whalley and Tessa Chester (now Rosi Re Beech) meets those requirements and includes a substantial book-list of general studies and works on individual illustrators. Tessa Chester appends a note on 'Reproduction Techniques', a subject whose complexity is fully explored by Bamber Gascoigne in his *How to Identify Prints* (Thames & Hudson, 1986). Fascinating insight into both the practicalities of illustrating children's books and the question of the graphic interpretation of texts can be gained from Sir Quentin Blake's *Words and Pictures* (Jonathan Cape, 2000).

INDEX by Author:

INDEX by Title:

INDEX by Chronology